BEGINNING GAME
ART IN 3DS MAX® 8

LES PARDEW AND
DAN WHITTINGTON

THOMSON

COURSE TECHNOLOGY

Professional ■ Technical ■ Reference

ISBN: 1-59200-908-5

Library of Congress Catalog Card Number: 2005929823

Printed in the United States of America

06 07 08 09 10 PH 10 9 8 7 6 5 4 3 2 1

Publisher and General Manager, Thomson Course Technology PTR:
Stacy L. Hiquet

Associate Director of Marketing:
Sarah O'Donnell

Manager of Editorial Services:
Heather Talbot

Marketing Manager:
Heather Hurley

Senior Acquisitions Editor:
Emi Smith

Marketing Coordinator:
Jordan Casey

Project Editor and Copyeditor:
Cathleen D. Snyder

Technical Reviewers:
David Franson and Kelly Murdock

PTR Editorial Services Coordinator:
Elizabeth Furbish

Interior Layout Tech:
Shawn Morningstar

Cover Designer:
Mike Tanamachi

CD-ROM Producer:
Brandon Penticuff

Indexer:
Kelly Talbot

Proofreader:
Dan J. Foster

Thomson Course Technology PTR,
a division of Thomson Course Technology
25 Thomson Place
Boston, MA 02210
http://www.courseptr.com

This book is dedicated to the many artists who have gone before,
upon whose foundation we have built.

Acknowledgments

I want to thank my wife, who has helped keep my wild brainstorms in check. To my wonderful kids, who kept me young, and to my grandkids, who make me smile. To my students at Salt Lake Community College, who have been my greatest teachers. Thanks to Les Pardew, who has been a great inspiration to my career.

—Dan Whittington

This book has been the culmination of a lot of work from a lot of people. I want to thank my wife and children for their support and love. I also want to thank all of the good people at Thomson Course Technology PTR for their dedicated help and encouragement. I want to give special thanks to Brent Fox for his technical help and to Cathleen Snyder for her editorial support.

—Les Pardew

ABOUT THE AUTHORS

Les Pardew was born and grew up in Idaho. His hometown was a small farming community where he learned the benefits of hard work. His graduating high-school class only numbered 33 individuals. From this small beginning, he has grown to become a recognized leader in interactive entertainment.

Les started his career in video games, doing animation for *Magic Johnson's Fast Break Basketball* for the Commodore 64. He went on to help create several major games, including *Robin Hood: Prince of Thieves, Star Wars, WrestleMania, NCAA Basketball, Stanley Cup Hockey, Jack Nicklaus Golf*, *Where in the World Is Carmen Sandiego?, Where in the USA Is Carmen Sandiego?, StarCraft Brood War, Tom Clancy's Rainbow Six*, and *Cyber Tiger Woods Golf*, to name a few.

Les is a video game and entertainment industry veteran with more than 20 years of experience. His artwork includes film and video production, magazine and book illustration, and more than 100 video game titles. He is the author or co-author of eight books, including *Game Art for Teens, Beginning Illustration and Storyboarding, Game Design for Teens, Mastering Digital Art, The Animation Reference Book, Basic Drawing for Games*, and *Game Art for Teens, Second Edition*. He is a business leader, founding two separate game-development studios. He is also a favorite speaker at video game conferences and events.

Les is also an accomplished teacher, having taught numerous art and business courses, including teaching as an adjunct faculty member at Brigham Young University's Marriott School of Management and ITT Technical Institute. He is the father of five wonderful children and the grandfather of one beautiful granddaughter. He loves being with his wife and children both at and away from home.

Dan Whittington was born in Santa Rosa, California, and raised in the Salt Lake Valley area. At the ripe old age of two, he began drawing cars and taking things apart. It was this passion for art, cars, and discovering how things work that turned tinkering with cars into a 20-year career as an auto mechanic.

In the fourth grade, Dan took up the violin and piano. Later, he found an interest in the accordion, banjo, and fiddle. An accomplished violinist and fiddle player, he played in several orchestras and was the president of the Utah Old Time Fiddlers.

Always sketching and doing freelance portrait work, an industrial accident in 1991 allowed Dan to pursue one of his first passions—art.

In 1992, while attending SLCC College, Dan was invited to apply for a position at Sculptured Software, where he launched his career in the video game world of 2D and 3D modeling and animation. He worked on such titles as *Mortal Kombat, MechWarrior, Turok, NBA Jam, WrestleMania, War Zone, Combat Medic, Snow Cross 2,* and *Need for Speed 2.*

As well as owning his own company, IMAGE Art & Design, he also teaches at SLCC as an adjunct instructor and was the catalyst that inspired SLCC to adopt the program Maya into their teaching curriculum.

Dan is married and has three children and four grandchildren.

Contents

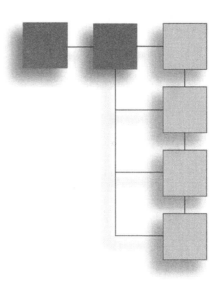

INTRODUCTION

Welcome to the incredible world of 3D art creation with 3ds Max 8. A fascinating new world of creative possibilities awaits you in this book. In its pages you will find techniques and methods for creating game art with one of the most powerful 3D programs ever created. You will learn to build objects, environments, and characters. You will also learn the basics of rigging and animating your game characters.

This book is for the beginning game artist who is new to 3ds Max 8 but may not be new to art. It covers the basic information you will need to know to begin using this amazing program. The book is, however, only the beginning. 3ds Max 8 has so many features and tools that no single book could ever hope to relate everything possible with such an extensive 3D application.

The concept of this book is to teach you by doing. Rather than bombarding you with every aspect of the program, we guide you through projects in which you learn the tools while you create models for games. The concept is like the process you go through when you move to a new city. You spend some time looking at maps and studying the lay of the land, but to really learn what the city is like you have to get in your car and drive around. The first things you learn are the routes to work, school, shopping, and other necessities. As you get comfortable with the area, you have more energy to explore because you know enough to find your way back home.

With this book we take the approach of teaching you how to do basic functions first. These basic functions help you to gain confidence with the location of the tools and features. As you become more confident with 3ds Max 8, we move on to show you how to use some of the more advanced features. In the end, although we don't cover everything, you should have a good foundation from which you can explore the rest of the program.

Why do we take this approach? Because after taking a serious look at the way most people learn to use 3ds Max on the job, we found that this is how they learned the program. 3ds Max is not something you can simply read about. You have to use the program to understand it. It is also a program that requires you to understand a lot of details. It is like learning a foreign language. You have to speak a language to learn it. You have to use 3ds Max to understand it.

The book is filled with example projects. These projects have very detailed step-by-step instructions. Each step is explained in detail, so just by following the instructions you will be building complex models and animating them.

In addition, you'll find a CD-ROM in the back of this book that contains trial versions of Corel Painter and Corel Paint Shop Pro, both helpful tools for the aspiring artist and animator.

We hope you like the instruction and examples in this book. We worked hard to give you real-world examples from games. The specifications for the models are accurate for the current industry. Any model you build following the instructions in this book could be used in a game. Good luck in your efforts. We hope this book helps you succeed as a great game artist and animator.

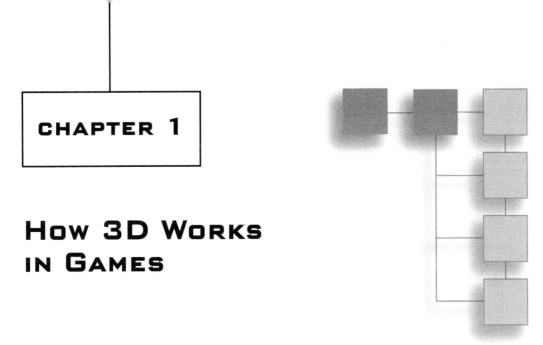

CHAPTER 1

How 3D Works in Games

Creating 3D art for games in 3ds Max is fun and exciting. This book is your gateway to the fascinating world of game art development in 3ds Max. In the following chapters, you will learn how art is made and used in games. You will also have a chance to create art yourself by following the many projects in each chapter. As you read each chapter and try each project, you will hopefully gain a better understanding of 3D game art development.

In this book we will only deal with game art, not art in general. Completing each project will require some level of artistic talent. Because you are interested in reading this book, we will assume you have some artistic skill. We will not go into the basics of drawing and painting. There are many books about those subjects, such as Les Pardew's *Basic Drawing for Games* (Thomson Course PTR, 2005), but in this book we only want to deal with the exciting world of creating 3D art for games.

The book contains step-by-step instructions on a number of topics. We have worked hard to be as detailed as possible so you can follow along with us; however, no book can provide every single step to every process in something as complex as game art development. The best way to use this book is to become familiar with the tools by reading the instructions that come with your art software. Once you are comfortable with the basic features of the art software, following the step-by-step instructions will be easier.

How Art Is Displayed

The best way to begin any discussion on game art is to clarify how art is displayed in a game. Most people play games on a computer, handheld device, or console game system. The pictures we see in games on these systems are made up of small, colored square dots of light called *pixels*. More precisely, a pixel can be defined as the smallest controllable segment of a display. Back when computer games first came out, the resolution of video-game pixels was very low, and they appeared as big blocks of color. As technology has advanced, the size of pixels has shrunk to the point that in some game systems it is difficult to see a single pixel.

Pixels are small dots of colored light that make up pictures on a computer screen. We are reiterating this because it is very important. In traditional art, artists work mostly with the reflected light of a painted surface. For games, artists work with pure light as it is displayed on a screen as opposed to painting on a canvas. This fundamental difference takes a little getting used to, particularly in the area of color (see Figure 1.1).

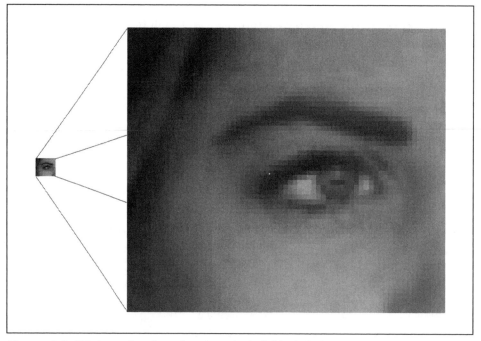

Figure 1.1 This image is enlarged to show the individual pixels.

A game artist uses colored light to create images. Most other forms of art are reflected light. For example, when a person looks at an oil painting, he sees colors that are reflected from light in the room. On the other hand, when a person looks at the same painting displayed on a color monitor or TV he is looking at direct light, not reflected light.

Reflected light is not as bright and vibrant as direct light; however, we live in a world of reflected light. When you are creating game art, it is important to remember that the art will look unrealistic or cartoon-like if you don't take care to reduce the intensity of the color to match how the object looks in real life.

Historical Overview of Computer Art

The first computer art goes back to even before the pixel was developed. Back when computers were in their infancy, the pioneers in the industry used printouts or a device called an *oscilloscope* rather than computer monitors. Some of the earliest computer games were TeleType games in which the players would send updates to each other as printouts.

As display technology advanced, digital graphics creation moved from the printer to the computer monitor. Early monitors were monochromatic and designed for text, not for graphics. Regardless, artists found ways to create art even if it was only in one color.

Most people mark 1963 as the origination of computer art, when Ivan Sutherland invented Sketchpad. Sketchpad allowed artists to use a light-pen device to work on vector images on a vector graphics display monitor. Vector graphics are lines and curves derived from mathematical formulas.

Later in that same decade, the raster image was invented and pixels came into being. A *raster* is the pattern of dots that form an image. Raster images are made up of horizontal lines of pixels, and the number of horizontal lines and the number of pixels in each line determine the resolution of the computer monitor.

The first raster images were very blocky because those early computers were not powerful enough to project very many pixels. You can see clearly the progress of raster images in the evolution of characters in games. Figure 1.2 shows a very early game character. The image is in one color and the pixels are very large. This character is only five pixels wide and five pixels high.

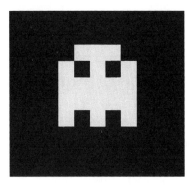

Figure 1.2
Early game characters were one color and very blocky.

The Move to Color

It didn't take long before scientists learned how to change the colors on computer monitors. Computers were still considered business or research tools, not art tools, but the artist was not to be denied. Programmers with interest in creating graphics on computers started writing programs to create computer art.

During this time another important event was taking place: The personal computer was introduced to the market. These early machines were not very powerful compared to the big mainframe systems, but they did do something that changed the face of computing forever. They put computers in the hands of millions of people, some of whom were interested in creating art. Many of these people were the ones who started writing graphics programs for the personal computer, which were the forerunners of the programs we use today.

Figure 1.3 shows another early game character. Notice that he has more pixels and different colors than the character in Figure 1.2. He is 16 pixels high and seven pixels wide.

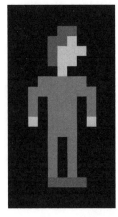

Figure 1.3
Early color game characters were limited in their number of colors.

This character has four colors. In those days many systems were limited in how many colors they supported. Some had set colors, such as the old IBM PCs. Others allowed some variations in color.

Progress was being made every day in computer graphics. With each succeeding year, systems were introduced that boasted higher resolutions and more colors. Figure 1.4 shows a game character with a 16-color variable set of colors, or *palette*. More colors meant artists could start shading their characters. Notice that the game character is starting to take on a sense of volume.

Figure 1.4
When variable colors became available, game characters started taking on a sense of volume.

In the late '80s, games were becoming more realistic, but they still looked blocky. The same thing was true for all computer art. Variable colors gave computer artists a chance to start creating more realistic digital pictures. During this time, desktop publishing was developed, the laser printer was invented, and people started to look at the computer as an art tool rather than just as a business machine.

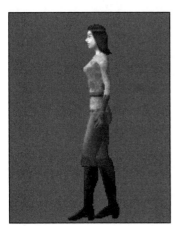

With a greater emphasis on graphics, personal computer systems entered a whole new path of evolution, bringing about better display systems and higher resolutions. The game characters went from being about 30 to 60 pixels high to around 200 pixels high, and displays went from 320×200 to 640×480 resolutions. Figure 1.5 shows a game character at about 180 pixels high.

Figure 1.5
Greater resolution meant more detail for computer game characters.

More Power Brings Better Tools

Once computers became popular for desktop publishing, the race to create better graphics tools started in earnest. Now developers had a real market for their programs because artists in large numbers were buying computers and software. This paved the way for companies such as Adobe and Corel to create software for personal PCs and sell the software directly to the general public rather than only to art-production companies.

Computer manufacturers and chip makers were intrigued by this new set of computer users. Artists wanted the fastest systems with the best graphics capabilities. They were driving the high end of computer usage and represented a substantial market for the most expensive machines.

Within a few short years the entire landscape of personal computers changed. System memory and processor speeds increased dramatically. Digital input devices, such as tablets, were developed. Computer monitors became larger. Graphics cards were developed, which gave computer systems added graphic punch. The rapid advances moved the personal computer from a tool for hobbyists to a tool for graphics professionals.

3D Makes Its Move

Three-dimensional computer art started in applications such as military simulators. The simulators were custom-built computers tied to hydraulic systems to simulate aircraft or vehicle motion. The first simulators were not photo-realistic, but they did give the trainee a feeling of being in a real environment. The advantage of these simulators was that the trainee could make mistakes without the danger of getting hurt or destroying valuable military vehicles or airplanes.

As graphic power increased, it soon became apparent that computer art could be used in both motion-picture and video-game productions. At first digital 3D art was used to augment physical models or to enhance special film effects. As time went on, however, digital 3D art started to be used more and more, until entire movies, such as *Toy Story* and *Dinosaur*, were done with computer art and no live actors.

Most of the initial 3D graphics for motion pictures were created on high-powered systems called *workstations*. These graphic workhorses were specially designed computer systems with the most powerful graphics hardware available. They were significantly more expensive than personal computers, and they ran specialized software that was also very costly. The workstation's life, however, was destined to be short-lived.

As more and more people purchased personal computers, the prices for computers started to fall. This was driven in large part by competition from computer and chip manufacturers to get computers into as many homes as possible and the fact that mass production made individual systems less expensive to build. So while personal computers were advancing daily in power and sophistication, they were also becoming more affordable. The more expensive process of building workstations had no chance of competing with the onrush of the PC.

As PCs became more powerful, high-end 3D software migrated from the workstation to the standard off-the-shelf PC. This move opened the door for computer artists everywhere to create beautiful 3D computer art.

Digital 3D art was also entering the computer and video game world. Home PC and video game consoles were rapidly gaining in power. In the mid-1990s, the video and computer game industry moved from primarily using 2D art to using 3D art for most games. Although they were very blocky at first, video games with 3D characters were readily accepted by the public. Game players liked the idea of games with 3D characters and environments.

PCs were not the only systems to advance rapidly in computing power. Video game systems were also becoming more powerful. By the late 1990s and early 2000s, game systems were capable of using almost lifelike graphics. Figure 1.6 shows a character from one of these systems.

Figure 1.6
3D characters replaced 2D characters in video games.

Figure 1.7 displays a timeline of the evolution of the game character to show how computer art has advanced over the years.

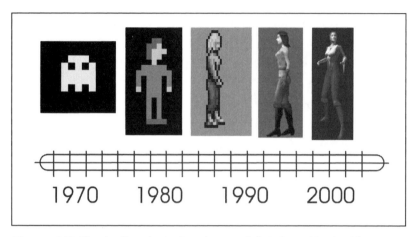

Figure 1.7 The timeline shows the advance of digital graphics in video games.

Moving forward, there are limitless possibilities for creating computer art. Many off-the-shelf PCs are powerful enough to handle complex digital composition. Software, such as Adobe Photoshop, Corel Painter, CorelDRAW, Alias Maya, Autodesk 3ds Max, and many others, has come down in price, as has hardware, effectively creating an environment that favors the artist. Artists are free to create incredible art with advanced tools, and the future looks like it will only get better for the computer artist.

2D and 3D Art

Artists use a variety of computer programs to create art for games. These programs fit into two basic categories—two-dimensional (or 2D) programs and three-dimensional (or 3D) programs. Two-dimensional programs are the easiest to understand because computer screens and video game screens are basically flat. A 2D art program directly manipulates pixels on screen. Many of these programs are very sophisticated, and some even simulate natural media, such as airbrushes, oil paints, or even watercolors.

Three-dimensional programs create virtual 3D objects used in the creation of 3D game characters and game worlds. 3ds Max is a great program for creating 3D art for games. It has a huge following with developers in the industry, to the point that almost every game artist who deals with 3D game art has to have at least a working knowledge of the program.

Because this book focuses on creating game art using 3ds Max, most of the information will relate to 3D art. However, a large part of 3D art for games is created in 2D art programs. We have included trial versions of some of these programs on the CD to help you get started.

Included on the CD for this book are several 2D programs:

- Corel Painter
- CorelDRAW Suite
- Paint Shop Pro

Hint

Take some time to explore and become familiar with the art programs on the accompanying CD-ROM. Each program is a professional tool. The better you understand these programs, the more you will gain from the projects in this book.

In later chapters, we will get into several specific exercises that deal directly with these programs. They are all programs that we use regularly in our own work, and each one is a true professional program.

Using Painting and Drawing Programs

Drawing programs go back to some of the first art programs ever created for computers. These programs are based on vector graphics and actually keep track of each line that is drawn. The CD contains CorelDRAW, which is a very powerful and complete vector-drawing program. Other good vector programs include Adobe Illustrator and Macromedia FreeHand.

Paint programs differ from drawing programs in that they are based on raster graphics rather than vector graphics. Some of the most popular painting programs are those used in photo manipulation. Photoshop is likely the most widely used paint program in the game industry. It is very powerful and has extensive tools and functions for working with photographs and art creation in general. The CD that comes with this book contains two programs that are comparable to Photoshop: Corel PHOTO-PAINT and Paint Shop Pro.

Game artists use painting programs to create 2D art for games. Two-dimensional art is often created by the artist from scratch instead of by manipulating other art or photographs. The CD that comes with this book contains a painting program—Corel Painter. This program is great for creating art. It has some very powerful features that allow you to use tools that simulate natural drawing and painting tools.

Drawing on a computer is much like drawing on paper, if you have the right hardware. I like to use a Wacom Intuos tablet. Figure 1.8 shows the Intuos tablet in use.

The tablet uses a stylus pen that weighs about the same as a pencil and feels a lot like one too. The stylus is pressure-sensitive so it reacts similarly to a real pencil. The tablet is nice because it can be held in any position, like a sketchbook.

New touch-screen technology is also available for those who want to work directly on the screen. Figure 1.9 shows the Wacom Cintiq tablet/monitor in use.

When you move the pen over the tablet, the cursor on the computer screen moves. Just as when you click with a mouse button, you can select or execute commands on the screen by touching the tip of the stylus to the tablet. Unlike the mouse, however, the stylus has a pressure-sensitive tip, which paint programs use to simulate the pressure the artist uses in drawing.

Figure 1.8 Use a tablet for digital drawing. (Photo courtesy of Wacom Technology. All rights reserved.)

Figure 1.9 New technology allows artists to draw directly on the screen.
(Photo courtesy of Wacom Technology. All rights reserved.)

If you are serious about creating art for games, I highly recommend getting a digitizing tablet because it helps make the drawing and painting process on the computer more natural. Don't worry if you don't have one, though. You can still complete the projects in the book because all of the art programs used in the projects work with a mouse.

3D Art in Games

Most video and computer games today use 3D art to create the game experience. To really understand how to create 3D art you first must understand how it is used in a game.

First of all, the image you are viewing on a TV or computer monitor is not really 3D because the display is a flat surface made up of pixels, as we discussed earlier. The images you are seeing are really pictures of a 3D game world viewed in rapid succession. In other words, the game system is processing a virtual 3D environment and creating images of the environment, which it sends to the display for viewing. It is actually a very complex process that takes a lot of computer processing power. Let's break it down a little so it is easier to understand.

The Vertex

The basic building unit of a 3D game is the vertex (or vertices for plural). A *vertex* is a single point in virtual 3D space. It has no dimension in virtual space; it is just a single point. It is in reality a location. To even begin to calculate a 3D object, the computer has to start with a location. From that location, the computer then can define other locations or vertices that define a 3D object.

The Polygon

Polygons are flat planes in virtual 3D space. Vertices make up the corners of a polygon plane. The lines that connect the vertices to make up the polygon plane are called *edges*. Figure 1.10 shows several polygons, vertices, and edges.

Because a polygon is a flat plane, it has no real thickness. It is simply a plane that indicates the joining of three, four, or many vertices. It is important to understand that polygons don't have any depth because polygons models are almost always hollow wire frames. *Wire frame* is the term used to describe a 3D model without surfaces. The wire frame consists of vertices connected by edges forming polygons. By arranging the polygons so they all connect to each other, the game artist can create what appears to be a 3D object. Figure 1.11 shows a simple human head created in polygons.

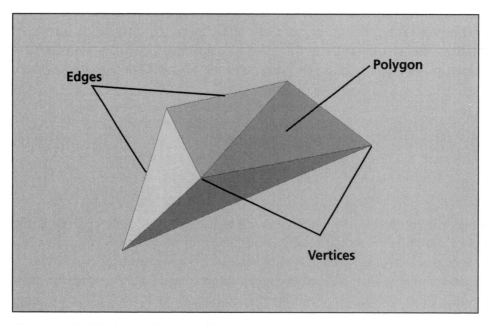

Figure 1.10 Polygons are flat planes in virtual 3D space.

Figure 1.11
Polygon models can appear to be solid.

Textures

Textures are 2D images that are applied to a three-dimensional model to give the model surface detail. In real life every surface has a texture. Sometimes the textures are only a color, while other times they might be very complex, such as the bark of a tree. Take a quick look around and study some of the many textures you see in everyday life. Figure 1.12 shows the simple polygon head from Figure 1.11 with a texture added.

Figure 1.12
A texture is added to the head model.

Figure 1.13 shows a wooden door. You could create this door using nothing more than color and geometry, but that would be an extreme waste of computer processor time that you could devote instead to more critical game needs. It would also be an extreme waste of your time. A better method would be to create the appearance of the wooden door in a 2D picture and paste that picture on a relatively simple object.

Figure 1.13
Adding a texture for the door can save processor time.

You will notice on close examination that every surface in nature has some qualities that you can fit into a few specific categories.

- Color
- Roughness
- Translucency
- Reflectivity
- Luminance

Each one of these qualities or attributes is part of what gives the surface the look and feel it has. To make a 3D model look believable in a game, the artist needs to capture the inherent qualities of the surfaces he is trying to depict by creating textures that match the surface as closely as possible. The metallic sheen of a kitchen appliance has a very different look than a weathered fencepost. The hard gray of a sidewalk is very different than the spiky look of the lawn right next to it.

Lighting and Reflections

An important part of developing realistic game environments is developing qualities and attributes you see in normal life. How an environment is lit will play a big role in how realistic that environment will look. Another important factor of an environment is its reflective nature. A shiny object should reflect what is around it.

Lighting

Lighting is used in a game to illuminate the game geometry; it is updated every frame so it simulates the real world. When designing the lighting for a game, you need to understand two important things—where and what. By where, I mean the location of the light. By what, I mean the type of light. Before you get into placing a light, you need to understand the types of lights used in games. Some of the more common lights are

- Point light
- Directional light
- Ambient light
- Colored light

Point Light

A *point light* is similar to the light given off by a light bulb. The light projects in all directions and is brightest near the source. The light from a point light diminishes with distance. Look at the light in Figure 1.14. Notice that the light gives off a strong highlight on the ball. The area around the light is brightest; the areas on the corners of the plane are darker.

Point lights are good for lighting a room or a local area outside where artificial light is used, such as a streetlamp at night.

Directional Light

Directional lights simulate the light of the sun. The sun is a bright light source that is millions of miles away. Its light rays are almost exactly parallel to each other as they hit the earth's surface. A directional light illuminates everything evenly. Look at Figure 1.15, and notice how the light on the plane is even. There is no darkening with distance from the light.

Figure 1.14 A point light is used to light a scene.

Figure 1.15 A directional light is used to light a scene.

Directional light is the most widely used light source in games because it is one of the easiest to calculate. It is also a light that you are comfortable with because you see it every day in real life. Directional light can be general, as in Figure 1.15, or it can be limited, like a spotlight. Limited directional lights are called *spotlights* or *conical lights.*

Ambient Light

An *ambient light* is a general light source that lights all surfaces in all directions. It is usually combined with a point or directional light to give a scene a more natural appearance. Ambient light is the result of light bouncing off one surface and then another. Most light in a home that comes through the windows is ambient light even when the sun is shining directly through the window. Because the nature of light is to bounce from one surface to another, shadows are not completely black. You might have noticed that the shadows in Figures 1.14 and 1.15 are almost completely black, which gives them a very unnatural look. In real life, light bounces off everything so almost all shadows have some light. Look at Figure 1.16, and notice that the shadows are much softer and the ball looks three-dimensional. The ambient light simulates the reflected light normally seen in real life.

Almost every scene needs to have some ambient light to make it look realistic. The only exception is a game set in deep space, where there is little or no reflected light.

Figure 1.16 An ambient light is used to light the shadow areas.

Colored Light

A *colored light* is not really a light; rather, it is an attribute of all the lights I have already discussed. Colored light is any light source that has a specific color. The scene in Figure 1.17 is lit with four separate colored lights. They are all point lights, but they each have a different color.

Almost every light source is a colored light. A fluorescent light is usually slightly blue, whereas a normal incandescent light bulb is yellow. The rays of the sun contain the full spectrum of light but they tend to be a little on the yellow side unless the sun is setting, in which case they can be very red and orange. When you are lighting a scene, use a light that fits the nature of the scene. For example, when you are doing an interior room, give it a slightly yellow light to simulate the incandescent light source.

Figure 1.17 Four colored lights are used to light this scene.

Reflections

A shiny surface looks shiny because it reflects its surroundings. The only way to get a true reflection on a surface in a game is to calculate it based on the angle of the surroundings and the game view, and then render the calculated image on the surface.

This usually has to be done for each ray of light; the process is called *ray tracing*. Ray tracing is impractical for much real-time game rendering because it takes up too much processor time. Some of the newer games on very high-powered systems use ray tracing in a limited form. In the absence of true reflections, game developers have come up with a few tricks that simulate reflective surfaces.

Specularity

Specularity is a surface property that helps define an object as shiny or dull. Shiny objects have well-defined highlights. These highlights are direct reflections of the light source. By placing a well-defined highlight on an object, you generally give the object a shiny appearance, even without a complete reflection.

Environment Maps

Some surfaces need more than just a specular highlight to look right. A shiny car, for example, needs to reflect its surroundings. One way developers have created the look of reflections without resorting to the time-consuming process of ray tracing is by using an environment map. An *environment map* is a texture that gets rendered onto a surface as a reflection. The texture is usually a close approximation of the environment the object is in, and it can be changed from time to time as an object moves. Figure 1.18 shows an example of an environment map.

Figure 1.18
An environment map

Rendered Reflections

Another trick for achieving reflective qualities in games is to build the reflection geometry. This method only works on flat surfaces, such as floors, but it is very effective in giving a scene a realistic reflection. Take a look at how this is done. The lamp shown in Figure 1.19 is sitting on a tile floor. There is an exact duplicate of the lamp directly below the lamp, but upside down. The floor is semitransparent so the lower model shows through the floor. The effect makes the floor look reflective and the objects move completely accurately for the reflection. This process obviously takes more polygons to create, but the effect is sometimes worth the extra geometry.

Figure 1.19
Games sometimes use actual
geometry for reflections.

Animation

Before 3D graphics became popular in games, all animation had to be drawn one frame at a time in 2D. With the advent of 3D graphics, a whole new world opened for animators. Now they could create animation in a 3D environment and view the animation from any angle. Animations became separate elements from the art, making it possible to do one animation and apply it to multiple characters.

Unlike 2D animation stored as picture files in a game, 3D graphics are stored as motion files, or they can be auto-articulated using software programs to drive the movement. Motion files can contain data on almost every attribute of a 3D model, including translation, rotation, size, color, and many others. There are basically three types of animation used in games—object animation, morphing animation, and bone animation.

Object Animation

Object animation is basically moving a 3D object model from one location to another. It is the simplest of all animations. The only thing object animation requires from the game system is computation of the object's location, rotation, and size from frame to frame. Object animation is sometimes done by the game programmers, but in many cases the artist will set up the animation in 3ds Max beforehand.

Morphing Animation

Morphing animation is mostly used for internal object movement animation where distortions of the vertices are needed, such as in facial animation for dialogue or expressions. Morphing animation is usually set up by the artist in 3ds Max and exported with the model information or as a separate morph file.

Bone Animation

Bone animation, or *joint animation*, as it is sometimes called, is the process of creating an internal object or character animation based on a system of bones and joints that make up a skeleton. Bone animation is by far the most complex of the three basic types of animation and is used for animating characters in games.

When setting up bone animation, the artist creates a skeleton for the model and then attaches the vertices of the model to the skeleton in a process called *rigging*. When a bone is pivoted on a joint, the attached vertices move with the bone. Vertices can often have more than one influencing bone. When more than one bone influences a vertex, it divides the movement between the two or more bones based on the percentage of influence from each bone.

Game AI

Game *AI*, or *artificial intelligence*, can mean a lot of things in game development, but for this chapter we will simply use it to refer to the game code that controls where and how environments, objects, and characters are displayed. In other words, games are controlled by a complex system of software. This software determines what the player sees at any given time during the game. It also reacts to any input from the player.

Bringing Everything Together

A lot things have to work together perfectly for even a single frame of a 3D game to be displayed. To get some perspective, think of it in these terms. A single setting in a game contains as many as 70,000 polygons. Each of these polygons has at least three vertices. Even if many of these vertices are shared, there could be as many as 100,000 vertices—or, in other words, specific virtual space locations. All of these virtual space locations have to be tracked by the game system, not just once but several times every second. Many of the most popular games run at 60 frames per second. That means that in one second of game play, the system is tracking six million vertices. But it doesn't stop there.

In addition to simply keeping track of all of these vertices, the system has to apply textures to each polygon. These textures have to be mapped to the polygons so that they stay in place. Every polygon in the game has either a color or a texture applied to it. Sometimes these textures have more information than just a picture. They might have multiple layers containing information about transparency, bump, specularity, diffusion, and other attributes. So the game is tracking complex textures on 70,000 polygons 60 times every second. But it doesn't end there either.

Everything in the game has to react to light. Every polygon not only needs to have a texture, it has to have lighting. Many games have multiple light sources and dynamic lighting that moves during the game. So not only does the game system have to track lighting on a polygon from one light source, it also has to calculate the effect of multiple light source effects on all polygons. But even then we still are not done.

At any given time in the course of the game, there is a significant chance that the view will change and elements in the view will be in motion. In other words, the game system has to track and calculate the new positions of all the vertices, polygons, textures, and lighting every frame. In addition, some elements are animating or moving independently of the view. Not only does the game system have to track where the moving objects are within the view, it also has to actually calculate those movements via the game AI as it reacts to whatever the player's input might be. Are you still with me?

All these game calculations have to be completed 60 times every second. Once everything is calculated, the scene can then be rendered to the display. Okay, let's think about the display, which is made up of individual pixels. During the rendering process every individual pixel has to be given information on brightness and color. If a game is running at 1024×768 resolution, it means that for every frame, brightness and color information has to be delivered to 786,432 individual pixels. That is more than 47 million deliveries every second of the game.

Are you beginning to see why 3D games are so complex? Can you see why a very powerful computer system is required to run 3D games?

Why is this so important to the artist? Well, understanding what it takes to display even a single frame of a 3D game will help you to plan and execute your art in such a way that you will be able to get the most out of the game you are creating. Because even the most powerful game systems have a limit on the number of calculations they can process at any given time, you have to set limits on the number of polygons, textures, lights, and animation processes. Sometimes these limits may vary. For example, you might have a need for a lot of specialized lights in a particular part of your game. To keep the frames running smoothly, you can reduce the number of polygons and textures in that area. Figure 1.20 shows the steps in the process of displaying a 3D game.

I think it is important for you to understand that this is only an overview of what it takes to run a 3D game. The entire process is actually much more complex. We haven't even covered things such as particle effects and physics models. The purpose of this whole chapter is to help you get a feel for the complexity and overall scope of creating a 3D game.

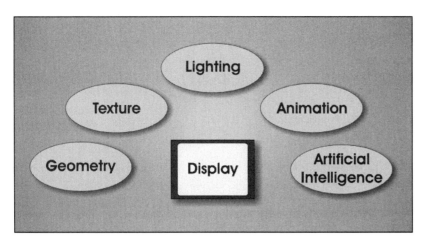

Figure 1.20 Displaying a 3D game takes many steps.

Summary

This chapter has been an overview of 3D art as it relates to games. In this chapter, we covered several important points.

- Displaying art in games
- The history of computer art
- 2D and 3D art programs
- Components of 3D models
- Textures on 3D models
- Lighting of 3D models
- Animation of 3D models
- Rendering 3D models to pixels

The 2D art programs used in this book are contained on the CD that accompanies the book. The programs include

- Corel Painter
- Paint Shop Pro
- CorelDRAW

Now that you have finished this chapter, you are ready to move forward and start to create great game art. Your only limitations will be those imposed by the game system and your own knowledge and talent. As you grow in your abilities, you will find a wonderful and rewarding world of creative expression. Your opportunities are limitless. Welcome to the world of game art in 3ds Max.

Questions

1. What are the small dots of colored light that make up the display of a game called?
2. We live in a world made up of mostly what kind of light?
3. What type of game was around before even the pixel was developed?
4. Who do many mark as the first inventor of computer graphics?
5. Why did many of the first computer games have very blocky graphics?
6. What did the advent of the personal computer do for computer artists?
7. When did the race for better graphics tools start in earnest?
8. What were the first uses of 3D computer art?
9. What are the two basic types of computer art programs?
10. How are drawing programs different than painting programs?
11. What is the advantage of a digitizing tablet?
12. What is a flat plane in virtual space called?
13. How can game artists give polygon models surface detail?
14. What type of light gives off a general illumination of all 3D geometry in a scene?
15. What is the surface property that helps to define a surface as shiny or dull?

Answers

1. Pixels
2. Reflected light
3. TeleType
4. Ivan Sutherland
5. The processors were slow.

6. It gave them their first chance to create computer art.

7. When computers became popular for desktop publishing

8. Military simulators

9. 2D and 3D

10. Drawing programs use vector graphics, whereas painting programs use raster graphics.

11. It lets the artist use a stylus like a pen.

12. A polygon

13. Apply a texture to the geometry

14. Ambient light

15. Specularity

Discussion Questions

1. Is the understanding of the origin of computer art important to the modern game artist?

2. Are 3D games more fun than 2D games? Why or why not?

3. What advantages do 3D games have over 2D games?

4. What makes 3D games so complex?

5. Why should an artist understand the complexities of 3D games?

Exercises

1. Create a chart showing the evolution of computer games from their beginning until now.

2. Calculate how many polygons could be used on a game system that can display 100,000 textured polygons per second.

3. Develop a production plan for your favorite 3D game system showing how many polygons you plan to use for the characters and environments.

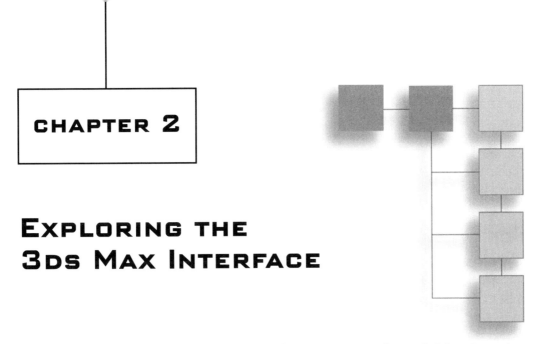

CHAPTER 2

EXPLORING THE 3DS MAX INTERFACE

One of the biggest challenges in any complex program, such as 3ds Max, is getting a grasp on where to find things, how to understand what they mean, and how they are named using the interface. But before you explore the Max interface, let's talk about what an interface is.

Early interfaces used to be referred to as GUIs (pronounced *gooey*) or Graphical User Interfaces. A GUI can be defined as a computer program that makes it possible for a person to communicate or interface with a computer through the use of symbols, visual metaphors, and pointing devices. Because a computer uses something called "machine language" (the elemental language of computers, consisting of a string of zeroes and ones), something was needed for the average person to interface with a computer in an easy-to-understand format. The earliest of these GUIs appeared in 1983 on the Macintosh. In 1985 Macintosh introduced the first GUI, which came to be known as Windows. This operating system also allowed users of DOS-based systems, or personal computers (PCs), the same capabilities as Macintosh users in terms of interfacing with the computer. Everything you see, use, or hear on the computer is using some type of interface that allows you access to the machine language of the computer. (The machine language is that deep, dark abyss of ones and zeroes that few people understand, unless they are computer programmers.) But that is another story.

What we will attempt to do in this chapter is explore the interface that you can use to access all the various commands in 3ds Max that allow you to create 3D art and animation.

3ds Max is a very powerful 3D art and animation tool. It is used by professional motion picture artists and animators to create many of the amazing 3D images, animations, and scenes used in movies and video games.

The trick for you, the artist, is to create and present these models, animations, and scenes seamlessly so the viewer does not realize he is viewing something scripted and created on a computer.

Familiarizing Yourself with the 3ds Max Interface

The first step to starting with any program is understanding the program and its interface. We are using 3ds Max as the 3D program for this book, so now you'll take a brief look at some of the menus, locations, and commands you will need to use to create visually stunning and believable models and animations.

The first look at the 3ds Max interface can be a little overwhelming. The sheer number of menus and icons seems endless, and it would take volumes of books to explain every feature in the program. Don't worry right now about learning every feature. The step-by-step instructions in this book are designed to help you understand a few of the features of the program that you need to create each project. As you work with 3ds Max, I hope you will become familiar with the features and come to love 3D modeling as much as I have. See Figure 2.1 for a visual representation of where many of the tools you will be using as you read this book are located.

Here is a brief explanation of some of the features of each of the tools shown in Figure 2.1.

- **Main menu bar.** This menu bar includes the following menus:
  - **File.** A standard Windows menu with typical open, close, import, and export functions.
  - **Edit.** Another standard Windows menu that contains duplicates of many of the main toolbar commands.
  - **Group.** This menu includes commands for managing combined objects.
  - **Views.** This menu includes commands for setting up and controlling the viewports.

- **Create.** This menu includes commands for creating objects.
- **Modifiers.** This menu includes commands for modifying objects.
- **Character.** This menu includes tools for working with bones, linked structures, and character assemblies.
- **Animation.** This menu includes commands for animating and constraining objects.
- **Graph Editors.** This menu includes graphical access to editing objects and animation.
- **Rendering.** This menu includes commands for rendering and for the environment.

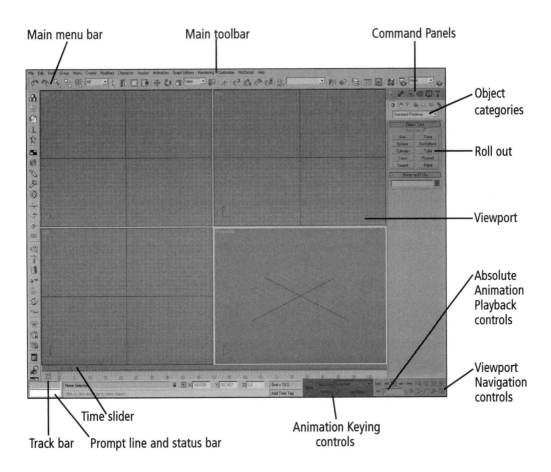

Figure 2.1 The 3ds Max window

- **Main toolbar.** This toolbar houses a collection of graphical shortcuts that you can easily find without using the main menu bar.

- **Command Panels.** These panels give you access to modeling and animation functions, such as:

  - **Create.** This panel contains all object creation tools, such as cubes and toruses.

  - **Modify.** This panel contains modifiers and editing tools for objects.

  - **Hierarchy.** This panel contains linking and inverse kinematics parameters used for animation.

  - **Motion.** This panel contains animation controllers.

  - **Display.** This panel contains object display controls, allowing the user to hide and freeze objects for easier modeling.

  - **Utilities.** This panel contains miscellaneous utilities.

- **Object categories.** This list includes such categories as Shapes, Lights, and Cameras.

- **Rollout.** This is where all the options are stored for the Object categories.

- **Viewport.** This is where you view and work with your scene.

- **Time slider.** This slider allows you to, when animating, scrub the animation back and forth, indicate a frame, or pick a frame to work on.

- **Track bar.** This bar indicates which frame the animation is on.

- **Prompt line and status bar.** These provide a quick reference for you, usually indicating which tool's icon you have rolled over, as well as display properties.

- **Animation Keying controls.** This section includes animation key controls and filters.

- **Absolute Animation Playback controls.** These controls play the animation forward and backward, and allow you to move frame by frame.

- **Viewport Navigation controls.** These include controls that allow you to perform such tasks as magnifying, rolling the camera, and panning or sliding the scene side to side.

Exploring the 3ds Max Interface in Greater Depth

Now we're going to take a more in-depth tour of the 3ds Max interface and try some of the available tools you will be using as you read this book.

You can begin by changing your four-pane viewport to a single viewport Perspective viewing mode (my preferred way of modeling). Right-click in the upper-left corner of any viewport over the panel indicator heading, and a new submenu will appear, as shown in Figure 2.2.

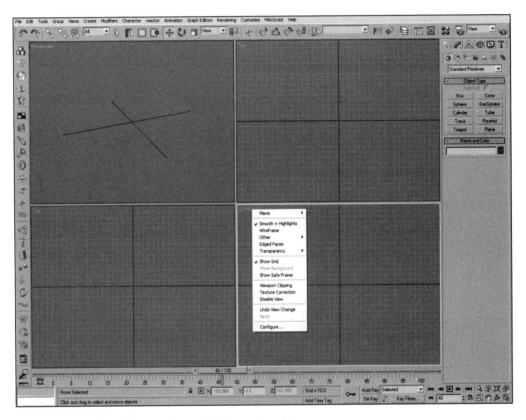

Figure 2.2 Right-click over the panel indicator heading.

Click on Configure in the submenu and in the Viewport Configuration window, click on the single-pane window icon (see Figure 2.3).

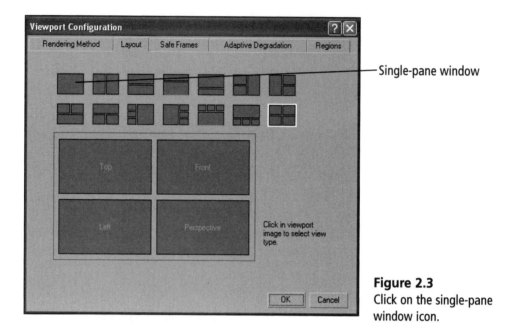

Single-pane window

Figure 2.3
Click on the single-pane
window icon.

Right-click in the large single pane and make sure that Perspective is checked, as
shown in Figure 2.4. Then hit Enter.

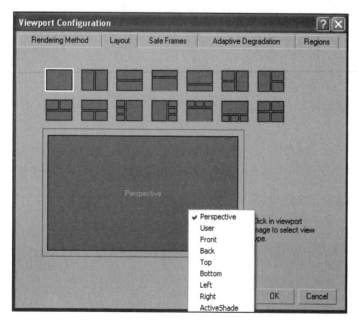

Figure 2.4
Select the Perspective option.

Your interface should now look like Figure 2.5.

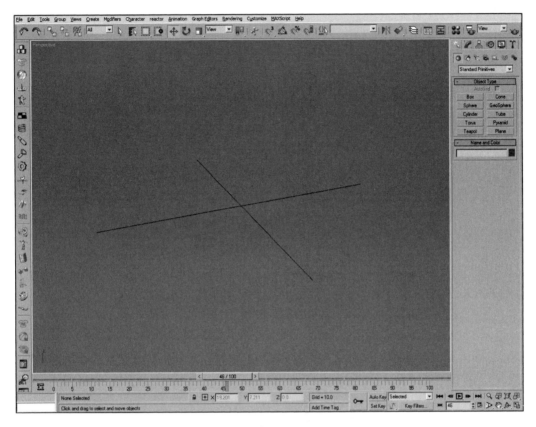

Figure 2.5 Reconfigure the viewports to a single Perspective viewport.

Note

You can set up your view-screen interface in any manner you want. I suggest experimenting and trying different settings to see which one works best for you.

Exploring the Command Panels

The Command Panels in the upper-right side of the interface provide a common area where most modelers find the tools for the majority of their basic modeling techniques. Most commands in this area are also located in the main menus. Using the Command Panels is easier because you can locate the tools you need using icons and symbols, which give you a quick reference.

Using the Create Tab

Begin by creating a primitive. Click on the Create tab in the Command Panel, as shown in Figure 2.6.

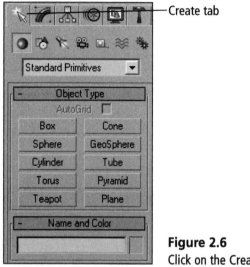
Create tab

Figure 2.6
Click on the Create tab.

Next, click on the Box icon, and then click in the viewport and drag to create the box in one direction. Then release the mouse button and pull out the box in another direction (see Figure 2.7).

Note

Create several boxes and notice that each time you create a new box, it appears as a different color.

These boxes you have created are called *primitives*, and they are used to start building models in 3ds Max. They basically give you a starting point. Experiment with the other icons on the Create tab and see what kind of primitives you can create. One way to focus on a particular primitive is to use the Select tool located on the main toolbar, select a primitive, and hit the Z key. This will focus in on the primitive selected.

Right-clicking on an object brings up a marking menu. When you select either the Move, Rotate, or Scale option, you can move the object using its respective tool selection to move it in space, as opposed to moving the camera around the object.

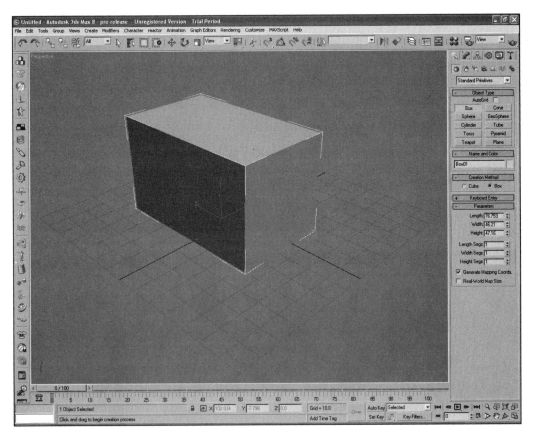

Figure 2.7 Create a box primitive.

Note

You can continue to make primitives until you right-click or select one of the Move, Scale, or Rotate tools.

You'll notice that these boxes are shaded. It is difficult to see the geometry contained in these boxes (in other words, vertices, segments, and polygons) without changing the viewing mode. Right-click on the word Perspective in the viewport, and then select Wireframe, as shown in Figure 2.8. Your objects should now look like the ones in Figure 2.8.

You can move the camera inside the viewport to take a look at these primitives from different angles. Use the middle mouse button to pan from side to side. Use the middle mouse button scroll feature to move in closer, or use the middle mouse button and the Alt key at the same time to rotate the camera around the scene.

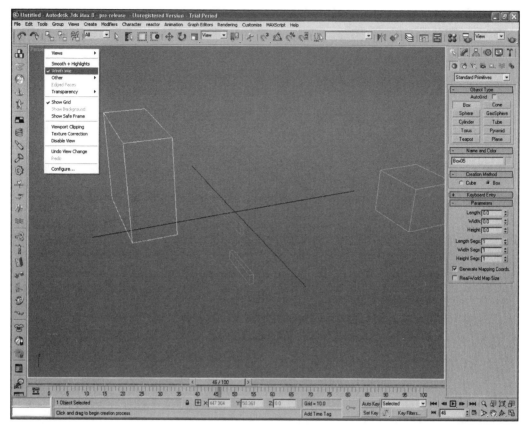

Figure 2.8 Select Wireframe to display objects in Wireframe mode.

There are also corresponding icons in the Viewport Navigation controls in the lower-right portion of the interface that allow you to effect the same controls.

To move around the interface using a three-button mouse, you can

- Use the middle mouse button scroll feature to move in, magnify, or roll the camera out and away.

- Hold down the middle mouse button and move the mouse side to side to pan the camera from side to side.

- Hold down Alt and use the middle mouse button to rotate the camera around the scene.

Using the Modify Tab

Next I want to talk about the Modify tab, located just to the right of the Create tab (see Figure 2.9).

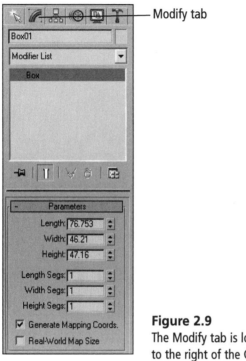

Modify tab

Figure 2.9
The Modify tab is located just to the right of the Create tab.

On this tab, you'll see all kinds of useful information about each of the box primitives you created, including the length, width, and height of each object, as well as the length segs, width segs, and height segs. The "segs" define how many segments or lines are in each box. Try entering some different numbers in the boxes or using the up or down arrows in the Parameters boxes to obtain different results.

Now go to the File menu and select New (or press Ctrl+N). Don't save any changes. In the New Scene dialog box, select New All, and then press Enter for your next exercise.

Create a box anywhere in the scene. By using the Modify panel and the Selection tool, you should have a box that has exactly the same dimensions, vertices, segments, and location as the one shown in Figure 2.10.

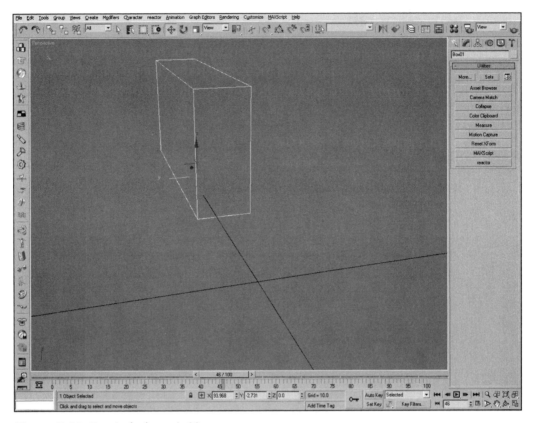

Figure 2.10 Here is the box primitive.

Return to the Create tab, and in the Parameters area, enter the values you see in Figure 2.11.

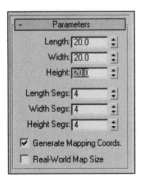

Figure 2.11
Enter values in the Parameters area.

You should have a box that looks like the one shown in Figure 2.12.

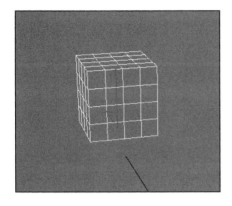

Figure 2.12
Enter the specific values in the Parameters
area to create a box like this one.

Now right-click on the box, and when the menu appears in the viewport, scroll to
the Move command and click on the small box next to it. Then enter the information shown in Figure 2.13 in the Move Transform Type-In dialog box.

Note

You can also access the Transform Type-In dialog box from the Tools menu or by pressing F12.

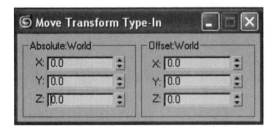

Figure 2.13
Enter information in the Move
Transform Type-In dialog box.

This centers the box in the world and on the grid. You box should now look like
Figure 2.14 and be located on the grid.

Right-click on the box again, choose Convert To from the menu, and select
Convert to Editable Poly (see Figure 2.15). This will allow you to edit as well as
select the type of editing you can do to the box.

Note

If you repeat this step again, you will see that Convert to Editable Poly is now highlighted in blue,
indicating that it is effective.

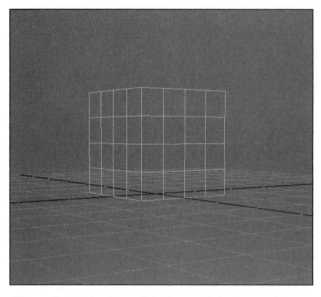

Figure 2.14 Your box will be located in its new position on the grid.

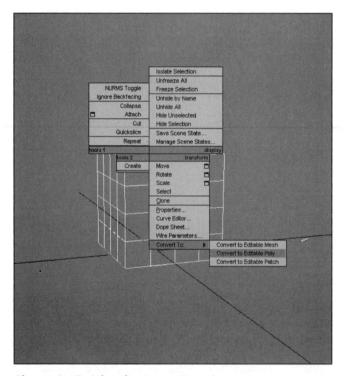

Figure 2.15 Select the Convert To options menu.

You'll notice that the menu has changed—a lot of new information has changed in the Modify panel. In addition, if you place your pointer over the Modify panel in the spaces between the buttons, you will also see that a hand appears, thus indicating that you can move the panel up and down, revealing more options by clicking over the area and dragging the hand up and down (see Figure 2.16).

Figure 2.16
The Modify panel has new information and new menus.

Working with the Subobject Mode Selection Tools

The next features I want to introduce to you are the Subobject Mode Selection tools. These are the primary tools used for modeling geometry. Put your mouse pointer over each of these in the highlighted area shown in Figure 2.17 and see which elements of the polygon they affect.

Figure 2.17
Hover your mouse pointer over the Subobject Mode Selection tools.

The tools include:

■ **Vertex.** A vertex is the smallest editable object in a polygon. It represents a point in space where you have two vertices between which you can draw a line, creating an edge. Selected vertices are shown in red (see Figure 2.18). You can select them one at a time or drag to draw a marquee around a section of vertices.

Note

The marquee will also select the faces on the other side of the polygon. If you rotate the camera around the object, you can observe this.

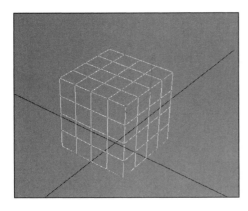

Figure 2.18
Selected vertices are shown
in red on your screen.

- **Edge.** An edge is formed by two connecting vertices. Selected edges are
  shown in red (see Figure 2.19).

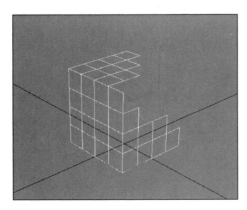

Figure 2.19
Selected edges are also
shown in red on your screen.

- **Borders.** This tool allows you to select all edges around a hole in the geometry.
  The Shrink and Grow buttons located below the icon are available for all
  subobjects (see Figure 2.20).

Figure 2.20
The Shrink and Grow buttons
are below the Borders icon.

- **Polygon.** A polygon is formed when three or more edges are joined, making a polygon, also commonly known as a *face*. There are several polygons on each side of this cube, which you can see in Figure 2.21.

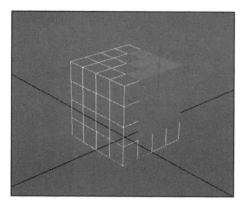

Figure 2.21
There are several polygons
on each side of the cube.

- **Element.** An element is the entire combined object, containing vertices, edges, and faces (see Figure 2.22).

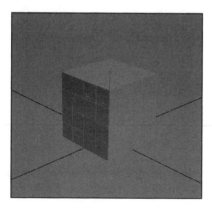

Figure 2.22
An element is the entire combined object.

This concludes our explanation of the basic building techniques for modeling. Next you'll find out how to add some textures and detail to make your work look finished.

Texturing

Texturing is the art of placing pictures or textures on a set of polygons or elements using a materials file to give the illusion that there is more geometry than there actually is. It also adds a great deal of detail and character to the model. You extend the realism of materials by applying textures to control surface properties, such as bumpiness, opacity, and reflection. The geometry used in video games is enhanced with texture maps. You can use almost any image file, such as one you might create in a paint program, as a map.

In Figure 2.23, the model on the left uses the default shaders, whereas the one on the right has the textures turned on.

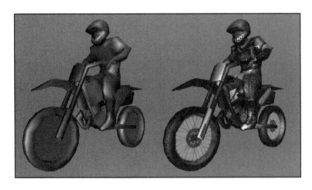

Figure 2.23
Here you see examples of
non-textured and textured models.

Now let's try a simple texturing technique. Right-click on the word Perspective in the upper-left window and choose Smooth + Highlights. Your box should now look shaded, as in Figure 2.24.

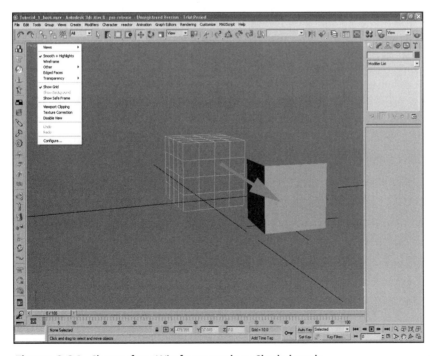

Figure 2.24 Change from Wireframe mode to Shaded mode.

Next, select your box using the Element tool and click on the Modifier List down arrow on the right side of the screen. Scroll down until you find the UVW Map option and click on it (see Figure 2.25).

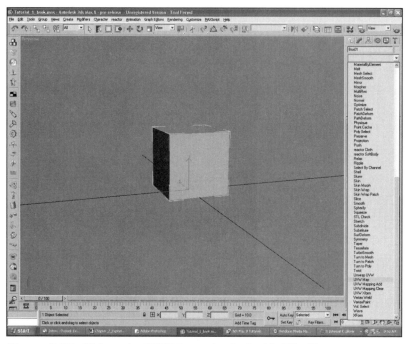

Figure 2.25 Click on the UVW Map option in the Modifier List.

Now click on the Utilities tab or the Hammer icon in the Command Panel, then click on the Asset Browser and select the file named tile.bmp (located on the CD-ROM that came with this book). Close the viewer. Next, drag the picture onto the box. Your box should now appear with the picture on it, similar to the example shown in Figure 2.26.

Now return to the Modify tab. Click on the Box radio button in the Parameters section, and you should have a box that looks like the one shown in Figure 2.27. Clicking on the Box button applies the texture to each of the six faces of the box in a uniform manner.

Try experimenting with the different radio buttons to see what effect they have on the cube.

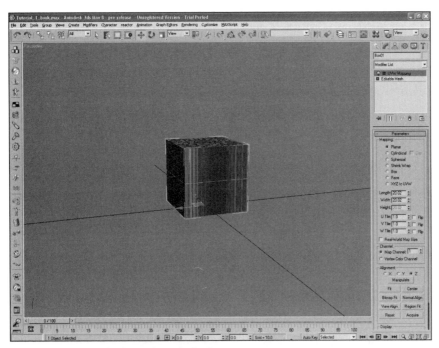

Figure 2.26 Apply the texture to the box.

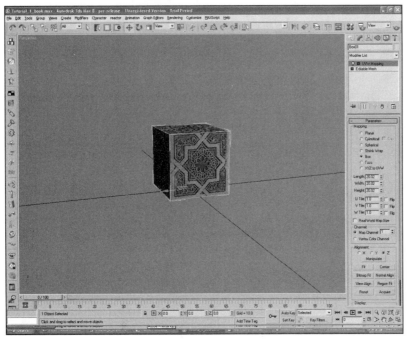

Figure 2.27 Select the Box radio button.

Animation

Next you'll take a brief tour of the animation tools available in Max.

Start by opening up a new scene. Set it up to view the Top viewport. You can set this view by pressing the T keyboard shortcut.

Next, create a floor for a ball to bounce on. Click on the Box icon in the Command Panel and make a box with a length of 50.0, a width of 100.0, and a height of 0.5. Leave the rest of the settings at their defaults. Now change to the Right viewport and create a ball with a radius of 30.0 and the segments set to 30. If you're not in Smooth + Highlights mode, switch to that now. You should now a have a scene that looks similar to what you see in Figure 2.28.

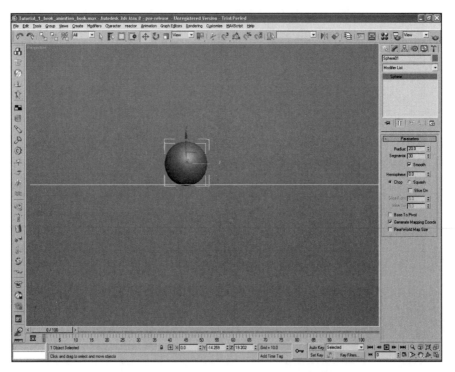

Figure 2.28 Create, scale, transform, and locate the ball primitive in the new scene.

Now you can move the ball up in preparation for its fall and consequent bounce. Change to the Right viewport and right-click on the ball. Using the Move dialog box, move the ball to the following coordinates (see Figure 2.29):

X=0.0, Y=130.0, Z=100.0

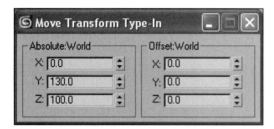

Figure 2.29
Enter the location in the dialog box.

The ball should now be transformed to the position shown in Figure 2.30.

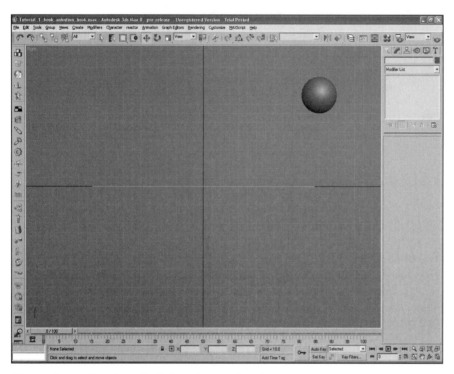

Figure 2.30 Transform the ball to the new location.

Confirm that you are on frame 0 and press the Set Key button on the lower portion of your interface. The slider bar will turn red, indicating that it is ready for key framing. Now hit the Set Key Frame icon (represented by a picture of a key), and a key frame should appear in the track frame (see Figure 2.31).

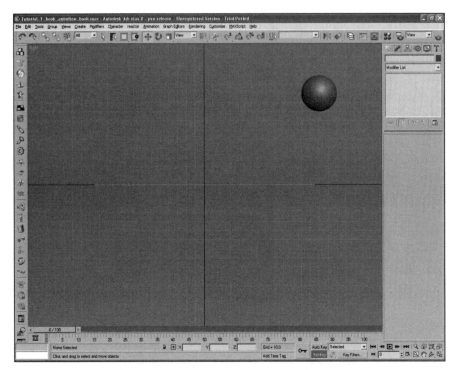

Figure 2.31 Use the Set Key function.

Now move the time slider to frame 30. Transform the ball to X=0.0, Y=42.0, Z=20.0, and press the Set Key button.

Now move the time slider to frame 16. Transform the ball to X=0.0, Y=66.0, Z=60.0, and press the Set Key button.

Move to frame 100 and transform the ball to X=0.0, Y=180.0, Z=80.0. Press the Set Key button.

If you play back the animation it looks very strange; it doesn't look like the ball is really bouncing. This is because 3ds Max is calculating the positions in a linear manner—from point A to point B in a straight line. It is up to you to add character and realism to the scene.

Note

You can play back the current progress of your animation at any time by pressing the Play button in the Absolute Animation Playback controls.

Now continue to set the frames as follows:

- Frame 1: X=0.0, Y=130.0, Z=100.0
- Frame 7: X=0.0, Y=93.0, Z=82.0
- Frame 16: X=0.0, Y=66.0, Z=60.0
- Frame 30: X=0.0, Y=42.0, Z=20.0
- Frame 50: X=0.0, Y=42.0, Z=78.0
- Frame 65: X=0.0, Y=−90.0, Z=90.0
- Frame 100: X=0.0, Y=−180.0, Z=44.0

You should now have an animation that is beginning to look more believable (see Figure 2.32).

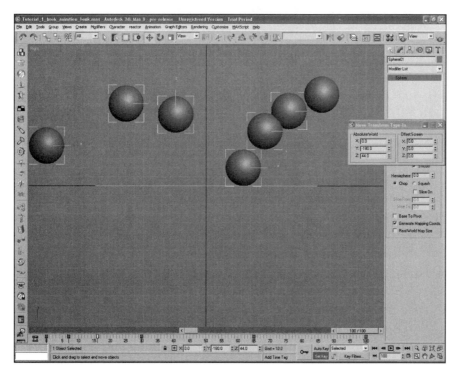

Figure 2.32 The ball has a series of key frames set.

Let's add some deformation to the balls in order to add to the realism. Go to frame 30, select the ball, and scale it to 60.0 in the Y axis. Transform the ball down so that the bottom of the ball hits the top of the floor. And, of course, press the Set Key button. At frame 40, reset the Y axis to 100.0. Because you don't want the ball to deform until it hits the floor, move to frame 27, scale the Y axis to 100.0, and press the Set Key button. At frame 40, rotate the ball in the Y axis to −126.0. Now if you play the animation, it looks like an old rubber ball bouncing on the floor (see Figure 2.33). You now have enough information to clean up the animation and adjust it to your liking. Try experimenting with different settings, key frames, and deformations on the ball.

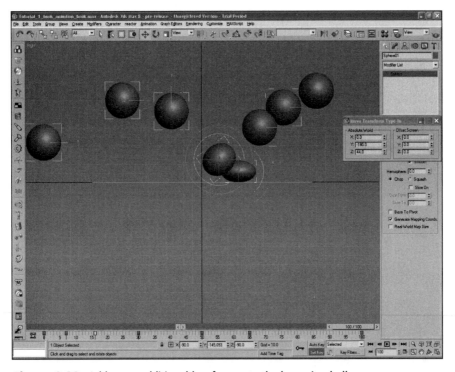

Figure 2.33 Add some additional key frames to the bouncing ball.

Summary

This chapter has been an overview of the 3ds Max interface. In this chapter, we covered several important points.

- Exploring the 3ds Max interface
- The Command Panels
- Texturing
- Vertexes, borders, edges, polygons, and elements used in 3ds Max
- Animation

These very basic exercises were designed to help you get a feel for the 3ds Max interface. As you progress through this book, you will learn more techniques and commands to build on as you make your own models.

Questions

1. What is a primitive?
2. How do you increase or decrease a selection?
3. How do you switch from Wireframe mode to Shaded mode?
4. What does GUI stand for?
5. Why must you use an interface to communicate with a computer?
6. What is texturing and why is it used in video games?
7. How do you start a new scene in 3ds Max?
8. How do you create a primitive?

Answers

1. An object used to start building a model in 3ds Max
2. By using the Grow or Shrink option in the Command Panel
3. Right-click in the viewport and select the type of view you want from the menu.
4. Graphical User Interface
5. A computer uses machine language and only understands ones and zeroes.
6. Texturing is the art of placing of pictures or textures on a set of polygons or elements using a materials file to give the illusion that there is more geometry than there actually is.
7. Select File, New from the main menu bar (or press Ctrl+N).
8. Use the Create tab and select one of the primitives, and then click in the viewport.

Discussion Questions

1. Why is it important for modelers to be good artists?
2. Why is it important for animators to be good observers?

3. How might you increase the realism of models in video games by using additional textures?

4. Without primitives, how would you start to build a model?

5. Why does it take a great deal of time to make animations believable?

Exercises

1. Try selecting different parts of geometry and using various move, scale, and rotate functions to see what you can make.

2. Try texturing a model that you make from any of the primitives you have modified.

3. Try the various views in the viewport and see what they do.

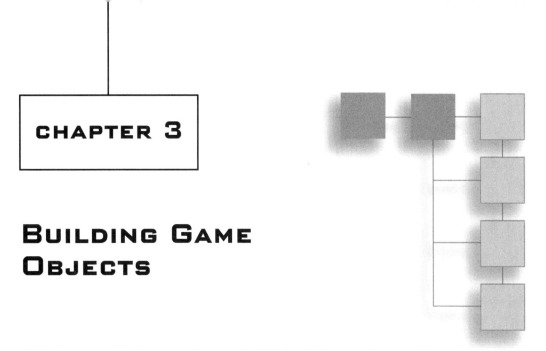

CHAPTER 3

BUILDING GAME OBJECTS

This chapter will show you how to build simple low-polygon objects that we will use to build a scene in Chapter 5. You will then use some very basic mapping techniques to add some textures to the objects. But you'll start by making an old rusty oil barrel.

When you start a new scene, there is nothing in the virtual world to work with. The first thing you need is a starting point. 3ds Max provides a number of primitives, which you can shape and alter. You'll notice in the Create panel, located in the Command Panel, there are several choices under Object Type. Try them out and see how they react in the viewports when you click and drag with the left mouse button. You might notice that it takes two clicks to make any of the primitives. One direction allows you to set the width, and another allows you to set the height. You can watch the specifics of the parameters in real time as you create them in the viewports. Sometimes you'll eyeball what you want, and other times you'll want to make things in a specific width and height.

Building an Old Oil Barrel

Now you can start building some objects to populate your world by building an old oil barrel, similar to what might have been used during World War II.

1. In the Command Panel, click on the Create tab and then click on the Cylinder Primitive button.
2. Starting in the Top viewport, click and drag to any width.

3. Observing in the Left viewport, drag the depth of the cylinder to approximately what a barrel might look like (see Figure 3.1).

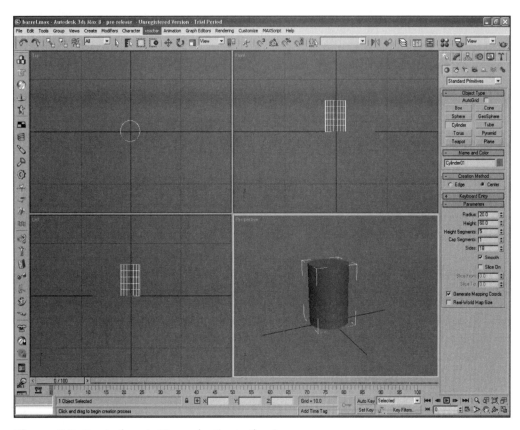

Figure 3.1 Create the primitive and estimate the size.

4. In the Parameters box, set Radius to 20.0, Height to 60.0, Height Segments
to 15, Cap Segments to 1, and Sides to 18, as shown in Figure 3.2.

5. Next to the Create tab in the Command Panel is the Modify tab. Click on
it to open it up. You will still see the same Parameters box that was in the
Create panel when you made the cylinder primitive.

6. Converting the model to an Editable Mesh is the next step. In any of
the viewports, right-click on the model. In the marking menu, select
Convert to, Convert to Editable Mesh. You will notice that the menu in
the Command Panel will change significantly, as shown in Figure 3.3.

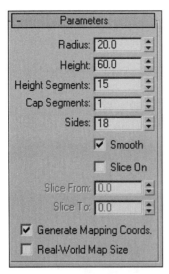

Figure 3.2
Define the primitive specs in the Parameters box.

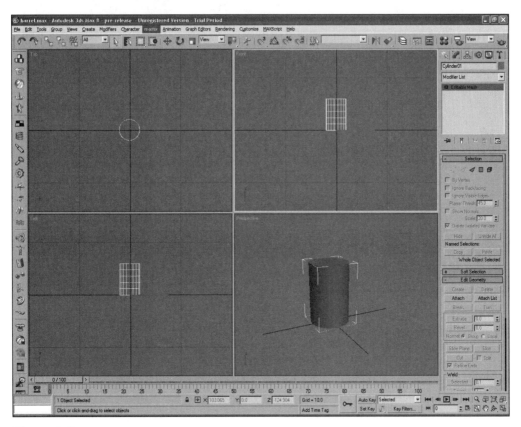

Figure 3.3
Convert the model to an Editable Mesh and notice the menu change in the Command Panel.

Note

Step 6 does not do the same thing as selecting Convert to, Convert to Editable Poly, which was mentioned in Chapter 2.

You might also notice that when you right-click on the model, you'll have additional options in the marking menus that were not previously available (see Figure 3.4). A *marking menu* is another interface that allows easy access to the same commands you find elsewhere in the other menus.

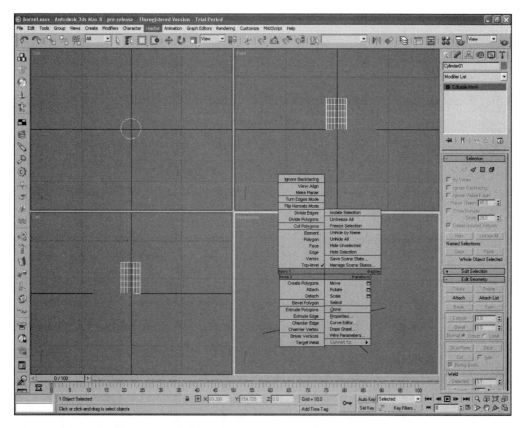

Figure 3.4 Right-click on the model to view the new, additional menus.

7. With the barrel selected, press the Z key. This will focus in on the selection—in this case, the barrel—in all the viewports.

8. Select Vertices from the marking menu.

9. Using the left mouse button, drag and make a selection box around several vertices (see Figure 3.5). You'll notice that the vertices turn red when they are selected.

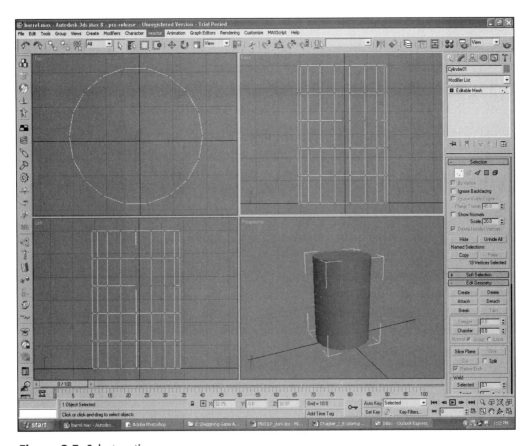

Figure 3.5 Select vertices.

If you rotate the model in the Perspective view, you'll notice that you have selected all the vertices in the back.

10. If you look in the Selection panel under the Modify tab, you'll see a check box that, when checked, allows Ignore Backfacing. Click to select that button.

11. Now try selecting vertices in the Side or Front viewport. You'll notice that you can only select the faces that face toward you—or "face the camera," as it is more commonly referred to. The camera is the interface that allows you to look at virtual space.

12. Above the Ignore Backfacing check box, there are five selection identifiers. They match the ones you bring up in the marking menus. Try using these various buttons. Select various components in the model and see what they do.

Referring back to Figure 3.4, you'll also notice that when you right-click on a selection, the marking menu gives you an option to move, rotate, or scale. You'll concentrate on these tools in this exercise.

13. Select Move, Rotate, or Scale. You'll notice that a gizmo appears (see Figure 3.6). This gizmo allows you to move, rotate, or scale your selection in one axis or all of the axes in the virtual space.

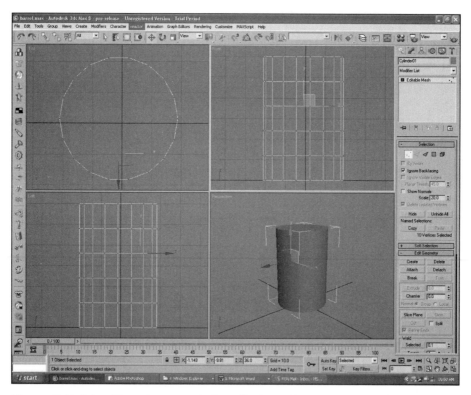

Figure 3.6 Select Move, Rotate, or Scale to display a gizmo.

If you move your cursor over one of the arrows or axes on the gizmo, you'll notice that gizmo highlights let you know you have an option at that point to make a change with the respective tool. If you select the gizmo in the Z axis, you move or scale things upward or downward along the Z axis. To scale in all axes, you need to select the yellow gizmo in the center (see Figure 3.7).

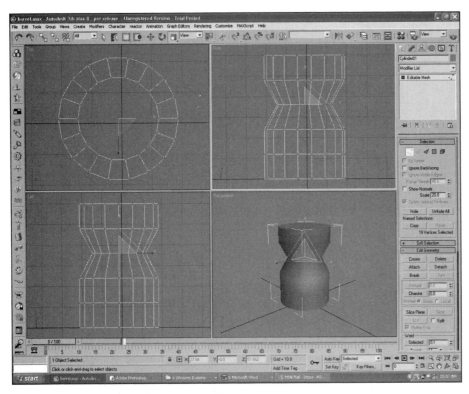

Figure 3.7 Select the yellow gizmo in the center.

Try experimenting with these options and get a feeling for what they do. It might seem odd at first, but before long you'll be doing these things without even thinking about them.

14. Using the Move tool, move the vertices so they look similar to Figure 3.8.

15. Next, using the Scale tool, shape the vertices to look like Figure 3.9.

    Now you have your barrel shaped. That's all there is to it. Now all you're missing is a texture.

16. In the Command Panel, click on the Utilities tab and open up the Asset Browser. Find the texture Oil_Barrel.bmp. Drag the icon for Oil_Barrel.bmp onto any of the viewports and over the barrel. And there you have it—the barrel textured (see Figure 3.10). This is a quick and simple way to model noncomplex objects and texture them. Of course, you must plan out your model and textures well in advance to make this work.

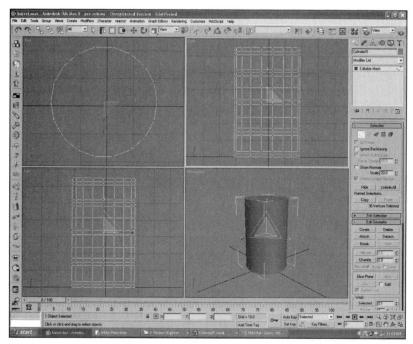

Figure 3.8 Move the vertices into position.

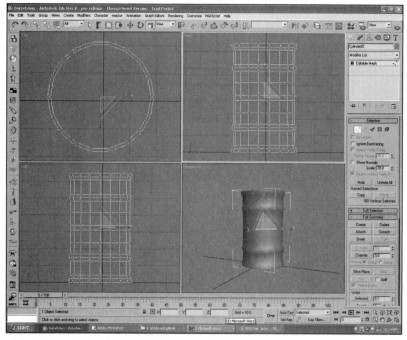

Figure 3.9 Scale the vertices.

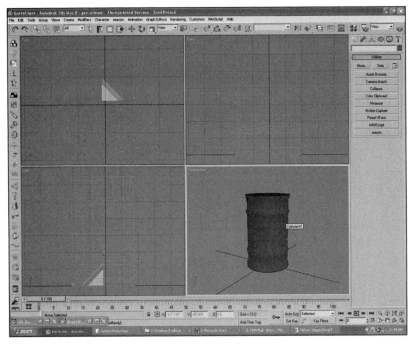

Figure 3.10 Now you have a finished barrel.

17. Save your scene as Barrel.max.

Building a Wood Crate

Next you'll build a simple wood crate.

1. Reset 3ds Max by selecting File, New from the main menu. In the New Scene submenu, select New All and click OK. This clears 3ds Max and allows you to start over with nothing residual in the new scene.

2. Use the Create menu to create a box with the following specifications:
   - Length: 50.0
   - Width: 50.0
   - Height: 50.0
   - Length Segs: 5
   - Width Segs: 5
   - Height Segs: 5

   I turned off the grid in each viewport by pressing the G key in each one (see Figure 3.11).

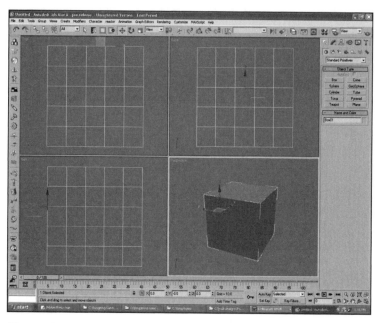

Figure 3.11 Create a primitive box.

3. Using the Vertex Move tool, slide the second-from-the-top row of vertices up with the top row of vertices in the Front viewport. Slide the second-from-the-bottom row so it aligns with the bottom row of vertices in the Left viewport. Move the two middle rows to the outside rows of vertices in the Top viewport (see Figure 3.12).

4. Now select each of the inner faces and move it slightly toward the middle of the box (see Figure 3.13). I changed to Wireframe view for clarity.

Note

You can change to Wireframe view for clarity in any viewport by placing your cursor over the title of a viewport, right-clicking to bring up a menu, and then selecting Wire Frame.

5. You will notice some faceting, or overlapping faces, in the Perspective Shaded view. This is because when you moved the vertices up, you overlapped some faces. You can fix overlapping faces by welding adjoining vertices (see Figure 3.14). At the bottom of the roll-down menu in the Edit Geometry box, there is a box called Weld. Inside that box is a button called Selected. Select all the vertices in the box. Leave the defaults and click on the Weld button. Notice the change in the Perspective view. This will make the box much cleaner and will fix any overlapping faces and duplicate vertices.

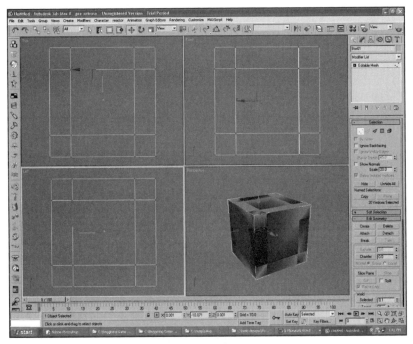

Figure 3.12 Move the vertices into position.

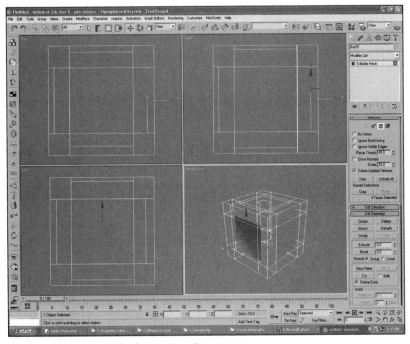

Figure 3.13 Move the faces inward.

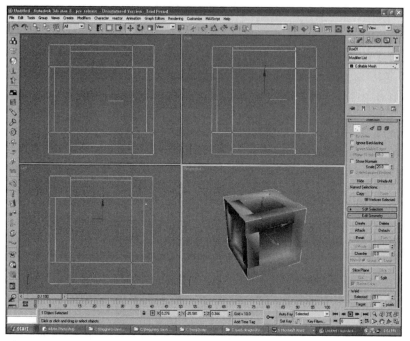

Figure 3.14 Weld the vertices.

6. Using the Asset Browser, assign the Wood_Crate.bmp texture to the box. You'll notice that this texture did not turn out quite as clean as the barrel (see Figure 3.15). That is because when you changed the location of the faces and welded them, you moved the UV coordinates. But you can easily clean this up.

7. In the main menu, select Modifiers, UV Coordinates, Unwrap UVW. In the Modifier, expand Unwrap UVW and select Face.

8. Select all the faces in the box, as shown in Figure 3.16.

9. In the Map Parameters section, select Box. Then, deselect to view the changes (see Figure 3.17).

10. Save your model as Crate.max.

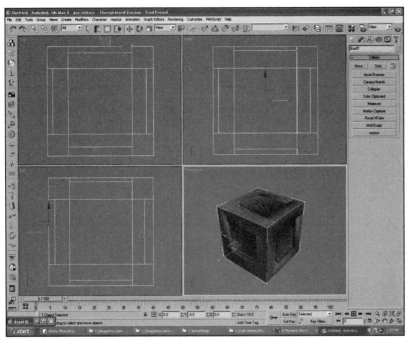

Figure 3.15 Apply Wood_Crate.bmp to the box.

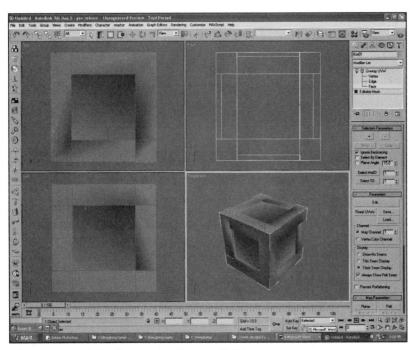

Figure 3.16 Select faces using Unwrap UVW.

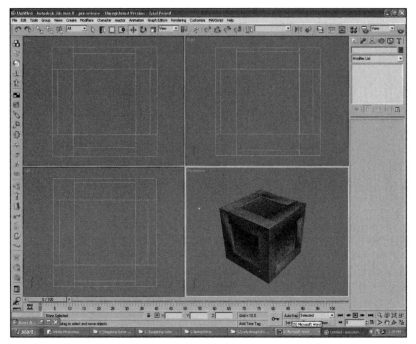

Figure 3.17 Now you have a finished crate.

Creating the Hangar

Next, you'll create a simple airplane hangar with an open door.

1. Using the Create menu, create a box with the following attributes:
   - Length: 50.0
   - Width: 50.0
   - Height: 40.0
   - Length Segs: 4
   - Width Segs: 4
   - Height Segs: 1

2. Shape the box to look like the example in Figure 3.18.
3. Using the Asset Browser, apply Hangar.bmp to the box (see Figure 3.19).
4. Select four faces on the front of the hangar, as shown in Figure 3.20.

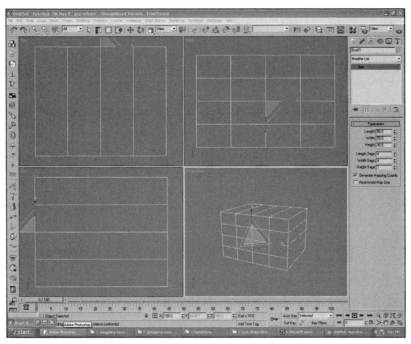

Figure 3.18 Shape the box.

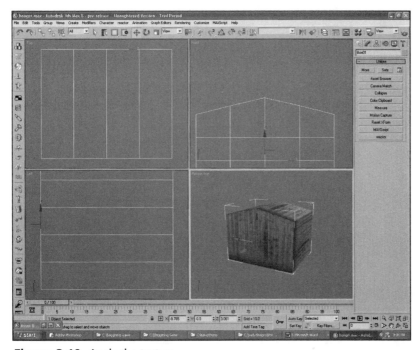

Figure 3.19 Apply the texture.

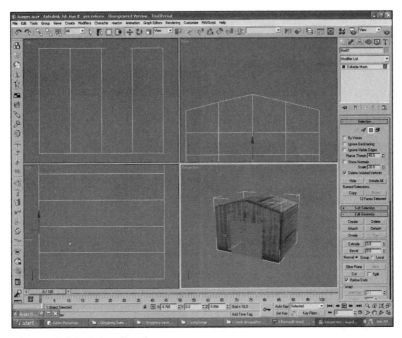

Figure 3.20 Select four faces.

5. Now delete those four faces, as shown in Figure 3.21.

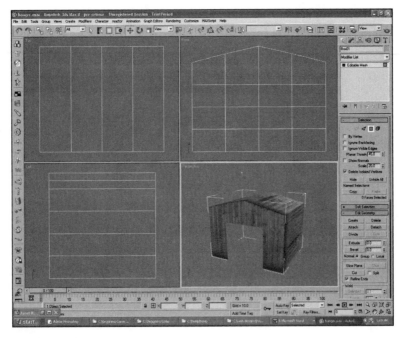

Figure 3.21 Delete the faces.

6. Do the same with the polys at the bottom of the hangar, as shown in Figure 3.22.

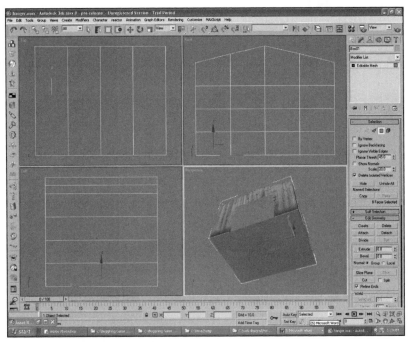

Figure 3.22 Select and delete these faces.

7. Making sure you don't have the Face Select option on, assign Unwrap UVW to the hangar. Apply the Box mapper in the Map Parameters section, and click on the Align Y button. You model should look like Figure 3.23.

You might notice if you look through the doors of the hangar that there appears to be no faces in the back of the hangar. However, when you rotate around the object, you observe that they are there. This is because the faces are being culled, or not rendered to the camera. This is very common in video games.

8. Often you will have to build double-sided faces in objects to see the inside from the outside. To do this, you first need to collapse the Unwrap UVW modifier in the Command Panel. Click the Collapse All button and, when prompted, select Yes.

9. Select Edit, Clone from the main menu bar.

10. Select Copy and click on Yes. This duplicates the hangar.

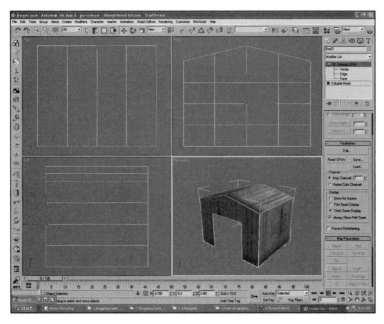

Figure 3.23 Your model should now look like this one.

11. Next, make polygons selectable and select all the polygons in the duplicated model (see Figure 3.24).

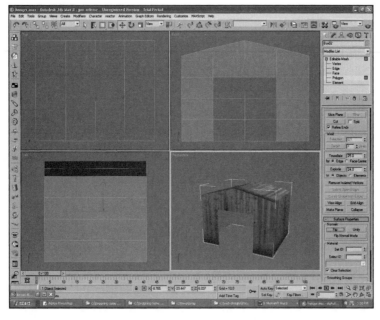

Figure 3.24 Select the faces.

12. In the rollout menu under Surface Properties, click on the Flip button. This reverses the normals on the duplicated model. Because you now have two models—one normal and the other turned inside out—you can see the inside of the hangar from the outside (see Figure 3.25).

13. Save your model as Hangar.max.

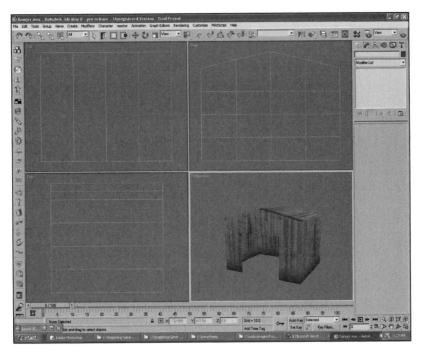

Figure 3.25 Reverse and deselect the normals.

Making Trees

Now you can make some simple trees for our scene.

1. Reset 3ds Max and start with a new scene.

2. Create a plane in the Left viewport with the following attributes:

- Length: 10.0
- Width: 6.0
- Length Segs: 1
- Width Segs: 1

3. Move the plane to the zero position and apply the Pine.tga texture to it (see Figure 3.26).

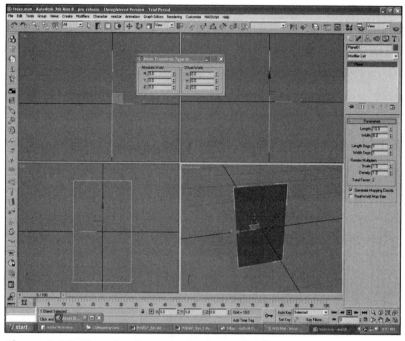

Figure 3.26 Move the plane primitive into position.

4. Using the Asset Browser, find the texture pine.tga. Open the Material Editor by pressing the M key and drag pine.tga from the Asset Browser to the first round ball or material sample.

5. Using the Asset Browser, locate pine1.tga.

6. Open the Map dialog box in the Material Editor and drag pine1.tga to the Opacity box.

7. Next, choose Edit, Clone and make a copy of the plane.

8. Convert the plane to Editable Poly and flip a face. Make sure it is visible on both sides before moving to the next step.

9. Make sure you have both elements selected, and choose Group, Group from the main menu to combine them into one object.

10. Using the Transform menu, rotate the new copy 45 degrees in the Z axis (see Figure 3.27).

11. Now group all the planes again. Clone and then rotate the duplicate 90 degrees.

12. Group them all again and, in the Command Panel, name the object pine_tree (see Figure 3.28).

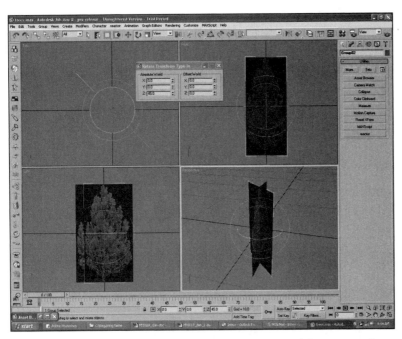

Figure 3.27 Move the plane primitive into position, and then group, clone, and rotate it.

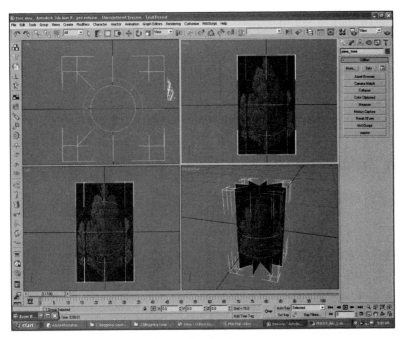

Figure 3.28 At last—you have a finished tree!

13. Save your model as pine_tree.max.

Summary

This chapter has been an overview of some very simple modeling and texturing techniques. In this chapter, we covered several important points.

- Setting up and modeling primitives
- Editable Mesh versus Editable Poly
- Marking menus
- The Ignore Backfacing option
- Textures on 3D models
- Gizmos
- Unwrap UVW modifiers
- Flipping normals
- Combining models
- Cloning

Questions

1. How many types of primitives are there in the Create panel?
2. Where is the Modify tab located?
3. What does pressing the Z key do?
4. Where do you find and select textures?
5. How do you reset 3ds Max for a completely new scene?
6. Name one way to fix faceting or overlapping faces.
7. When making a building, how can you see the inside from the outside?
8. What does the Group command do?

Answers

1. Ten, located under the Create Primitives tab
2. Next to the Create tab in the Command Panel
3. Focuses in on a selection
4. In the Asset Browser
5. Choose File, New from the main menu.

6. By welding overlapping faces together

7. By building double-sided faces

8. Makes different objects into one object

Discussion Questions

1. What other options does Unwrap UVW allow?

2. Where can you edit faces and vertices in Unwrap UVW?

3. When cloning objects, what is the difference between a copy and an instance?

4. When texturing an object, what do cylindrical, spherical, planar, and box mapping do?

5. Why do they call a gizmo a gizmo?

Exercises

1. Try adding some trim to the hangar.

2. Create your own texture for the barrel and apply it using some of the different mappers.

3. Add the words "Dangerous Materials" to the wood-crate texture and observe what happens when you apply it.

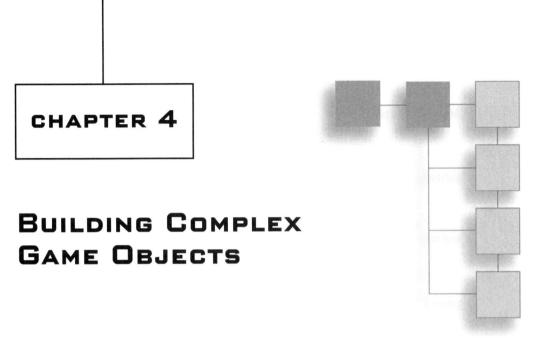

CHAPTER 4

BUILDING COMPLEX GAME OBJECTS

This chapter will show you how to build a complex object using several different primitives and techniques. I don't intend to give you an error-free lesson; rather, I will guide you through some of the pitfalls you might encounter when building complex game objects, as well as show you techniques you can use to create stunning models. You will be armed with enough information to make your game models acceptable for programmers and game platforms.

This chapter will deal with building complex game objects. It will cover the following topics:

- How to set up the airplane scene
- How to create an airplane fuselage, radiator housing, spinner, wings, and landing gear
- How to clean up the airplane model
- How to mirror the geometry to finish building the airplane
- How to texture the airplane

Modeling a P-51 Mustang Airplane

In this section you will create the exterior of a classic airplane, the P-51 Mustang. You'll use primitive objects and modifiers to create the parts. Viewport background texture bitmaps will act as reference guides to help you shape your model.

Setting Up the Scene

If you haven't already, start with a new scene and save it as Mustang. One of the first things you want to do before you set up any complex scene is to have some sort of drawing or sketch to start with. The more accurate the drawing, the easier it is to model professionally. Next, build reference planes in the three axes. This allows more accurate modeling and saves time. I have three orthographic sketches of a generic P-51 Mustang on the CD in the back of this book, ready for you to use. You can start by setting up your patterns using planar polygons.

To create a reference plane, follow these steps.

1. From the Create menu, choose Standard Primitives, Plane. Click and drag an area in the Top view and create a plane that has a length of 400 and a width of 400. Length Segs and Width Segs should each be set to 1.

2. From the Main toolbar, choose the Move tool.

3. On the status bar, set the position values in X, Y, and Z to 0. This places the pivot point on the world origin and centers the pattern plane. Press the Z key to frame the plane in the viewport.

Now apply a reference image:

1. Turn on Smooth + Highlights.

2. Click on the Utilities tab and open up the Asset Browser.

3. Search for the Top view of the Mustang sketch and drag and drop it on the top reference plane you just created.

Now create two additional reference planes for the side and front profiles. Repeat the procedure you just finished to create additional reference planes based on the Front and Left views. The width and height of these planes should reflect the sizes of the reference images that will be assigned to them. Therefore, the reference plane you build in the Front view should be 134 in length by 400 in width, and the reference plane you build in the Left view should be 134 in length by 400 in width. Notice the lengths and widths are the same. When you are finished, you should have reference planes that look like the ones in Figure 4.1.

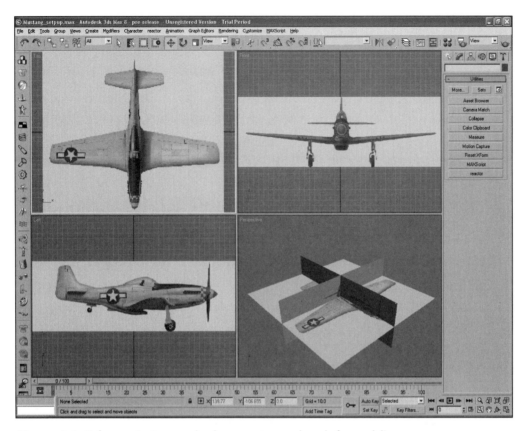

Figure 4.1 Reference textures and polys are set up and ready for modeling.

Once the reference planes are in place, you should freeze them to avoid accidentally moving them around.

1. Right-click one of the reference planes, open the submenu, and choose Freeze Selection.

2. Save your file as Mustang _01.max. It is important to save often. I generally use a numerical system to designate saved objects. You can use whatever works best for you.

Note

The Save dialog box includes a button labeled with a plus sign that you can use to easily increment the save number.

Creating the Fuselage

You can use many different modeling approaches to build the fuselage. For now, follow these steps to create the fuselage using a primitive cylinder.

1. In the Front viewport, draw a cylinder from top to bottom, approximately the length of the fuselage. You can view your progress in the Left viewport.

2. Right-click on the cylinder and set the Absolute values in X, Y, and Z to 0. This places the cylinder on the world origin and centers it. Press the Z key to frame the plane in the viewport.

3. On the Modify tab in the Parameters rollout, set the Height Segments to 10, the Cap Segments to 1, and the Sides to 18. This is a good place to start. You will be editing these as you go. If you change the Left viewport to Wireframe, you can view the segments and polygons that make up the cylinder.

4. Continue to move and scale the cylinder until you have an element that looks like Figure 4.2

5. In the Name and Color rollout, type **fuselage**.

Now would be a good time to save your project. Press Ctrl+S to save the scene.

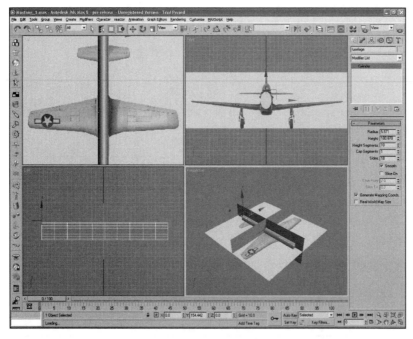

Figure 4.2 Now you have the cylinder with Height Segments of 10, Cap Segments of 1, and Sides of 16.

Shaping the Cylinder into a Fuselage

Next you'll change the cylinder profile so it begins to take shape and resemble a fuselage.

1. Activate the Left viewport and make sure the fuselage is selected.

2. Press the Z key. You'll zoom in on the cylinder and frame it in the Left viewport. You'll need this to perform some sub-object editing to the vertices that make up the wing.

3. Right-click on the cylinder and choose Modifiers, Mesh Editing, Edit Mesh from the menu bar. This allows you to perform sub-object editing to the vertices that make up the fuselage.

4. Change the Left viewport to Smooth + Highlights.

Note

You can also turn on Edged Highlights to help see the faces.

5. In the Selection rollout, click the Vertex button. Observe the cylinder in the Left viewport with vertex selection on (see Figure 4.3). Each tick you see is actually a vertex. When you want to select and move vertices, you need to drag a selection window around them. Otherwise, you will only select one vertex, rather than all of them. Then you can use the Move, Rotate, and Scale commands to shape the vertices.

Figure 4.3 The vertices appear as blue ticks at the intersections of the polygons of the cylinder.

6. Draw a selection window around a set of vertices (see Figure 4.4).

Figure 4.4 Selected vertices are displayed in red. You can add to your selection by holding down the CTRL key and dragging around other vertices.

Note

If you click on a selected vertex using the ALT key, the vertex will be deselected.

7. Using the Left viewport, select vertices and use the Move and Scale tools to shape your object to look similar to Figure 4.5.

8. Now continue in the Top and Front viewports until you have an object that looks like Figure 4.6. Don't worry about the main wing or horizontal stabilizers at this point. You will create those later in this chapter.

9. Save your model as Mustang_02.max.

Figure 4.5 You can see the modeled cylinder in Left viewport.

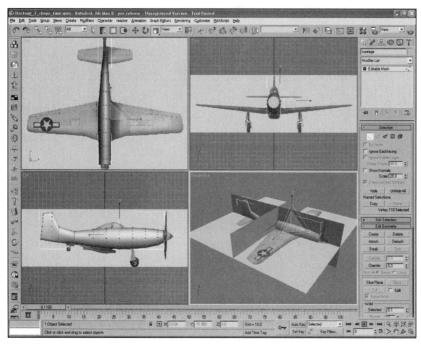

Figure 4.6 The molded cylinder is starting to take shape.

Completing the Fuselage

One common way of modeling is to cut the model in half (or remove or delete half the geometry on one side of the model) and, once the model is roughed in, clone it, rescale it, turn it inside out, and then reattach or weld it. This reduces your modeling time by working on one side at a time, and it makes your model fully symmetrical during the final stages of completion.

View the rear of the model in the Perspective viewport, and notice the tail section has one large poly that is used to cap the original cylinder, highlighted in green (see Figure 4.7). Now you need to weld the vertices around this section, centering them for your next operation—cutting the model in half.

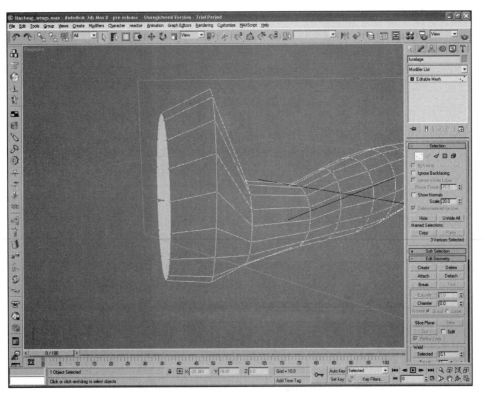

Figure 4.7 You can see the end cap used for the original cylinder.

1. Select two end vertices, corresponding to each other, on either side of the cap and side (see Figure 4.8).

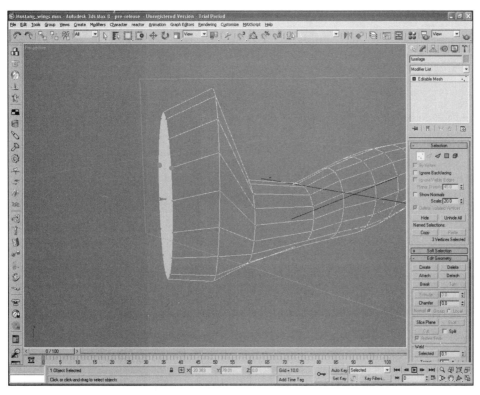

Figure 4.8 Select corresponding vertices.

2. In the Modify panel, under Weld, turn your tolerance up (in the box next to Selected) to 100. Then click the Selected button to weld the two vertices together. This merges two or more vertices into one. Continue doing this until the cap is welded and you have one nice seam down the middle of your model (see Figure 4.9).

3. In the Top viewport, select half of the polygons on the left side of the fuselage and delete them (see 4.10).

4. In the Left view, you need another row of polygons to shape the vertical stabilizer. Change to Polygon mode and select the Cut option in the Command Panel.

5. In the Modifier panel, under the Geometry option, click the Cut button. Place the cursor over the top segment until a plus sign appears and then click with left mouse button.

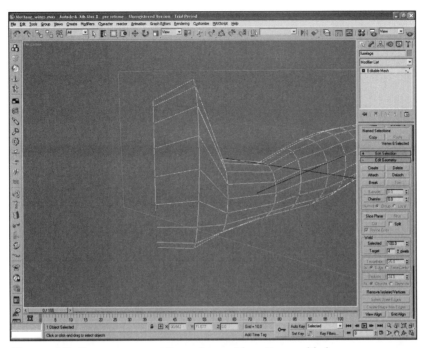

Figure 4.9 Here you can see the end cap with vertices welded with a single seam down the middle.

Figure 4.10 This model has deleted polys.

6. Continue down the stabilizer in the middle of each segment, being certain to click on every segment as you go. As you pass each segment, you'll notice the cursor changes to a plus sign. This lets you know when you have a legitimate place to cut. It is important that you don't miss a segment, or you'll end up creating odd geometry, holes, or stray vertices in your model that you must clean up later.

7. Continue down the rudder to the bottom of the fuselage. Press the Esc key or right-click to finish the cut. You will now notice you have just cut the faces of the polygons you clicked on. I've changed to Wireframe for clarity in Figure 4.11.

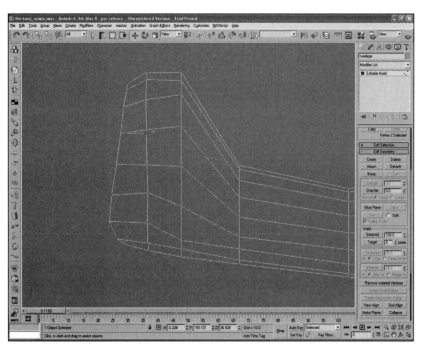

Figure 4.11 You can see the cut face in the vertical stabilizer.

8. Continue shaping the rudder, moving vertices and cutting faces where you feel it is appropriate. Change from Wireframe to Shaded mode frequently to check your work.

Sometimes your work will look fine, as it does in Figure 4.12. But moving around in the other viewports, you might notice that some of your work is behind the working plane and hidden in the Left viewport.

Figure 4.12 Some vertices are behind the working plane and look fine when viewed from the side.

9. In a case such as this, you can simply go to the Top viewport and move the tail vertices over so they are visible in the Left viewport, rather than hidden behind the working plane. You can then move them where you want them in relationship to the pattern (see Figure 4.13).

10. As you progress, you might find you need to reduce vertices or make two into one. In this case, select Target Weld and drag a vertex to the target vertex until a plus sign appears (see Figure 4.14). Release the mouse, and the two vertices will be welded into one.

11. Continue working on the vertical stabilizer, taking care not to move any of the vertices in the center of the model where you deleted the selection. Move around the model often using the Perspective viewport. This makes for very professional-looking models.

12. Take several good looks around your model (see Figure 4.15). Views down the length of a model often reveal vertices that are out of position.

Figure 4.13 The vertices have been moved to the visible area in front of the working plane.

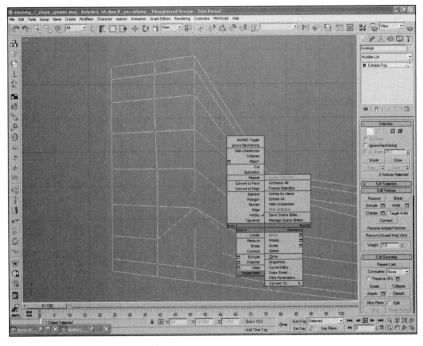

Figure 4.14 Drag and weld vertices.

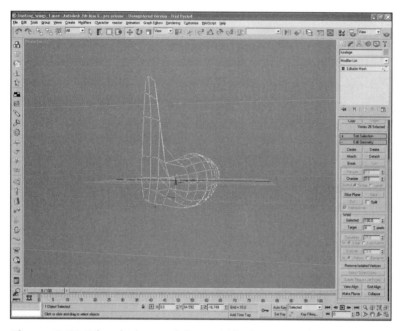

Figure 4.15 Take a look around the model in the Perspective viewport.

The structure I came up with is displayed in Figure 4.16.

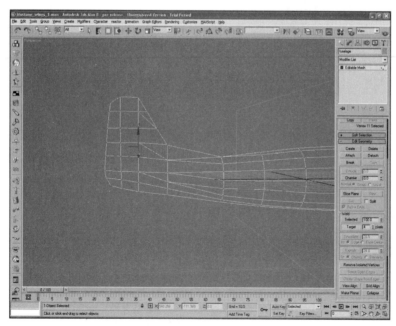

Figure 4.16 Here is a view of my stabilizer.

When I viewed the model in Shaded mode, I noticed I had some holes in my model—or, more to the point, I had some polys missing from my model (see Figure 4.17).

Figure 4.17 My geometry is missing faces.

13. 3ds Max has an option that allows you to rebuild missing polys. Right-click on your model and choose Create Polygons (see Figure 4.18).

14. In any missing face, click on any vertex. After the plus sign appears, click around each vertex in the missing poly and back to the one you started with. It should take a total of five clicks to complete the poly. You might notice, as I did, that nothing seems to happen. You probably built a poly with the normal pointing away from the camera. You can confirm this by rotating around the model and seeing the poly from the back side. Select the face again, and then click the Flip button, located in the Modify panel under Surface Properties. This will reverse the poly normal to the correct direction (see Figure 4.19).

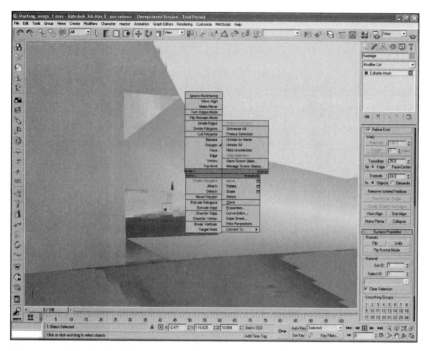

Figure 4.18 Scroll to the Create Polygons menu.

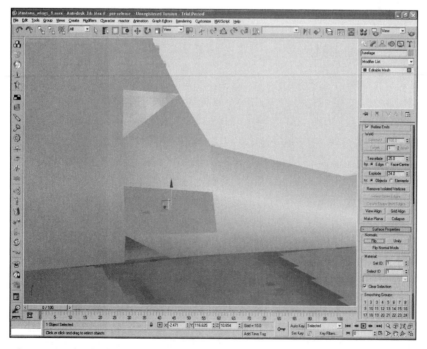

Figure 4.19 The face normal is reversed.

15. If you move back from the model, you will notice some strange or hard-looking edges in the faces you just filled in using the Shaded mode (see Figure 4.20). Again, there is a solution for this. In Element mode, select the model. There is a Smoothing Groups tool near the bottom of the Command Panel. Click the Auto Smooth button, which will smooth normals in the entire model in a uniform manner (see Figure 4.21).

16. Save your model as Mustang_03.max.

Figure 4.20
Notice the faces with hard edges.

Figure 4.21
The model was smoothed using the Auto Smooth button.

Creating the Radiator Housing

To create the radiator housing, you will use a version of the extrude function called Inset. The most common way of extruding faces is to use the Extrude button. However, in this case it creates some unwanted geometry.

1. Using the pattern for your guide and switching to Polygon subobject mode, select the three faces in the area of the radiator housing (see Figure 4.22).

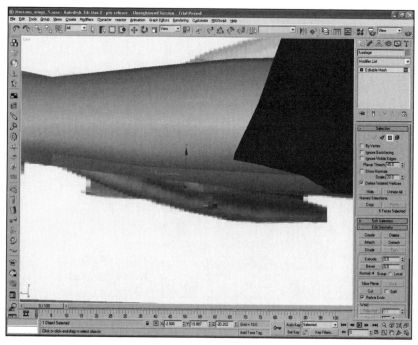

Figure 4.22 Select the polygons.

2. Right-click on the model and choose Convert to, Convert to Editable Poly from the menu (see Figure 4.23). (This is different than using Convert to, Convert to Editable Mesh, and it brings up different commands in the Command Panel.) Under the Edit Polygons rollout in the Command Panel, find the Inset button and click on the submenu button to the right of it. This will bring up another submenu.

3. Set the Inset amount to 0 and select Apply. Using the Move tool, move the newly created polys downward (see Figure 4.24). It is also beneficial to switch to Shaded mode during this phase, if you so desire.

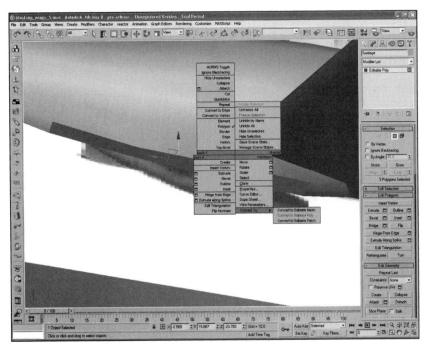

Figure 4.23 Choose Convert to Editable Poly from the menu.

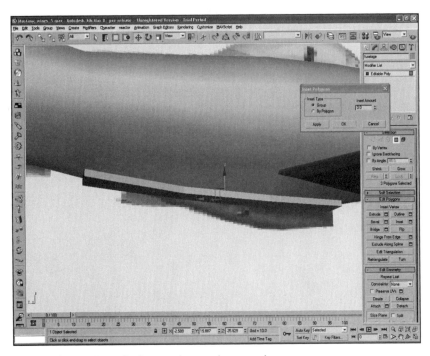

Figure 4.24 Move the inset polygons downward.

4. Repeat the process (see Figure 4.25).

5. Select the poly in the lower-front portion of the housing you created and repeat the process again, pulling this poly forward (see Figure 4.26).

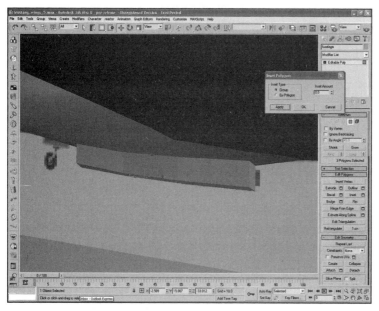

Figure 4.25 Repeat the Inset command.

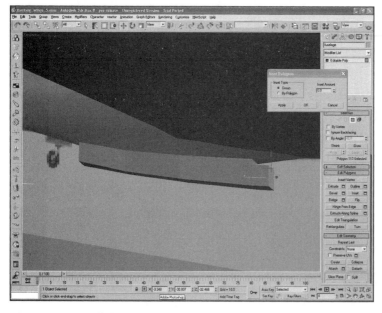

Figure 4.26 Pull the poly forward.

6. Now, using the methods discussed earlier, shape the radiator housing to your liking (see Figure 4.27).

7. If you rotate the model and view it from the back side, you will notice some polys facing inward from the polys you just extruded using the Inset tool (see Figure 4.28). These need to be deleted, so select and delete them (see Figure 4.29).

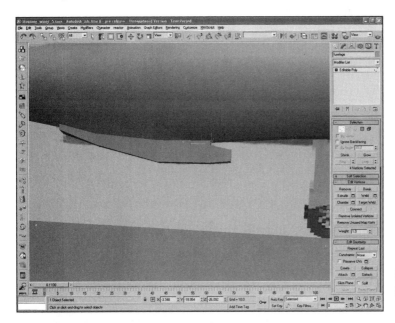

Figure 4.27
Shape the radiator
 housing.

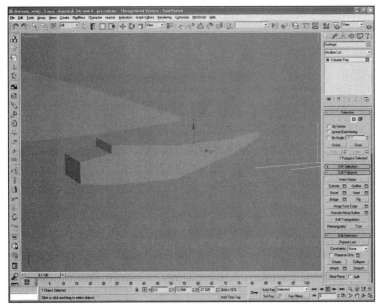

Figure 4.28
These polys are
facing inward.

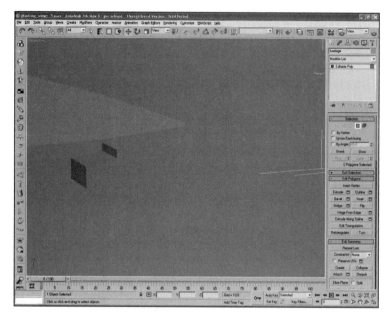

Figure 4.29
Delete the unneeded polys in the fuselage radiator housing.

8. Using the Cut, Weld, and Inset tools, create the canopy.

9. Continue shaping your model until you are happy with the results. Figure 4.30 shows the model with the radiator housing and canopies modeled. The Edged Faces option is used to display the model in this example.

10. Save your model as Mustang_04.max.

Figure 4.30
Now you have a completed fuselage with radiator housing and canopy.

Cleaning Up the Model

Carefully rotating around the model and checking each section, I noticed I had some undesirable polygons and geometry in the tail section when I welded and deleted the fuselage tail section (see Figure 4.31). Removing small, unwanted polys will reduce your polygon count and make your model clean and nice.

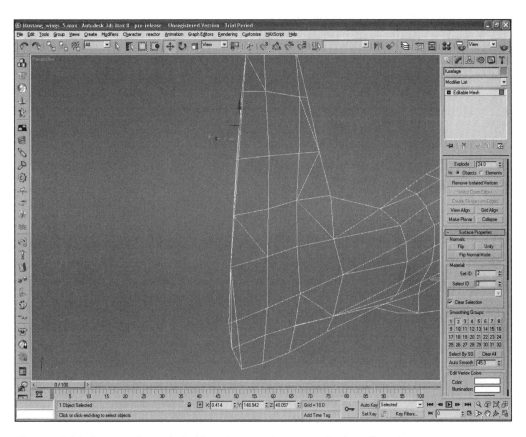

Figure 4.31 Remove the undesirable polygon and geometry in the tail section.

1. Carefully select these undesirable polygons (see Figure 4.32). If that doesn't work, try making a large box around many of them and using the Ctrl key to deselect the ones you don't need. Then, delete them (see Figure 4.33).

2. Save your model as Mustang_05.max.

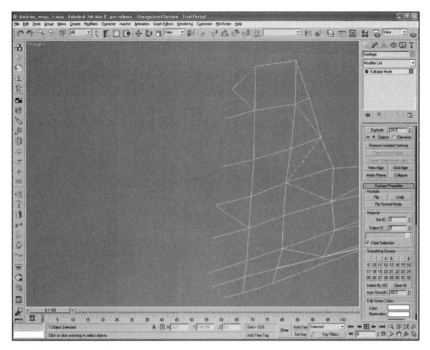

Figure 4.32 Select the undesirable polys.

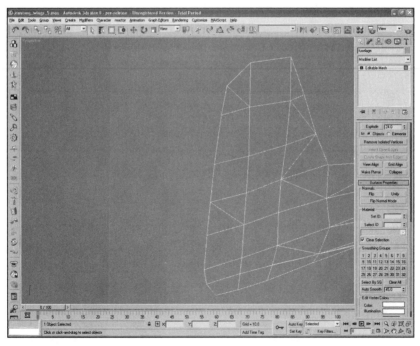

Figure 4.33 The polys have been deleted from your model.

Creating the Spinner

In the next phase of building the Mustang, you will work on the spinner. You'll be starting with a cylindrical primitive and using the Modify panel to create a hemisphere. You'll also use some tricks to help you locate the spinner in space closer to its final destination.

1. Open the Create panel. In the Object Type rollout, click to turn on Sphere.

2. Turn on AutoGrid by selecting the check box below Object Type. Now move the cursor over the surface of the end of the cylinder. This creates an axis tripod that follows your cursor, showing you where the sphere will be drawn.

3. In the Parameters rollout, turn on Base To Pivot. This lets you draw a sphere off the end of the cylinder.

4. In the Front viewport, move your cursor over the end of the cylinder and draw a sphere. It doesn't matter at this point what size sphere you draw; you will adjust the parameters after you draw it.

5. Edit the parameters as follows:

- Radius=14.6

- Segments=16

- Hemisphere=0.5

   Now instead of a sphere, there is a hemisphere (see Figure 4.34).

6. Now you need to finish shaping the spinner. Convert the spinner to an Editable Poly mesh. Using the same methods discussed earlier, select vertices and move and scale them to match the shape of the spinner (see Figure 4.35). Take care to keep the circumference of the spinner perfectly round. Because the spinner is very simple and already symmetrical, you won't need to delete half like you did with the fuselage.

Note

When using the Scale tool, select the yellow handle in the middle of the Selection tool, as opposed to an axis. This scales the vertices uniformly.

7. Save your scene as Mustang_06.max.

Figure 4.34 The hemisphere is in position for shaping.

Figure 4.35 The modeled hemisphere is in the shape of the spinner.

Creating the Main Wing

In this section, you'll be introduced to some taper modifiers that will make it possible for you to taper vertices without having to move each one and line them up as you go.

1. Hide the spinner and freeze the fuselage. This will make modeling the wing easier.

2. Create a box and place it in the scene, as shown in Figure 4.36. Remember that when modeling for any game, try to keep the number of polygons to a minimum.

    - Length=70.0
    - Width=166.0
    - Height=9.5
    - Length Segs=4
    - Width Segs=3
    - Height Segs=3

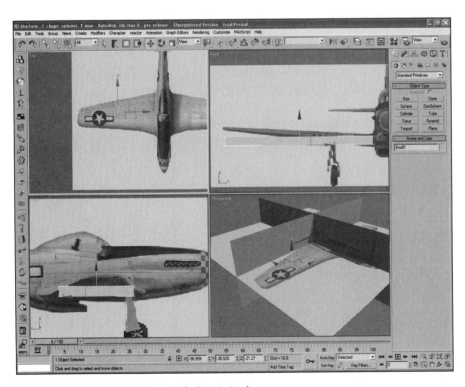

Figure 4.36 Create the box and place it in the scene.

3. In the Left viewport, shape the wing into a teardrop shape or a fully symmetrical wing, as shown in Figure 4.37. Don't forget to convert the element to an editable element.

Figure 4.37
Shape the box into
a symmetrical wing.

4. Move to the Top viewport and continue shaping the wing using the pattern (see Figure 4.38). You will need to move the wing up in the Z axis, above the pattern plane, to view the wing from the Top viewport.

Figure 4.38
Shape the wing
in the Top viewport.

5. In the Front viewport, select Modifiers, Free Form Deformers, FFD 2×2×2 from the main menu. A box with control points will appear around the wing (see Figure 4.39).

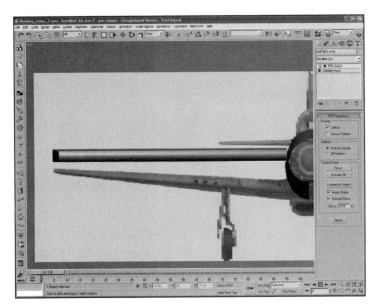

Figure 4.39
FFD 2×2×2 is
around the wing.

6. Right-click and select the control points. Selecting the outside control points of the FFD box, right-click again and select Scale. Scale the control points close together to match the pattern. Scale the wing root outward (see Figure 4.40).

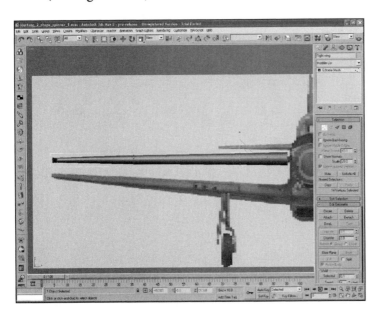

Figure 4.40
Scale the control points
around the wing.

7. Using the same control points, move them into position in the Front viewport (see Figure 4.41).

Figure 4.41
Move the scaled control points into position in the Front viewport.

8. In the Modifier List in the Command Panel, right-click on the FFD 2×2×2 modifier, select Collapse All, and select Yes. This will collapse the stack and commit the changes you made with the Free Form Deformer.

Creating the Wing Fillets

In this section, you're simply going to alter the root of the main wing to create the wing fillets.

1. Make sure the wing is converted to Editable Polys and select the inside polys (see Figure 4.42).

2. Using the Inset command, move and scale the vertices until you have something that looks like Figure 4.43. Don't forget to smooth the wing.

3. Convert the model to Editable Mesh and turn the Auto Smooth up to 100 (see Figure 4.44).

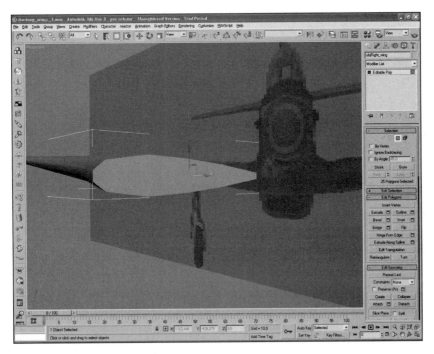

Figure 4.42 Select the polys.

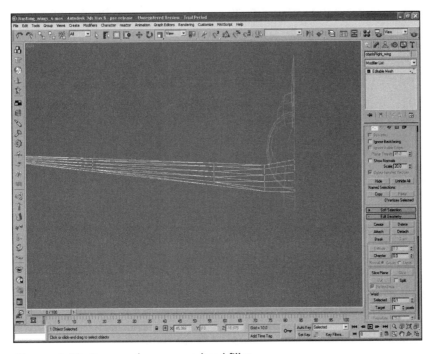

Figure 4.43 Now you have a completed fillet.

Figure 4.44 And now you have a smoothed wing with a completed fillet.

4. Repeat this process for the horizontal stabilizer (see Figure 4.45).
   Don't forget to delete the inward-pointing faces that will not been seen.

Figure 4.45 This model has the main wing, horizontal stabilizer, and spinner completed.

5. Take the time now to name each of the objects created in the chapter in the Command Panel. Then save the model as Mustang-07.max.

Building the Landing Gear

Now you'll take a few minutes to create the landing gear. One timesaving technique is to use the Clone method. This allows you to make copies of geometry, rather than model each gear independently.

1. Using the Create Torus command, create a torus. Use the specs below and move it into position (see Figure 4.46).

   ■ Radius 1: 8.5
   ■ Radius 2: 3.0
   ■ Rotation: 0.0
   ■ Twist: 0.0
   ■ Segments: 16
   ■ Sides: 9

2. Select the inside polygons that you will use to create the rim (see Figure 4.47).

Figure 4.46 Create a torus.

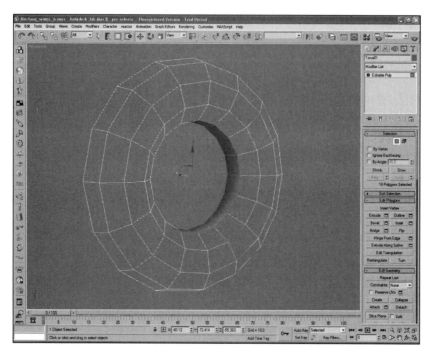

Figure 4.47 Select the polys for the rim.

3. Convert the torus to Editable Poly and select the Bevel command from the Edit Polygons roll-down menu (see Figure 4.48). Use the setting 5.537 for the height and –0.338 for the outline amount, and then close the window.

4. Select the vertices on either side of the axle at the center of the rim and weld them into one vertex. Repeat this procedure for the other side. This will collapse the inner vertices, making one on either side of the rim. Name this Main Landing Gear Wheel.

5. Now for the strut. Create a cylinder using the following values (see Figure 4.49).

   ▪ Height Segments: 5

   ▪ Cap Segments: 1

   ▪ Sides: 18

6. Move, rotate, and scale the vertices into their respective positions, checking each in the Side, Front, and Top views (see Figure 4.50). Name this Main Landing Gear Strut.

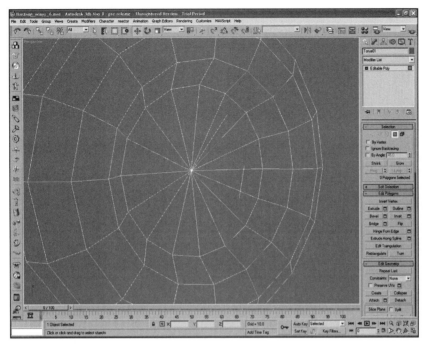

Figure 4.48 Bevel and shape the inner polys to make the rim.

Figure 4.49 Create a cylinder.

Figure 4.50 Model the landing gear strut and move it into position.

7. Now you need to create the landing gear doors. Create a box using the following values.

   ■ Length Segs: 4
   ■ Width Segs: 1
   ■ Height Segs: 1

8. Move, scale, and rotate the box into position and shape it to your liking (see Figure 4.51). Name this Main Landing Gear Door.

9. Repeat the procedure for the tail landing gear or try cloning the wheel and strut by choosing Clone from the Edit menu to save some time (see Figure 4.52). Rename the wheel and strut according to their parts.

10. Now, using all the techniques you have used so far, see whether you can create the massive four-blade propeller used by the P-51 Mustang (see Figure 4.53). Be sure to give it a name in the Command Panel to avoid confusion later.

11. Save your model as Mustang_08.max.

Figure 4.51 Create the main landing gear door. (Model is shown with Edged Faces on.)

Figure 4.52 Complete the tail landing gear.

Figure 4.53 Complete the four-blade propeller.

Mirroring the Geometry

Now it is time to mirror the geometry of the fuselage, wing, and horizontal stabilizers to further complete the model.

1. Select the fuselage. In the Modifier List, select Symmetry. In the Parameters box, deselect the Slice Along Mirror option. This will mirror the geometry, set the correct axis and placement, and weld the vertices along the seam (see Figure 4.54). Collapse the Modifier List.

2. Repeat the procedure for the main wing (see Figure 4.55).

3. Repeat the procedure again for the rear stabilizer. As you can see in Figure 4.56, this does not work well for the rear stabilizer. Undo this command.

   What you can do instead for the rest of the rear stabilizer and any other geometry that needs to be mirrored is clone, transform, and scale.

4. Start with the main strut. Select, clone, and make a copy of it. Right-click and open the submenu and change the X value to a positive. This will move the strut to the other side of the plane (see Figure 4.57).

Figure 4.54 Mirror the fuselage.

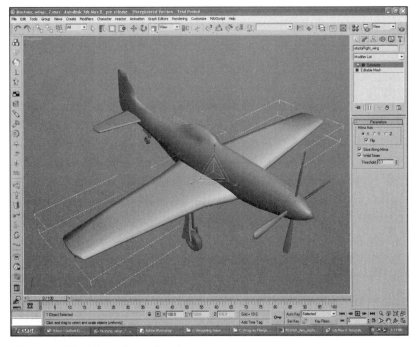

Figure 4.55 Mirror the main wing.

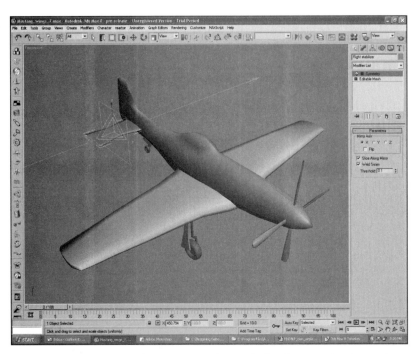

Figure 4.56 Following the same procedure as before improperly mirrors the rear stabilizer.

Figure 4.57 Clone the main strut.

5. Next, open the Scale submenu. Put a minus sign in for the X value (see Figure 4.58). This turns the geometry inside out and reverses the normals.

Figure 4.58
Scale the main strut
in the negative X.

6. Repeat this procedure for the rear elevator, main wheels, main gear doors, and rear landing gear doors (see Figure 4.59).

Figure 4.59
The rear elevator, main
wheels, main gear doors,
and rear landing gears are
in position.

In Figure 4.60, you can see a seam down the middle of the fuselage. This will have to be corrected.

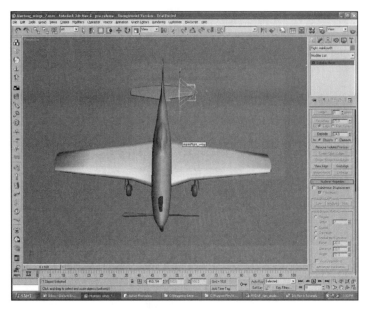

Figure 4.60
You will have to correct the seam in the fuselage.

7. Hide everything except the fuselage. Change to Edged Faces mode and focus in on a section of the gap. Select two vertices at a time and use the Weld function to weld the vertices along the gap (see Figure 4.61). Remember, you might have to increase your tolerance for the selected vertices to weld.

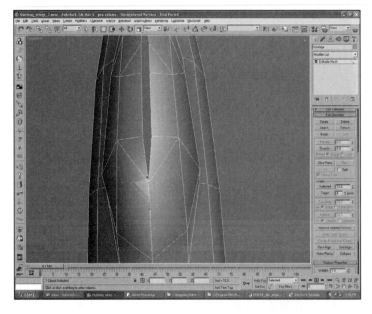

Figure 4.61
Weld the vertices.

8. Check the entire fuselage for gaps; smooth and weld as necessary (see Figure 4.62).

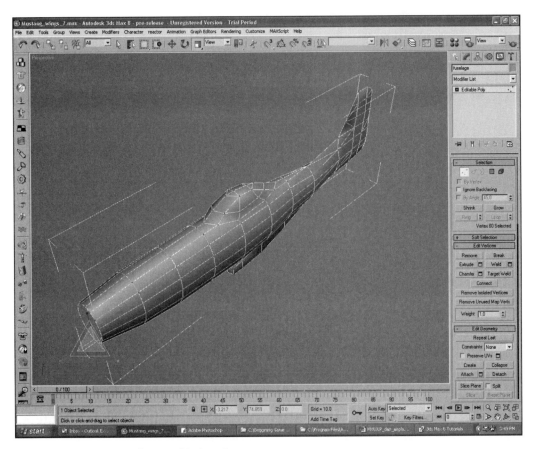

Figure 4.62 Now you have welded vertices.

9. Now take some time to look at your model and make sure it looks how you want it to. Many times after mirroring models, they look skewed and skinny. Now is the time to adjust anything that looks out of place. In my model, I noticed the radiator housing was too narrow, so I widened the vertices at the top and bottom of the radiator housing and adjusted it to be more to my liking (see Figure 4.63).

10. Save your model as Mustang_09.max.

Figure 4.63 I adjusted the vertices.

Putting It All Together

You might notice that when you select any parts of the Mustang and try to move them, they move independently and are not one model. You need to hook these separate pieces together to create one model or hierarchy.

1. Click on the Select and Link button, located on the Main toolbar (see Figure 4.64).

Figure 4.64
Click on the Select and Link button.

2. Next, select the main wing and click and drag it to the fuselage. You'll notice that a dotted line appears, and when you reach the fuselage a plus sign appears (see Figure 4.65).

Figure 4.65
A dotted line appears
when you drag the wing
to the fuselage.

This creates a hierarchy that attaches the wing to the fuselage. You can check this by clicking on the Select by Name icon in the main menu and checking the Display Subtree box at the bottom of the dialog box. In Figure 4.66, you can see that the main wing is now a subset of the fuselage.

Figure 4.66 Select by Name shows the existing hierarchy.

3. Continue adding all the separate pieces until you have one hierarchy tree under the fuselage. In my example, I put the propeller blades under the spinner and the spinner under the fuselage (see Figure 4.67). This allows me to rotate the blades and propeller together, independent of the fuselage.

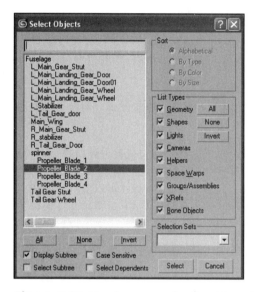

Figure 4.67 Here is an example of my hierarchy.

You can check your work as you go along by selecting the fuselage and using the Move or Rotate command. Everything that is attached will move together and objects that are not won't (see Figure 4.68). If you accidentally move one of the pieces, you can always return the object back to its original position by using the Undo command.

4. Save the model as Mustang_10.max.

Note

Most programmers will ask you to turn in your model with all the pieces grouped. Select all the pieces except the spinner and propeller blades. Select the Group command in the main menu and name the group "fuselage." Next, select the spinner and blade, group them and name them "propeller." Then, using the Select and Link button, select the propeller and drag the link to the fuselage. Your hierarchy should look like Figure 4.69

Figure 4.68 Check the model hierarchy.

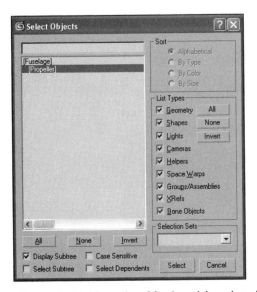

Figure 4.69 Hierarchy of final model ready to be exported

You will notice that now there is no way to select the individual sections of the plane and move them independently, with the exception of the propeller, which we made a separate group. In addition, if you look at the Rotate, Scale, and Transform locations, they are all reset to zero or blank. This is necessary when you export the model to the programmer. However, I would wait to do this final grouping until the model has been fully textured and is ready to be exported. Do not save the model at this time. It will be easier to texture if you leave the pieces ungrouped.

Texturing the Mustang

Now you'll add a texture to the parts of the Mustang. This will add a great amount of detail and increase the realism of the model.

1. Begin by selecting the fuselage. Open the Asset Browser and, under the Utilities tab, find and select the texture mustang.tif.

2. Press the M key to open the Material Editor. Drag the mustang.tif texture from the Asset Browser to the first material window (see Figure 4.70).

3. Next, drag the material you just created from the Material Editor to the fuselage (see Figure 4.71).

Figure 4.70
Assign the texture to a material in the Material Editor.

Figure 4.71
Assign the material
to the fuselage.

4. Close or minimize the Asset Browser and the Material Editor.

5. Make sure you have the fuselage selected and, in the Modifier List, select
   Unwrap UVW. Open the sub-object level in the Unwrap UVW stack and
   select Face. Turn off Ignore Backfacing. Select all the faces of the fuselage
   by dragging a box around the fuselage (see Figure 4.72).

Figure 4.72
Use the Unwrap UVW
modifier and select the faces.

6. In the Parameters section, click on the Edit button to open the Edit UVWs window (see Figure 4.73).

Figure 4.73 Open the Edit UVWs window.

7. At this point you have not told the program how you want the material mapped to the fuselage. This is why it looks the way it does in the Edit UVWs window. In the Map Parameters section, select Planar, and then select Align X (see Figure 4.74).

You'll notice that the UVWs in the Edit UVWs window changed to something you might have seen before from a Side view of the fuselage. But in this case, it is assigning UVWs to the model using an Orthographic Side view of the fuselage. As you might notice, the UVWs appear over a checkered background.

8. In the Edit UVWs main menu, find the drop-down that says CheckerPattern (Checker), open it, find Map #4 (mustang.tif), and select it. (The map number might be different for your exercise.) This will place mustang.tif in the window (see Figure 4.75).

Figure 4.74 Assign the Planar map to the fuselage.

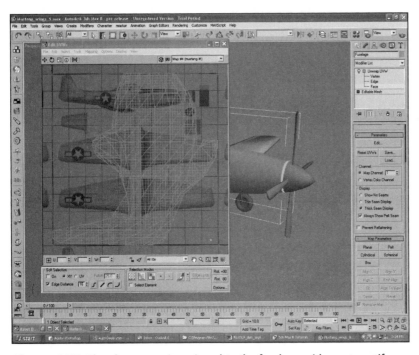

Figure 4.75 The planar map is assigned to the fuselage with mustang.tif
visible in Edit UVWs window.

9. Right-click in the Edit UVWs window and, using the Freeform gizmo, rotate and scale the selected UVWs to fit the Side view of the fuselage in the Edit UVWs window (see Figure 4.76). Make sure you deselect the Planar button in the Map Parameters menu; otherwise, you will have trouble moving the UVWs. This takes some getting used to. You use the same mouse commands that you used to move around in the viewports before to move around in the UVWs window.

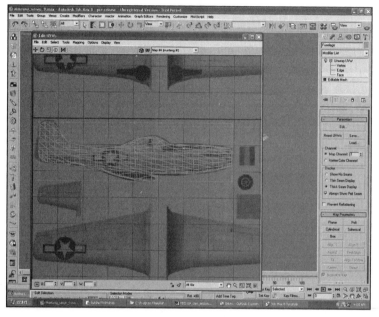

Figure 4.76 Move, rotate, and place UVWs over the Side view of the fuselage.

10. Now take a look at your work. Minimize the Edit UVWs window and deselect the fuselage by clicking anywhere in the viewport except over the fuselage. Your plane should now look like Figure 4.77.

Note

If you try to select the Editable Mesh in the Command Panel, you will get some undesirable effects.

11. You might also notice that the texture you applied to the model does not look as clean as it does in the Edit UVWs window. Hit the Teapot icon in the Main toolbar and do a quick rendering of the scene. This will help you see the applied texture clearly (see Figure 4.78).

Figure 4.77 Your plane should look like this one.

Figure 4.78 Render the scene to see the applied texture.

12. Now repeat this procedure for the main wing, except leave backface culling on. Select the faces from the Top viewport, assign mustang.tif to the top of the wing section top faces, and then do the same for the bottom (see Figures 4.79 and 4.80). Make sure you convert to Editable Mesh for each section you are texturing; otherwise, you will have trouble getting the Unwrap UVW selection to function. You won't need to reopen the Asset Browser each time you repeat this procedure, either—just drag the material from the Material Editor to each section as required.

Figure 4.79 UVWs are assigned to the top half of the main wing in the Edit UVWs window.

Figure 4.81 shows a view with the main wing completed.

13. Continue assigning the materials to the various pieces of the model and texture them accordingly. Figures 4.82 through 4.84 show examples of my final model. Of course, the level of detail depends on how many polygons and textures are allowed in a particular game.

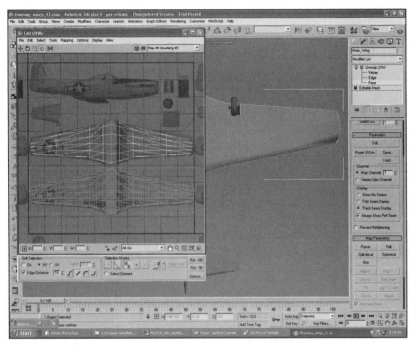

Figure 4.80 UVWs are assigned to the bottom half of the main wing in the Edit UVWs window.

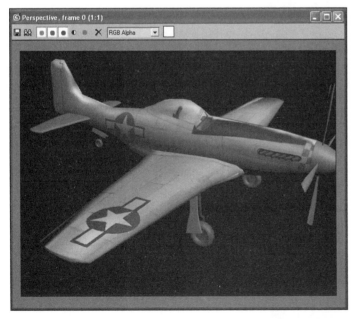

Figure 4.81 Here is a view of the textured main wing.

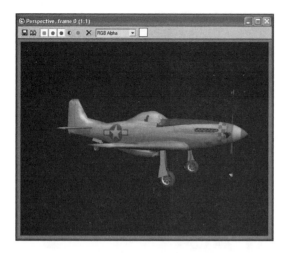

Figure 4.82
Here is a side view of the completed model...

Figure 4.83
...and a bottom view...

Figure 4.84
...and a top view.

Group the entire model into two separate groups—one for the fuselage, wings, gear, and stabilizer, and the other for the propeller blades and spinner. Link the spinner and propeller group to the fuselage. Make sure you can rotate the spinner independently from the fuselage.

14. Save your model as Mustang_final.max.

Summary

This has been a very rudimentary lesson on modeling and texturing a complicated model. Try altering the mustang.tif texture in your favorite paint program and see what you can come up with. You might try modeling and adding additional geometry, including exhaust stacks.

This chapter has been an overview of complex 3D modeling and texturing as it relates to games. In this chapter we covered several important points.

- Setting up the viewports with background images to help build the model
- Using primitive objects as the basis for each part of the airplane
- Editing the model at sub-object levels
- Using modifiers to alter geometry
- Welding vertices using the Vertex Weld modifier
- Using features in the Edit UVWs window
- Using the Edit Normal modifier
- Applying textures to objects
- Applying the UVW modifier
- Using simple planar-mapping techniques

Now that you have finished this chapter, you are ready to create your own complex game art. You have created models using simple primitives. And, you have demonstrated how great textures can add an immense amount of detail to a model without increasing the geometry.

Questions

1. What is the advantage of using reference planes to create models?
2. Once you have the reference planes in place, why would you want to freeze them?

3. What keyboard shortcut do you use to frame a selection in a viewport?

4. What color do vertices appear when they are selected?

5. Why would you want to cut a model in half?

6. What does the Weld Vertices option do?

7. When cutting faces, how do you know when you have reached a legitimate place to cut?

8. What does the Inset command do?

9. What is one way to select hard-to-select polys?

10. What type of modifier can be used to taper objects?

11. What must you do to any primitive before you do any sub-object modeling?

12. Where do you find the command to mirror geometry?

13. What hierarchy do you use to export your models?

14. What keyboard shortcut is used to open the Material Editor?

15. What keyboard shortcuts can you use in the Edit UVWs window?

16. What does the Teapot icon on the Main toolbar do?

Answers

1. They allow more accurate depiction of the model and save time.

2. To prevent moving them around by accident

3. The Z key

4. Red

5. It reduces your modeling time and makes the model fully symmetrical when duplicated, mirrored, and welded during the final stages of completion.

6. It combines two or more vertices into one.

7. The cursor changes to a plus sign.

8. It is a way of extruding faces.

9. Select several around the one you need and use the Ctrl key to deselect the ones you don't.

10. Free Form

11. Convert to Editable Mesh or Editable Polygons.

12. Under Edit on the main menu bar

13. What your programmer specifies

14. The M key

15. The same ones you use in the viewports

16. Provides a quick rendering of the scene

Discussion Questions

1. What would be the result of not smoothing the geometry before exporting a model to a game?

2. What are the pros and cons of using Orthographic or Perspective view for modeling?

3. Why don't games use a large variety of materials on models?

4. Why is it important to use some type of hierarchy?

5. Why is important to use the exporting methods required by the programmer for each model?

Exercises

1. Create a different version of the P-51 Mustang by painting on the texture and rendering the results.

2. Many versions of the P-51 were used in different missions. Research them and change the geometry of your model to fit the different types.

3. Try modeling by moving edges instead of vertices.

4. Using the Weld and Merge functions, see how far you can reduce the number of polygons before your model begins to look choppy.

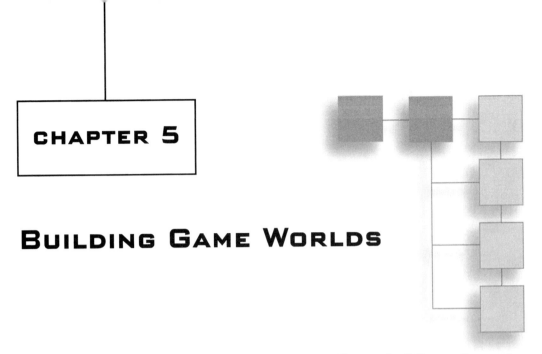

CHAPTER 5

BUILDING GAME WORLDS

This chapter will explain game-world creation. It will cover building and texturing a world, along with using 3ds Max as a world editor. What you'll do is apply a height map and a texture map to a plane. A height map is simply a black-and-white texture that, when used as a height map, will move vertices up or down, depending on how dark or light the texture is. You'll apply a texture map to the plane map to give the model some realism.

Creating the Terrain

The first thing you'll do is create the world's terrain.

1. Start by making a plane in the Top view (see Figure 5.1). Set the attributes as follows:

   - Length: 1000.0
   - Width: 1000.0
   - Length Segs: 50
   - Width Segs: 50

   Leave the rest of the attributes at their defaults.

2. Convert the plane to Editable Poly.

3. In the Modifier menu, select Displace.

4. In the Parameters box, click under Bitmap in the None box.

5. When the new dialog box opens, find and select Height_map.bmp.

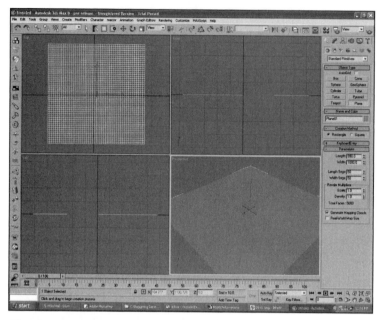

Figure 5.1 Create a plane for the terrain.

6. In the Displacement section of the Parameters rollout, enter 100.0 in the Strength field. This applies the height map to the terrain (see Figure 5.2).

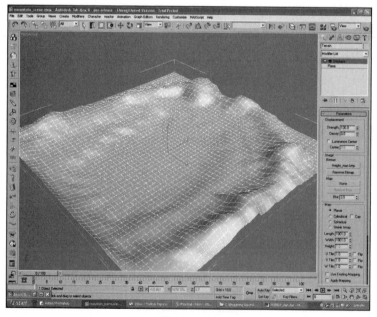

Figure 5.2 Apply the height map to the terrain.

7. Open the Asset Browser and apply Texture_map.bmp to the plane (see Figure 5.3).

8. Save the file as Terrain.max.

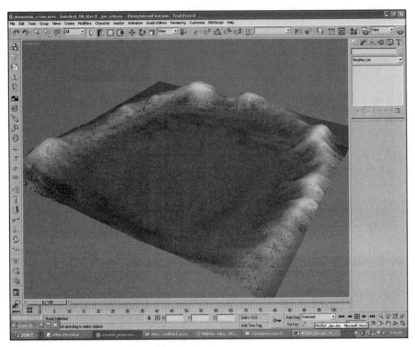

Figure 5.3 Apply the texture map to the terrain.

Creating the Sky Box

Next you can create a very simple, low-poly sky box. The sky box will be a background for your scene. It will include a texture for the sky with clouds. This box will not be an actual box, though; it will be a hemisphere. The term "sky box" originally came about early in game development, when they were made of five-sided boxes. This made for a very low-polygon sky box for the early game platforms.

1. Freeze the terrain. Don't forget to set the option in the Display tab to make the terrain visible when frozen.

2. Next, make a sphere with the following attributes:
   - Radius: 1000.0
   - Segments: 20
   - Hemisphere: 0.5

See Figure 5.4 for an example.

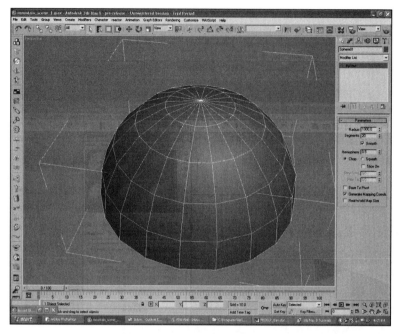

Figure 5.4 Create a hemisphere for a sky box.

3. Delete the faces in the bottom of the hemisphere, as shown in Figure 5.5.

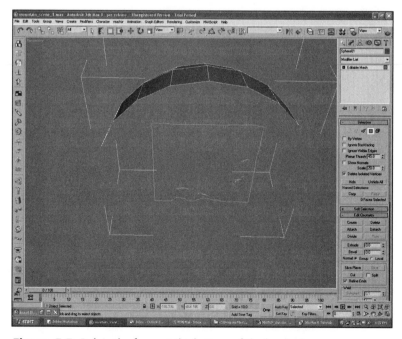

Figure 5.5 Delete the faces at the bottom of the hemisphere.

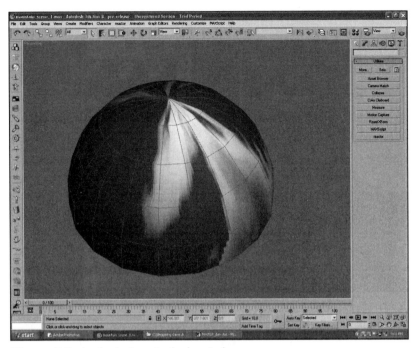

Figure 5.6 Apply sky.bmp to the hemisphere.

4. Using the Attribute Browser, apply sky.bmp to the hemisphere (see Figure 5.6).

5. From the Modifier Stack, apply UVW Mapping.

6. Select Cylindrical in the Parameters section.

7. In the Alignment section, choose Z and click on the Fit button (see Figure 5.7).

8. Collapse the stack and convert to Editable Poly.

9. Reverse or flip the normals so the sky box faces inward (see Figure 5.8).

10. To make things a bit easier to see, add a light. Choose Create, Lights, Standard Lights, Omni from the main menu.

11. In the Top view, click and place the light in the middle of the scene. In any of the other viewports, move the light upward to about the middle of the sky box (see Figure 5.9).

12. Do a test render and have a look (see Figure 5.10).

13. Save your scene as terrain_01.max.

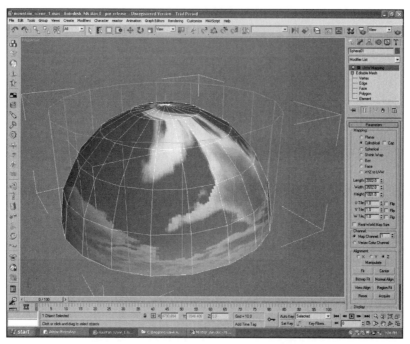

Figure 5.7 Apply the Cylindrical mapper, and align and fit your hemisphere.

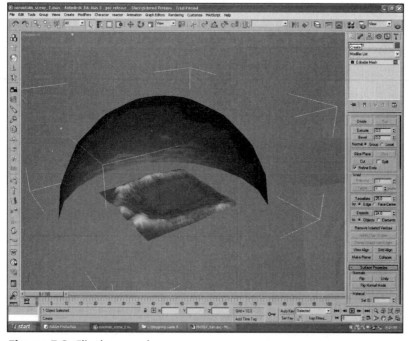

Figure 5.8 Flip the normals.

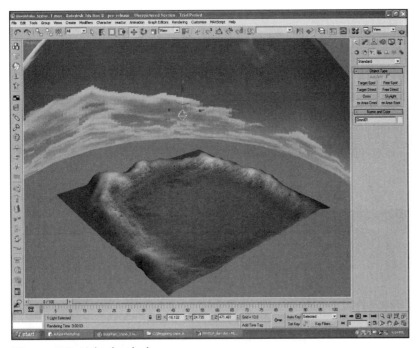

Figure 5.9 Light the sky box.

Figure 5.10 Do a test render.

Creating the Runway

Every airplane needs a place to take off and land. Now you will create a runway just for that purpose. The methods I will introduce here are the same ones you can use to make roads, sidewalks, and various other items in a scene.

Now is a good time to either freeze or hide the sky box to make viewing easier and so you don't accidentally select it.

1. Create a plane with the following attributes:
   - Length: 200.0
   - Width: 20.0
   - Length Segs: 30
   - Width Segs: 4

2. Place the runway slightly above the terrain (see Figure 5.11). I rotated mine slightly.

3. Convert it to an Editable Poly and pull the sides down slightly.

4. Now move the runway so it sits with the edges slightly below the terrain (see Figure 5.12).

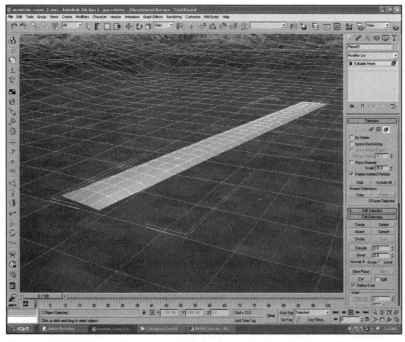

Figure 5.11 Rotate the runway slightly above the terrain.

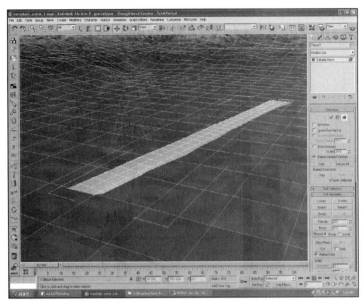

Figure 5.12 The edges should be slightly below the terrain.

5. Select one row of the center section of the runway and apply the center_line.bmp to it, as shown in Figure 5.13.

   You'll notice the texture is somewhat distorted.

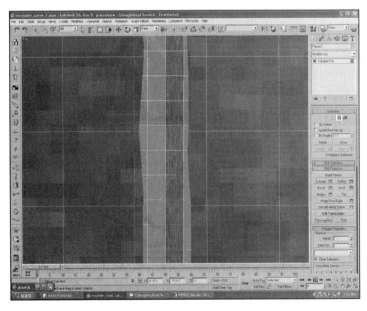

Figure 5.13 Apply center_line.bmp to the runway.

6. Now apply a UVW Map to the same faces to which you just applied center_line.bmp, and in the Parameters menu, select Face (see Figure 5.14).

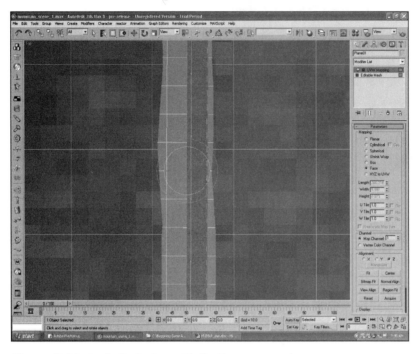

Figure 5.14 Apply the texture with the Face command.

7. Now, with the faces selected, put a minus sign in front of the 1.0 in the U Tile box in the Parameters menu. This will reverse the UVWs in the U direction (see Figure 5.15).

8. Repeat for the other side of the runway and, since it is correctly aligned, don't adjust the U Tile this time (see Figure 5.16).

9. Now continue on with the edges using the edge.bmp until you have a runway that looks like Figure 5.17. I decided to hide the terrain for this section.

10. Every runway needs some end markers to let the pilots know where the beginning and end of the runway are located. Using the techniques you already know, apply end_marker.bmp to the runway (see Figure 5.18).

    Your scene should now look something like Figure 5.19.

11. Save the file as terrain_02.max.

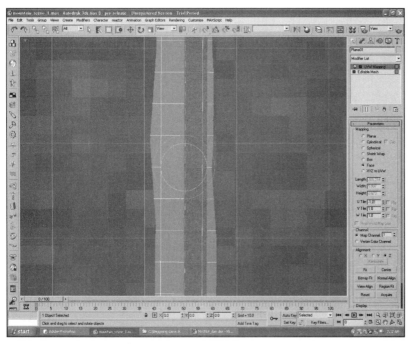

Figure 5.15 Reverse the UVWs.

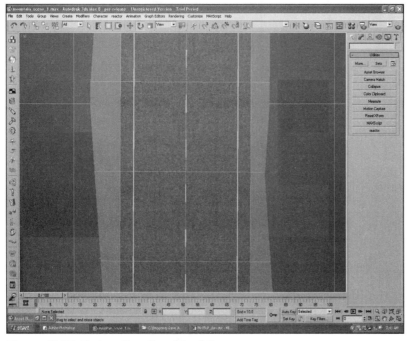

Figure 5.16 Texture the other side of the runway.

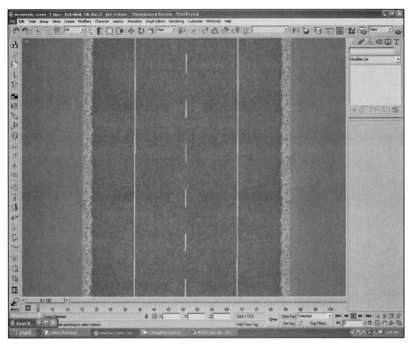

Figure 5.17 Apply the edge.bmp texture to the runway.

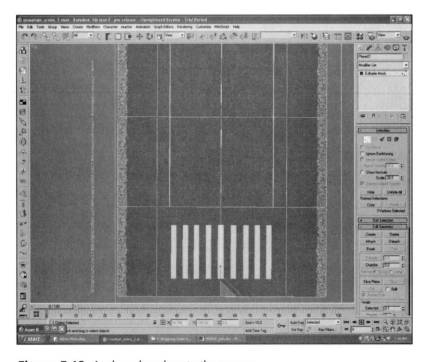

Figure 5.18 Apply end markers to the runway.

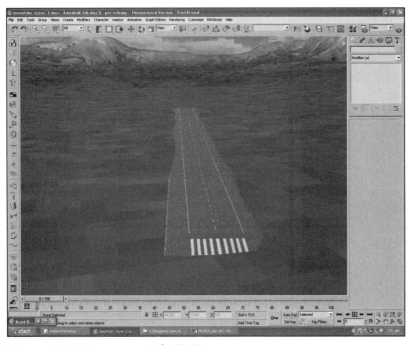

Figure 5.19 Your runway is finished.

Putting It All Together

The next step to complete the scene is to import the Mustang, the trees, and the hangar. Once imported, you can clone and place them in the scene to create a stunning level.

1. Choose File, Merge. The Merge dialog box will open. Find the tree.max file and select it. Another Merge dialog box will open (see Figure 5.20).

2. You can either use the All button to select what you'd like to import or click on the pine_tree file to import it. Once it is imported, open the dialog box in the viewports and set the transparency to Best. You might have to move and scale the tree to locate it above the terrain (see Figure 5.21).

3. Now clone the tree and place the clones in the scene to your liking (see Figure 5.22). Because of the varying terrain you'll need to position each tree at the appropriate height above the ground. The number of trees you can duplicate and have in your scene depends on your game platform. You might notice a slowdown in your computer. The speed at which your computer can render the amount of polygons and textures in a scene depends on how robust your computer is.

Figure 5.20 Open the Merge dialog box to select the file.

Figure 5.21 Merge the tree with the scene.

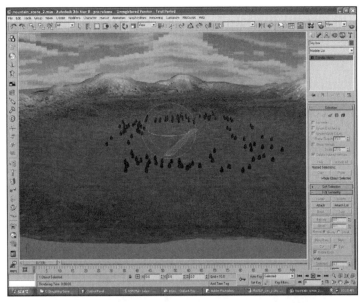

Figure 5.22 Clone the tree and move the clones in the scene.

4. Next, merge the hangar, barrel, and crates (see Figure 5.23).

Note

You'll need to scale the hangar, barrel, and crates to their respective sizes.

Figure 5.23 Import and merge the hangar, barrel, and crates.

5. Now clone the Mustang, and then merge, scale, and position the clones to your liking (see Figure 5.24).

6. Save your scene as terrain_03.max.

Figure 5.24 Merge, scale, clone, and position the Mustangs to your liking.

Summary

This chapter has provided you with a brief overview of how to merge objects into one scene and create a simple level using 3ds Max. In this chapter, we covered several important points.

- Using a height map to create terrain
- Creating a runway and altering the UVWs
- Creating a sky box
- Merging or combining separate files into one
- Adding a light to the scene

Questions

1. What is a height map?
2. What can you do to make a scene easier to see?
3. What does the minus sign do in the U Tile box?
4. How can you create a light for the scene?
5. How do you import other objects into a scene?
6. If you put too many objects in a scene, what can happen to your computer?
7. When you bring other models into a scene, what is one important thing you need to do?

Answers

1. A black-and-white texture that, when applied to a plane, moves the vertices up or down depending on how light or dark the texture is.
2. Create an omni light.
3. Reverses the UVW coordinates in the U direction
4. Choose Create, Lights, Standard Lights, Omni from the main menu.
5. Select Merge from the main menu.
6. It may slow to a crawl, depending on how many objects you have and how robust your computer is.
7. Scale them to the correct size.

Discussion Questions

1. What one thing could you do to save time and avoid having to scale each item you bring into a scene?
2. Why do too many objects and textures in a scene slow the video game down?
3. What can you do to the terrain in the scene in this chapter to make it appear more precise and less pixelated?
4. Why is using a height map a good idea? How does it save time?

Exercises

1. Create a different height map and try out different textures on your terrain.

2. See how many trees and objects you can place in your scene before you notice a slowdown in your refresh rate.

3. Try making your own sky textures from photographs.

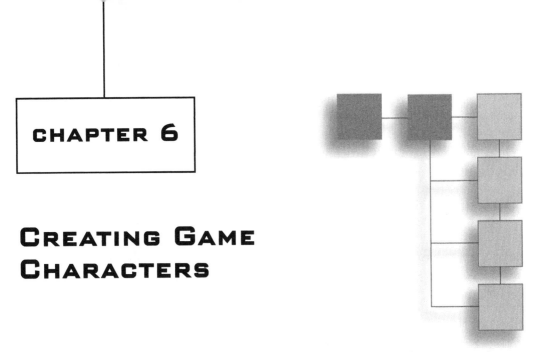

CHAPTER 6

CREATING GAME CHARACTERS

Creating good game characters is one of the most satisfying and fun aspects of game art. Like the actors and actresses in a motion picture, characters are the focus of attention. They are the performers on the stage of the game. Often the player is connected to the game through the game characters. Thus, creating good character art is very important.

This chapter will deal with character design and construction. It will cover the following topics:

- What game characters are
- What types of characters are in games
- Where you can get ideas for characters
- How you can draw character templates
- How you can build a character model

Game Characters

With the possible exception of some puzzle games, almost every game has characters. A game character is an intelligent person, creature, or machine in a game. Some game characters are beautiful; some are ugly. Some are stylized cartoon characters, while others are very realistic. There is almost as much variety in game characters as imagination will permit.

Game characters include all intelligent people or creatures in a game. *Intelligent* means that the character is either controlled by the player or by the game software. The specific software that controls characters in games is called *artificial intelligence*, or *AI* for short. AI in games is becoming increasingly complex, to the point that the player can interact with AI-controlled characters as if they were real.

Characters in games are becoming more and more lifelike. They don't just run around and shoot things—they can also have emotions. An angry character will not just attack with sword drawn; he will also have facial expressions and body language to emphasize the attack. He might yell at you or even call other game characters to help him fight. This increase in sophistication has increased the demands on designers and game artists to develop interesting and engaging characters.

Types of Game Characters

Games have many different types of characters, which can be broken into the following categories.

- Player characters
- Non-player characters
- Enemies

Each type of character can be further broken down into subtypes. Player characters can be controlled by a single player or, in the case of a multiplayer game, they can be controlled by many players. Non-player characters—or *NPCs*, for short—can be allies, facilitators, or decorations. Enemies can be rivals, and they can be aggressive, passive, or traitorous. These breakdowns are only a few of the many ways to categorize characters in a game.

Player Characters

A player character is controlled by a player. In many games there is only one player character—the one being controlled by you, the player. Some games, such as real-time strategy or team sports games, have the player control multiple characters at once with the assistance of sophisticated AI. In these team games, the player might control individual characters directly, but most of the time the player characters are doing their jobs as assigned by the game.

The amount of control the player has over a character will depend on the type of game being played. For example, a fighting game will give the player a lot of control over the character. The player will be able to control the movement and actions of the character in detail. Adventure games are similar in that the player will be able to control the character's actions to navigate through the world. Other games, such as real-time strategy games, give the player control over position and assigning jobs. The RTS character then intelligently acts upon the environment and game events.

Multiplayer games have several player-controlled characters in a single game. Some of these games are made up entirely of player-controlled characters. A multiplayer game might have hundreds of player-controlled characters. Many multiplayer games allow players to customize their characters; some even go so far as to include a character editor with the game. Character editors are challenging for the game artist because the artist has to create characters with multiple variations in costume, hair, body size, and accessories.

Non-Player Characters

Technically, any non-player-controlled character is a non-player character; however, it is useful to think of enemies as a separate group. Enemies are distinct in that players have to react very differently to them than they do to other characters in the game. I'll talk about enemies later.

NPCs are usually not overtly hostile to the player. They might be indifferent or have very limited reactions to the player, but they are not generally hostile.

Some games are filled with NPCs. Team sports games, for example, have NPCs that play the role of teammates, cheerleaders, spectators, announcers, and so on. Although they might not necessarily try to kill the player character, the opposing team is better classified as an enemy because their goal is to defeat the player.

Adventure games provide probably the best examples of NPCs in a game. In an adventure game the player interacts with several NPCs on many different levels. Some of the characters in the game might be helpful to the player by providing information or items. Others might be indifferent but helpful in their own way, such as store clerks or other types of merchants. Some characters might be nothing but decorative, giving no useful information and acting only as distractions.

In some games the NPCs change roles depending on the actions of the player. For example, an indifferent merchant might change to an ally if the player completes a quest or helps solve a problem. The merchant might also become an enemy if the player tries to steal something from his or her shop.

When designing characters, the concept artist needs to understand what the character's role is and create a character that fits that role. A sleazy police informant should not wear a three-piece suit. A military guard should not be slightly built. An opposing linebacker should not be obese. Characters need to fit their roles. Players should be able to tell a lot about your characters just from the characters' designs.

Enemies

Enemies are all non-player-controlled characters that try to keep the player from winning the game. The opposing team in a sports game is an enemy. The evil creatures in a horror game are enemies. The other drivers in a racing game are enemies. The vicious alien trying to kill the player in a first-person shooter is an enemy.

In some games enemies are very intelligent and cunning, whereas in others they might just be aggressive. In a football game, the opposing team might be very good at play calling and disguising play coverage. In a shooter, the enemies might be very good at ganging up on the player. In a fighting game, the opponent might have several combo moves.

In designing enemies, the look of the character is often as important as what the character does in the game. The characters should be intimidating, causing the player to feel a sense of accomplishment when he or she defeats them. Sometimes the intimidation is from an imposing physical appearance; other times it is subtler, such as in a quiz game where the opponent needs to appear intelligent.

Building Characters

Characters are some of the most complex models in games for a couple of reasons. First, a game character is the focal point of the game. Players will be looking at the character more intently than at any other element in the game. The second reason is that characters tend to be organic rather than mechanical. A human character, for example, is made up of many curves, which are difficult to create from flat polygons. Because of their complexity, I will be very detailed in the exercises that follow.

In this first section, you will explore creating a model sheet to use as a template. Next, you will cover building the character. Last, you will explore how to apply textures to the character. I chose a human character because it is the most common character in games, but more importantly, because it is the measure by which art directors choose who they will hire. Learning how to build great characters will go further in helping you get a job in the game industry than knowing how to build any other game element.

Character Templates

Character illustrations are great, but they often don't give the model builder enough information to create the character model. A critical piece of artwork for the concept artist to create is the *model sheet*, which can be used as a template for creating the character model.

What Are Model Sheets?

A *model sheet* is a template created by the concept artist to help the development team create accurate models of the designed characters. The model sheet is an orthographic rendering of the character drawn from different views. Each view is designed to give the development team vital information about the character.

Many characters in games today are very detailed. Games are getting closer and closer to reality in their graphics. Features such as cloth movement, facial animation, specular lighting, bump mapping, and transparency, which were impossible only a few years ago, are commonplace today. The movement to realism in characters is putting a lot of pressure on the concept artist and the development team to create better and better characters. The model sheet is the vital link between the concept artist and the development team.

Model sheets are a form of art borrowed from the motion-picture animation industry. When animators started drawing characters, they had to keep the characters looking consistent in all the scenes. Back then, all the frames of animation were drawn by hand. The problem became even more daunting when multiple artists worked on the same character. To help solve the problem, the industry came up with a system for helping the animators to keep their drawings consistent. A big part of that system was the model sheet.

Model sheets are also used extensively in the comic book industry. Comics, like motion-picture animation, have several artists working on the same character. Although the requirements for consistency are not as rigorous in comics as in motion-picture animation, they are still fairly rigid.

Unlike motion-picture animation and comics, games do not have as much hand-drawn art. Instead, games primarily use 3D models. The advantage to using a 3D model is that the character is consistent because the same model is used throughout the game. However, the need to keep the game character consistent with the designed character is still important. The model sheet helps take care of that need.

Model sheets are in many ways similar to drafting plans. The character is seen from different angles in isometric views. *Isometric* means without perspective. In other words, the view is flat to the viewer, without distortion for distance. Isometric drawings are more accurate than perspective drawings because the elements can be plotted directly from view to view.

Drawing a Character Template

A good template starts with a front view of the character. The character should have its legs separated and its arms out straight. Some modelers prefer to have the character's arms straight out to the sides like an airplane, but I prefer to have them down a bit because most of the time a character's arms will be down. Figure 6.1 shows the front view of a character in Corel Painter. Placing the arms out from the body will make it easier to attach a skeleton to the character for animation.

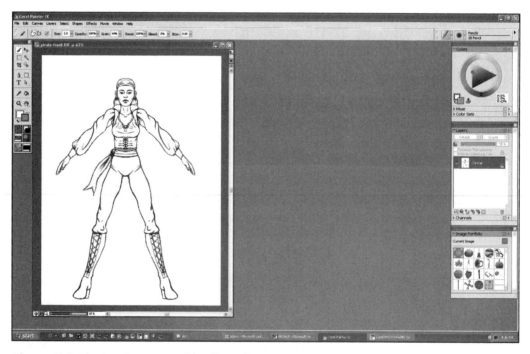

Figure 6.1 The template starts with a front view.

I like drawing characters in Corel Painter because I can adjust and change things in the drawing without having to worry about the paper surface when erasing. Figure 6.1 shows a drawing of a pirate girl in Painter. Notice the position of her arms and legs. Also notice that the flowing part of her sash is out away from the body.

A good template needs a front, side, and back view of the character. Each view needs to fit exactly over the others, so I like to use Painter's Tracing Paper function with the Clone function to help me build the other views.

1. First, select Clone from the File menu to create a clone image of the front view.

2. Minimize the original front view. Click on the clone image to activate it.

3. Next, choose All from the Select menu.

4. Now go to the Edit menu and select Clear. This will remove the front view image from the clone picture.

5. The little icon in the upper-right corner of the image window, directly below the close button, is the Tracing Paper switch. Click on it. The front-view drawing will be ghosted in below the drawing surface.

I use the Tracing Paper image to guide me in drawing the back view. Figure 6.2 shows the back view drawn over the front view.

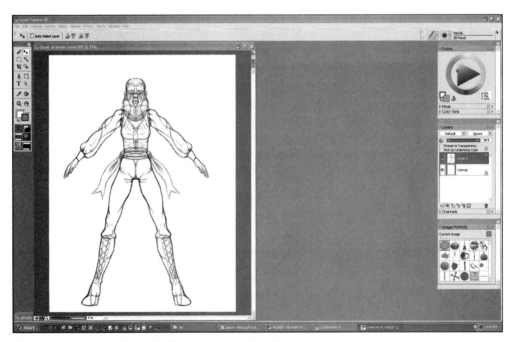

Figure 6.2 The back view is drawn over the front view.

When the back view is ready, the Tracing Paper button can be switched off, as shown in Figure 6.3.

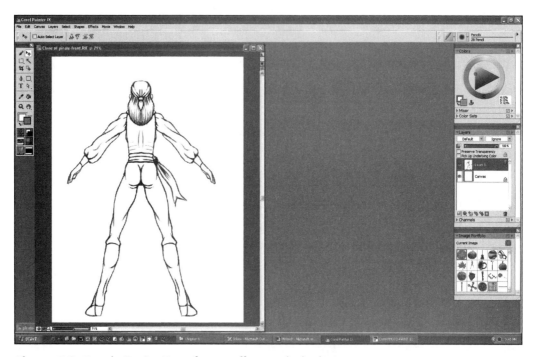

Figure 6.3 Turn the Tracing Paper feature off to see the back view.

The back view and the front view should line up directly with each other. This is because the two views will be used as modeling templates, and the edges have to match exactly. Even though the edges match, the drawings are quite different. Figure 6.4 shows the two drawings side by side.

I used the same approach for drawing the side view, as shown in Figure 6.5.

The side view is more complicated than the back view because the drawing is not an exact duplicate of the front; rather, it uses the front view to line up all of the drawing elements. Figure 6.6 shows the side view without the Tracing Paper turned on. In each view, every element of the figure must line up with the other views.

The front, back, and side views are the three main views for creating human characters. In some cases a top and bottom view might also be desirable. Figure 6.7 shows the three finished pictures together. Each picture needs to be saved separately to make a template.

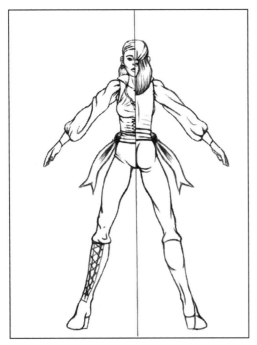

Figure 6.4
The drawings are very different.

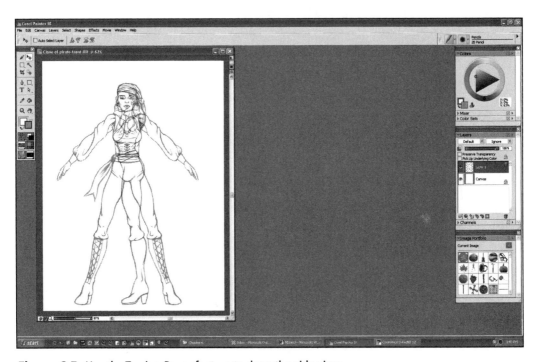

Figure 6.5 Use the Tracing Paper feature to draw the side view.

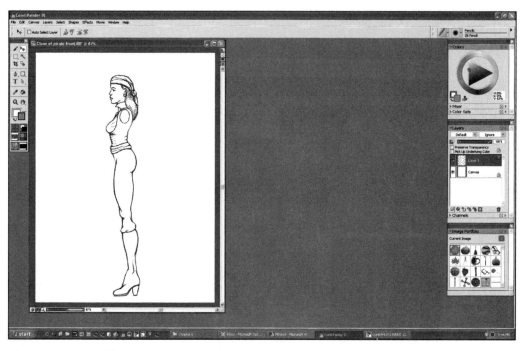

Figure 6.6 Turn off the Tracing Paper to finish the drawing.

Figure 6.7 All three drawings should line up with each other.

Character Modeling

Character modeling is a complex process requiring a great deal of time and skill. The character modeler is creating a complex model that needs to be able to look good and move correctly. He also needs to build the model with as few polygons as possible. Although game systems are continuing to become more and more powerful, they are still limited. The limitations on the systems require the game artist to work within a polygon budget for each character.

Polygon Budgets

A *polygon budget* is a limit on the number of polygons that an artist can devote to building a character. As a beginner you need to understand the importance of a polygon budget. Polygon budgets are created by taking the total processing power of the game system and dividing it among the processing needs of the game. For example, a racing game might have the following processing needs.

- Game AI
- Physics model for cars
- Audio
- Graphics

Graphics are just one of the elements that requires processing. Within the realm of graphics are several different processing requirements.

- Animation systems
- World geometry
- Textures
- Character (automobile) geometry
- Special effects

After the total processing requirements for each facet of the game are determined, you can calculate the initial polygon budget. For example, suppose that in creating an adventure game, the portion of processing allocated to characters is 10 percent of the total processing power. If the game system can render 500,000 textured polygons per frame, then the polygon budget for characters will be 50,000 polygons. That isn't 50,000 polygons per character; rather, it is 50,000 polygons for all characters that will ever be on screen at the same time. Thus, if the game limits the number of onscreen characters to 10, then the budget for individual characters will be 5,000 polygons. On the other hand, if the game is designed to have up to 50 characters on the screen at one time, then the polygon budget for each character will be 1,000 polygons. Often the artist doesn't come up with the polygon budget. It is usually given to him by the project manager.

This example is a very simplistic view of determining a polygon budget. In actual game development, there are many variables that we didn't take into account, such as level-of-detail systems and important versus non-important characters. Artists use a number of tricks to make the most of the polygons in their budgets. The scope of this book won't allow me to go into them, so it is best to just remember to be as frugal with your polygons as possible.

Polygon Counter

3ds Max has a utility called the Polygon Counter that helps artists maintain polygon budgets. This utility keeps track of the number of polygons in individual objects and in the scene. It also gives the artist a graphic view of how close he or she is to the polygon budget limits. The limits can be adjusted by the artist prior to starting the modeling process.

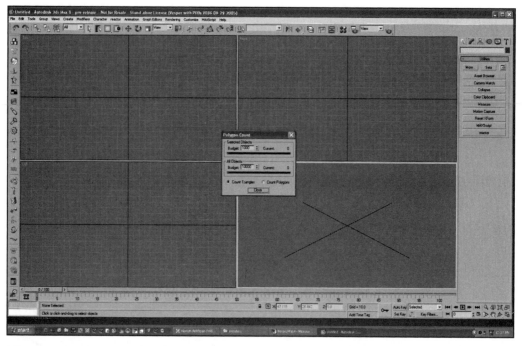

Figure 6.8 Create a single polygon plane.

The Polygon Counter is located under the Utilities tab, which is located on the upper-right side of the screen and is represented by a hammer icon. To bring up the Polygon Counter, click on the Utilities tab and then click on the More button to bring up a list of utilities. Select Polygon Counter from the list (see Figure 6.8).

Building a Template

The first part of building a character in 3ds Max is loading the template you created earlier. The process is quite simple, so it should not be hard to follow along.

1. Click on the Create panel. It is the tab in the upper-right corner of the screen that looks like an arrow with a light behind it.

2. Click on the Create Primitive icon. It looks like a grey ball, and it is located just below the Create tab.

3. Now click on the Plane button in the Object Type rollout, as shown in Figure 6.9.

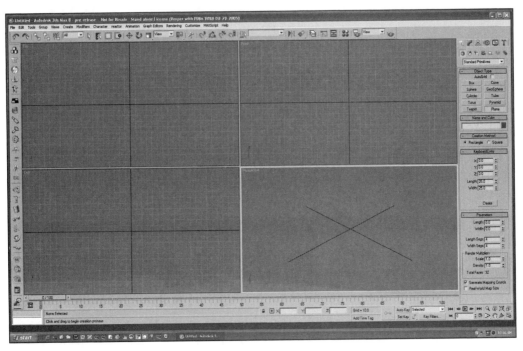

Figure 6.9 Click on Plane in the Object Type rollout.

4. Set the attributes in the Parameters rollout as follows (see Figure 6.10).

- Length: 100
- Width: 100
- Length Segs: 1
- Width Segs: 1

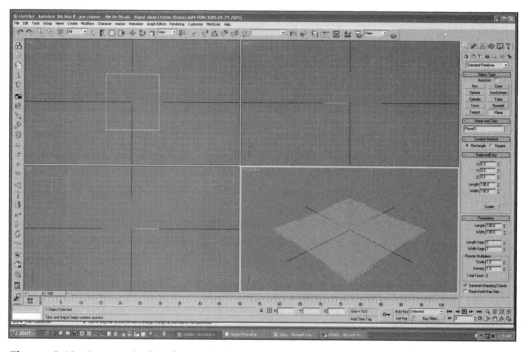

Figure 6.10 Create a single polygon plane.

5. Bring up the Material Editor, as shown in Figure 6.11.

6. Click on the first Sample Slot, and then click on the Maps rollout to bring up the map options.

7. Find Diffuse Color on the list and click on it to bring up the Material/Map Browser, as shown in Figure 6.12

8. The template is a bitmap file, so double-click on Bitmap in the list to bring up the Select Bitmap Image File dialog box.

9. Load in the front view of the character template.

10. Now apply the material to the plane and make it viewable, as shown in Figure 6.13.

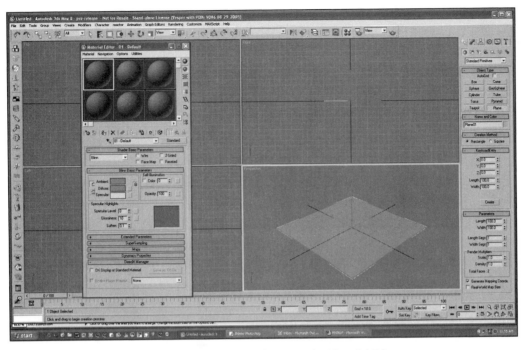

Figure 6.11 Click on the Material Editor icon to bring up the Material Editor.

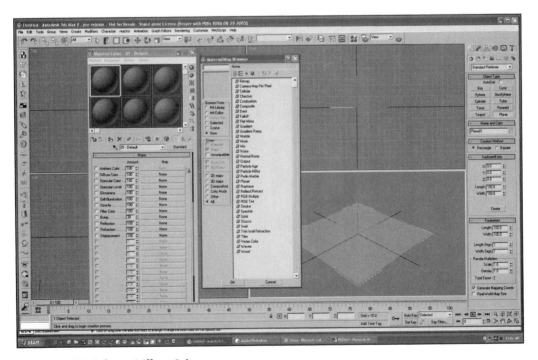

Figure 6.12 Select a Diffuse Color map.

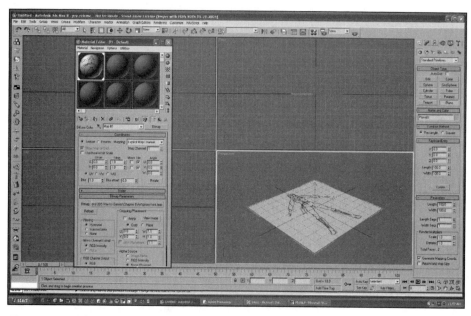

Figure 6.13 Apply the material to the plane.

11. Use the Rotate tool to rotate the polygon up 90 degrees, as shown in Figure 6.14.

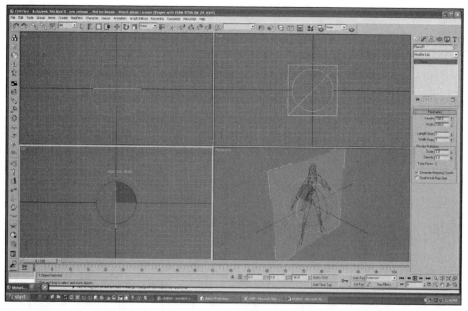

Figure 6.14 Rotate the plane up 90 degrees.

12. Create two more materials and load the side and back views of the template, as shown in Figure 6.15.

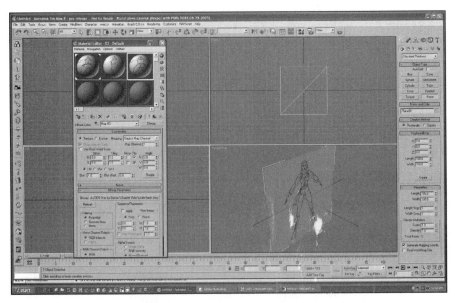

Figure 6.15 Load the other two views of the template.

13. Now create a new single-poly plane and make it perpendicular to the original plane, as shown in Figure 6.16.

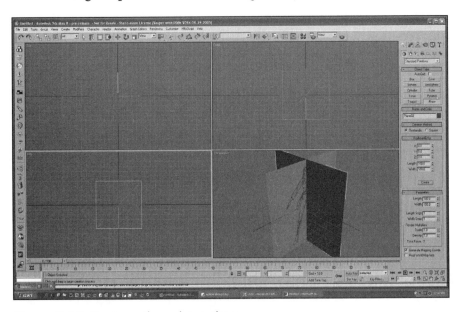

Figure 6.16 Create another polygon plane.

14. Apply pirate-side.bmp to the new material. Notice that it is facing the wrong direction, as shown in Figure 6.17. You could flip the image in 3ds Max, but it is just as easy to flip the original image in a 2D paint program and then reload the texture. You will need both later.

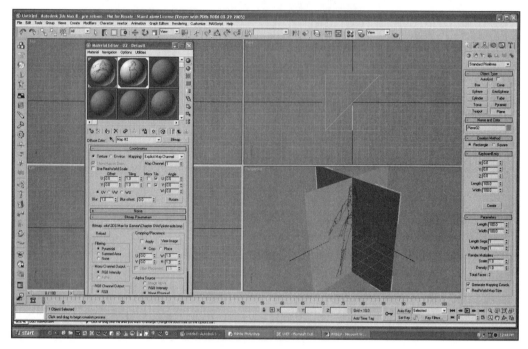

Figure 6.17 The map is not facing the correct direction.

15. Flip the map so that it is facing the correct direction (see Figure 6.18).

16. Create another single-polygon plane. If you made all the template pictures the same size and the polygon planes the same size, the template should line up perfectly.

17. Apply the back view template material to the new plane.

18. Bring up the Rotate Transform Type-In dialog box by right-clicking on the Rotate tool.

19. Now rotate the new plane so that it is facing in the opposite direction from the front view template, as shown in Figure 6.19.

20. Bring up the Viewport Configuration dialog box from the Customize menu and change all views to Smooth+Highlights, as shown in Figure 6.20.

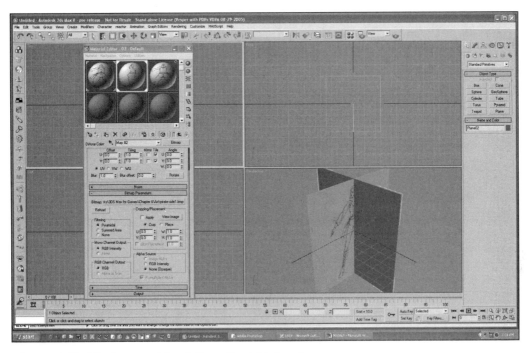

Figure 6.18 Flip the material so it faces the right direction.

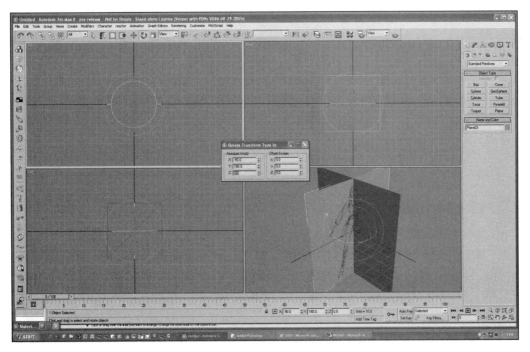

Figure 6.19 Rotate the new plane so it faces to the back of the template.

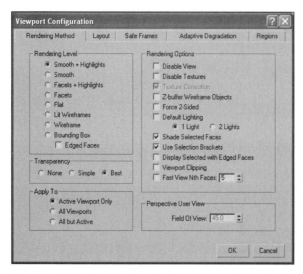

Figure 6.20 Change the shading mode to Smooth+Highlights.

21. Change the upper-left viewport to Back view instead of Top view by right-clicking on the viewport label in the upper-left corner of the viewport, as shown in Figure 6.21.

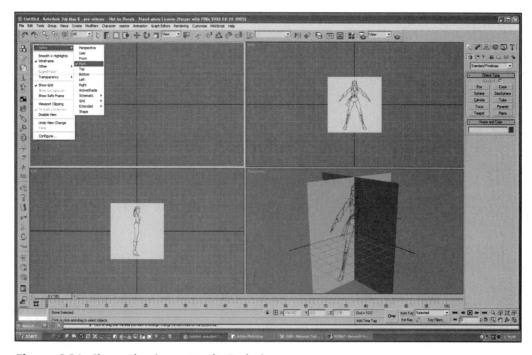

Figure 6.21 Change the viewport to the Back view.

Now the templates are all loaded into 3ds Max, and you are ready to start modeling. The templates should look like the ones in Figure 6.22.

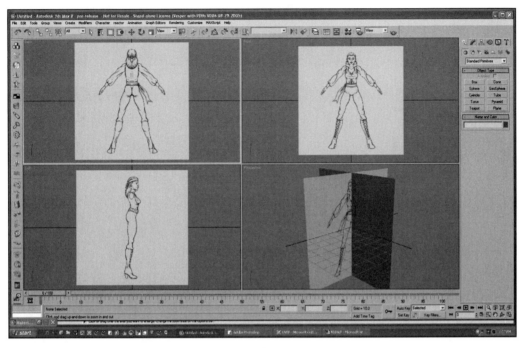

Figure 6.22 The templates are all loaded into 3ds Max.

Starting the Model

A good way to create models in 3ds Max is to start with a primitive object and build by modifying the object. You will start this model with just one primitive object, a box. This is only one of many approaches for building models. There are almost as many ways to build a model as there are modelers.

In this example, you will only be creating half of the model and then mirroring it to get the other half.

1. Create a box with the following attributes (see Figure 6.23).

   - Length: 2.0
   - Width: 2.0
   - Height: 2.0
   - Length Segs: 1
   - Width Segs: 1
   - Height Segs: 1

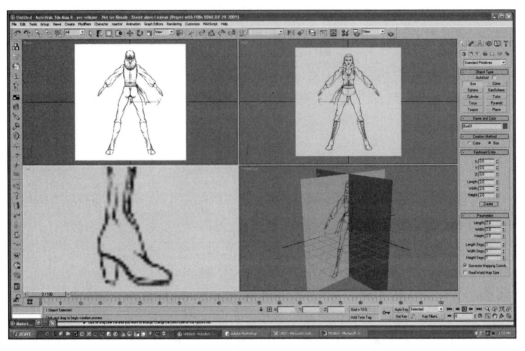

Figure 6.23 Create a box.

2. Now you need to convert the object to an Editable Mesh. Click on the Modify tab, represented by the icon that looks like a bent pipe. Changing the object to Editable Mesh makes the object editable so you can build with it.

3. Make sure the box is selected, and then click on Edit Mesh from the Modifier List.

4. Now click on Vertex in the Selection rollout. This puts the mesh in Subobject mode. Move the vertices of the box to line up with the toe of the boot, as shown in Figure 6.24.

5. Right-clicking on the object will bring up a quadmenu. In the lower-right portion of the menu, click on Properties. This will bring up the Object Properties dialog box, shown in Figure 6.25.

6. From this small box at the toe of the character you will be extruding the entire character model. To see what you are doing, turn on the See-Through option in the Object Properties dialog box.

7. Change the selection mode to Polygon by clicking on the red square in the Selection rollout.

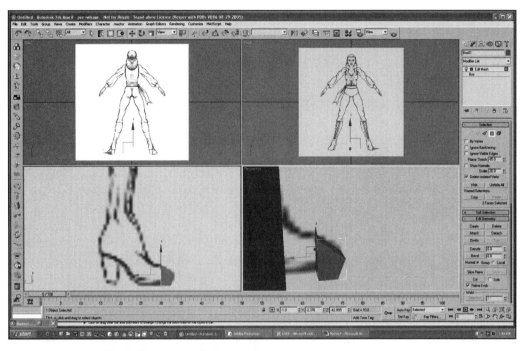

Figure 6.24 Modify the box to match the template.

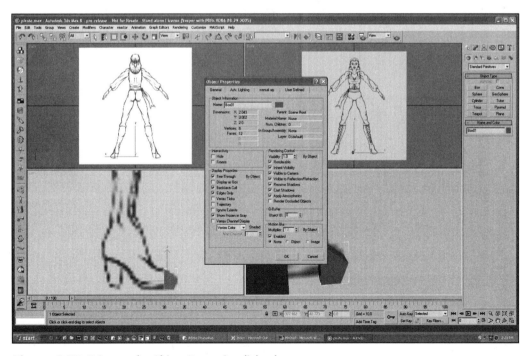

Figure 6.25 Bring up the Object Properties dialog box.

8. First you will be extruding the boot. Select the polygon facing the inside of the boot, and then click on Extrude in the Edit Geometry rollout.

9. To extrude the polygon, place the cursor over the selected polygon in one of the viewports and watch for the cursor to change into the extrude cursor gizmo. Now click on the polygon and drag up to extrude out and down to extrude in. You will want to extrude the polygon toward the back of the boot. Extrude the polygon until it lines up with the ball of the character's foot.

10. Now adjust the vertices to follow the contour of the boot in the Side view.

11. Continue to extrude and adjust vertices going up the boot. You will need to do this several times to follow the contour of the boot (see Figure 6.26)

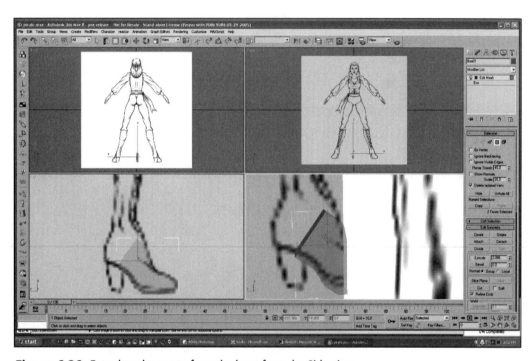

Figure 6.26 Extrude polygons to form the boot from the Side view.

12. When you get to the ankle, extrude twice to cross the foot to the heel.

13. Adjust the vertices of the extrusion across the foot so they line up with the heel on the bottom of the boot and the ankles on the top.

14. Now extrude the heel of the boot down from the boot.

15. Adjust the vertices of the heel, as shown in Figure 6.27.

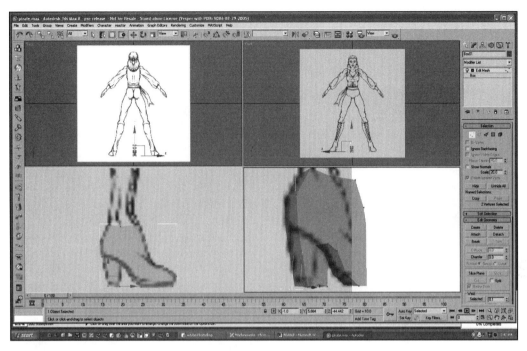

Figure 6.27 Adjust the vertices of the heel.

16. You should now have two polygons at the top of your model that you can use to extrude the rest of the leg. Go back to Polygon in the Selection rollout and select the top two polygons.

17. Extrude them upward, following the contour of the leg. Be sure to make your extrusions smaller around the knee so the model will animate better.

18. Continue extruding the leg from the Side view until you reach the hip area.

You will notice that the leg runs down the center of the X axis, yet the template shows the character with her legs at an angle. Your next step in the project will be to line the leg model up with her left leg in the template. Before you move the model, however, you need to change the template. By building the leg vertically first and then rotating it out, the angles of the joints in the leg are correct.

For the rest of the modeling you will need to change the template to a box template with its faces facing in.

1. First select the Front view template and move it 50 units in the Y axis by right-clicking on the Move tool and changing the Absolute World Y number to 50.

2. Next take the Back view template and move it −50 in the Y axis.

3. Now move the Side view 50 in the X axis. The template is now ready (see Figure 6.28).

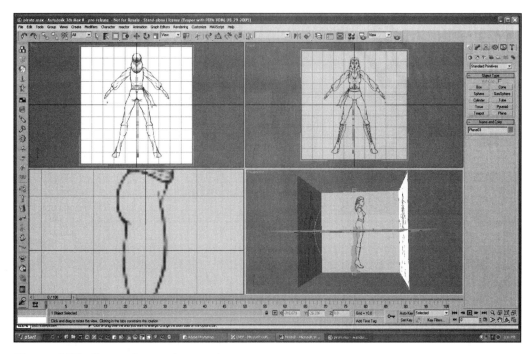

Figure 6.28 Change the template to a box.

4. It will be easier to expand the width of the leg in from the Front view, if the front and back vertices do not directly cover the middle vertices of the leg. In the Side view, select the middle vertices from the ankle up and scale them outward a little in the X axis, as shown in Figure 6.29.

5. From the Side view, select the leg model and move it over so the foot lines up with the girl's foot in the template. From there, rotate the leg until it lines up with the template, as shown in Figure 6.30.

6. Notice that the leg is now too short and doesn't reach the girl's hip. Use the Scale tool to scale the leg up until it reaches the hip, as shown in Figure 6.31.

7. Now you are ready to continue modeling the character. Move the middle vertices of the leg out to follow the contour of the template from the Front view, as shown in Figure 6.32.

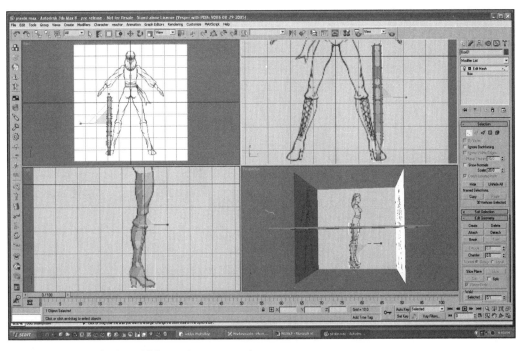

Figure 6.29 Scale the middle vertices outward.

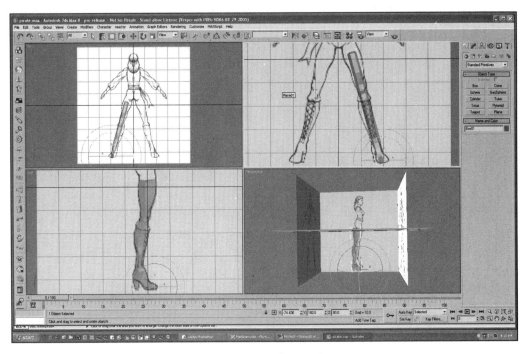

Figure 6.30 Rotate the model of the leg to match the template.

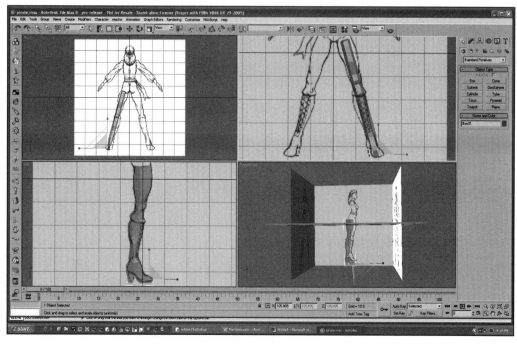

Figure 6.31 Scale the leg up to fit the template.

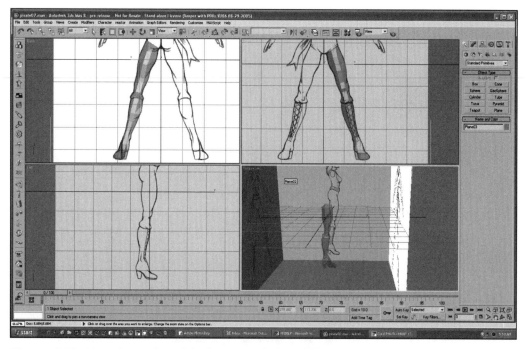

Figure 6.32 Move the vertices of the leg to match the template.

Modeling the Torso

The first step to modeling the torso is to create the hip and crotch area.

1. Select the top two polygons of the leg and extrude them upward just a little bit, as shown in Figure 6.33. This will help with the animation later.

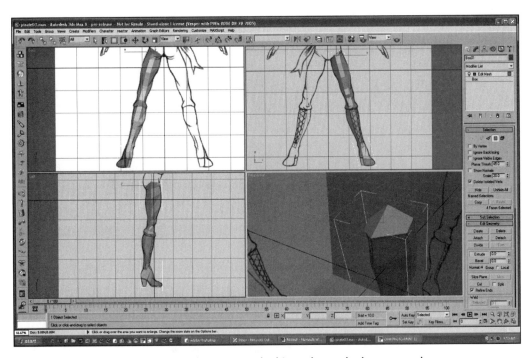

Figure 6.33 Select the top two polygons near the hip and extrude them upward.

2. Now extrude the polygons again and move them upward to near the top of the hipbone in the template.

3. Use the Scale tool to flatten the polygons vertically, and then readjust them using the Move tool. They should now look like Figure 6.34.

4. Now select the inside polygons of the hip area and extrude them toward the center of the template, as shown in Figure 6.35. Flatten these polygons as well.

5. Move the polygons to the center, as shown in Figure 6.36.

6. Adjust the vertices so they line up with the template around the crotch area.

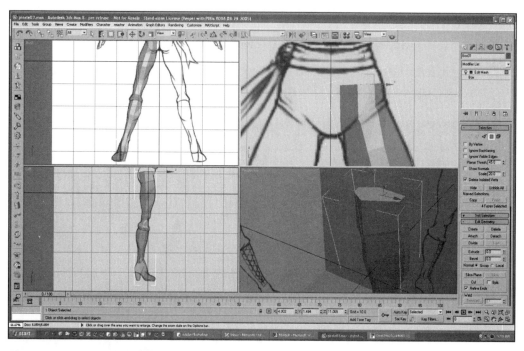

Figure 6.34 Extrude and flatten the polygons.

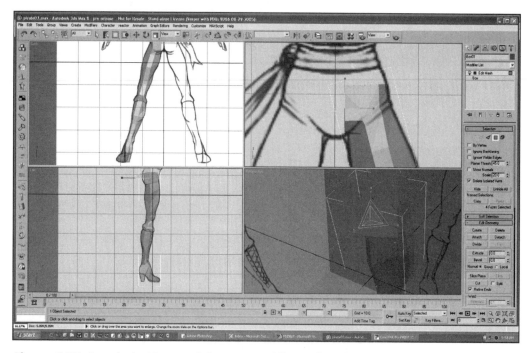

Figure 6.35 Extrude the hip toward the center and flatten the polygons.

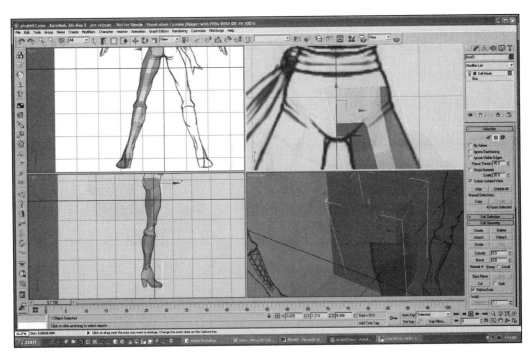

Figure 6.36 Line the polygons up with the center line.

Hint

When building a symmetrical model, there is no need to create the entire model from scratch. It is much easier to achieve symmetrical models if you only build half of the model and then use the Mirror tools to create the other half. This procedure will result in perfectly symmetrical models every time.

7. Now you can continue extruding the polygons upward, as shown in Figure 6.37.

8. Next extrude the midriff and ribcage, ignoring the breasts for now.

9. When you get to the shoulders, move the vertices to match the template, as shown in Figure 6.38.

10. Now you can extrude the arm, but first you need to adjust the vertices of the shoulder to match the shape of the arm, as shown in Figure 6.39.

11. As you did with the hips, extrude the arm polygons only a small amount, as shown in Figure 6.40.

12. Extrude down the length of the arm. Make sure you extrude smaller units around the elbow area for better animation.

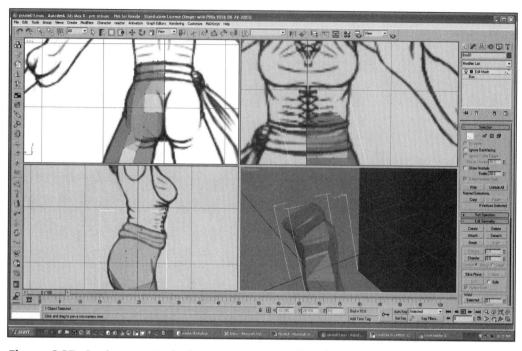

Figure 6.37 Continue to extrude the upper polygons to form the hips of the character.

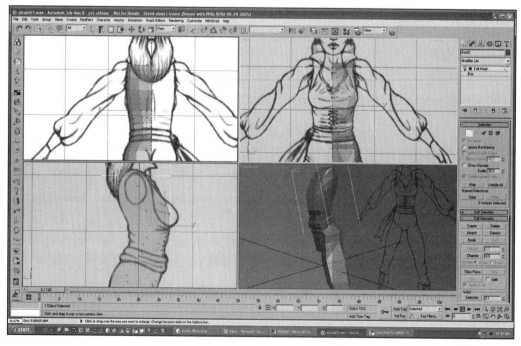

Figure 6.38 Make the geometry follow the template from each view.

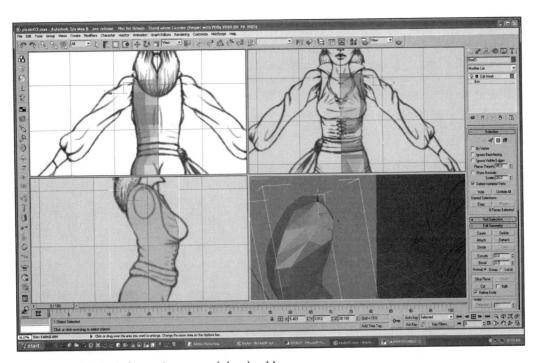

Figure 6.39 Move the vertices around the shoulder.

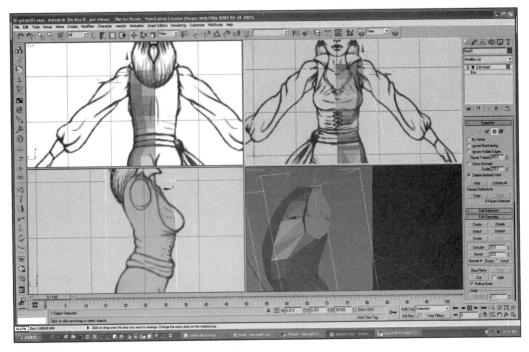

Figure 6.40 Make the first extrusion small.

Hint

The animation of the arm will work better if the extruding polygons are perpendicular to the arm. Rotate the extruded polygons to be perpendicular to the arm.

13. Adjust the vertices in the Front view to fit the contours of the template, as shown in Figure 6.41.

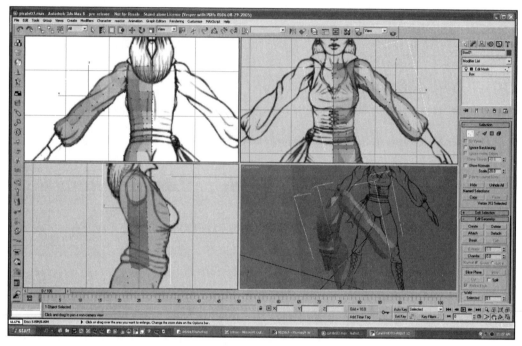

Figure 6.41 Make the arm follow the contours of the template.

14. Now extrude down to the palm of the hand.

15. When you have finished extruding, go back and move the vertices to follow the template from the Front view around the hand.

16. Next, swing around the hand in the Perspective view and shape it so it looks like a palm, as shown in Figure 6.42.

17. Now the arm needs to be expanded in the Y axis because it is too narrow. Select the vertices of the arm and use the Scale tool in the Y axis only to expand the arm (see Figure 6.43).

18. Next will be the breast. Shape the polygons around the base of the breast and extrude and scale the breast, as shown in Figure 6.44.

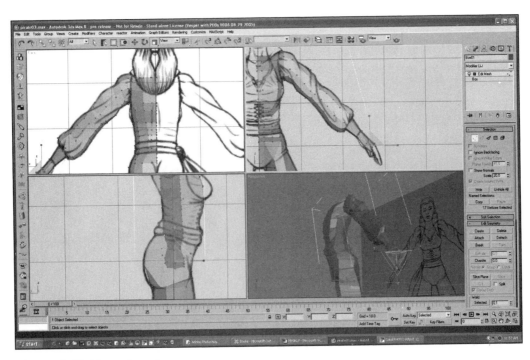

Figure 6.42 Shape the palm.

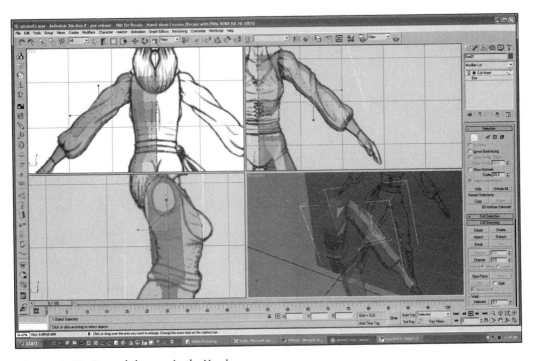

Figure 6.43 Expand the arm in the Y axis.

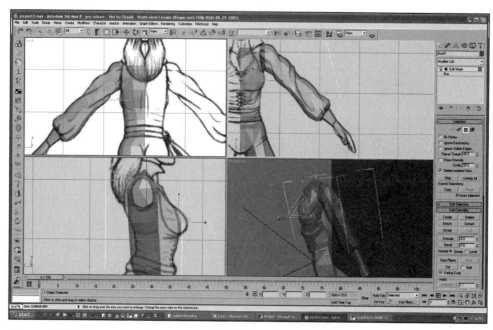

Figure 6.44 Shape the polygons around the base of the breast.

19. Extrude and scale the breast twice more, as shown in Figure 6.45.

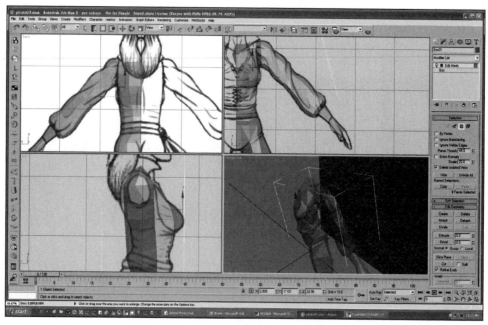

Figure 6.45 Scale the breast with every extrusion.

Give the model one final pass, looking at it in the Perspective view, to round the shapes and make it look more natural.

Building the Head

The head is probably the most complex part of a character model, with all of the facial features and hair. Some artists prefer to build it as a separate model and attach it later. In this example I will show you how to create it from the base model. You will be building the head from the neck up.

1. Adjust the polygons of the neck so they fit the base of the character's neck.

2. Extrude the neck polygons up following the template, as shown in Figure 6.46.

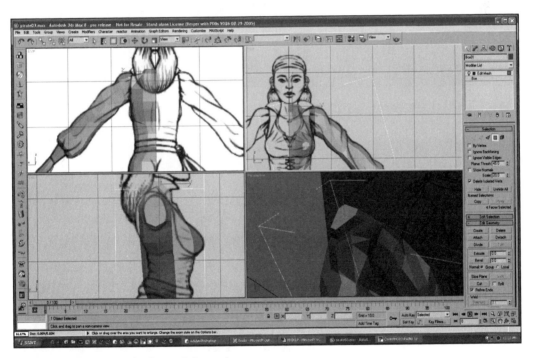

Figure 6.46 Start at the base of the neck.

3. Extrude the polygons again and pull them up to the jaw, as shown in Figure 6.47.

4. Extrude again to form the base of the jawbone.

5. Now select the polygons at the front of the jaw and extrude them toward the chin, as shown in Figure 6.48.

Figure 6.47 Extrude the neck polygons to the jaw.

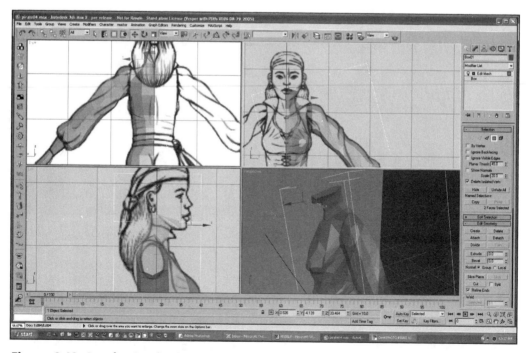

Figure 6.48 Start forming the chin.

6. Extrude the chin polygons one more time to reach the chin, as shown in Figure 6.49.

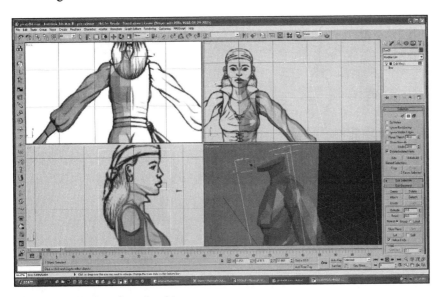

Figure 6.49 Complete the chin.

7. Shape the polygons of the chin to follow the jaw line back to the ear.

8. Now you can select the top polygons of the head and extrude them upward to the mouth, as shown in Figure 6.50.

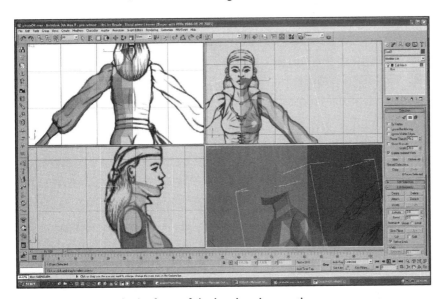

Figure 6.50 Extrude the faces of the head to the mouth.

9. Continue extruding the polygons of the head in small increments to the top of the lips, the bottom of the nose, and so on—all the way to the top of the head, as shown in Figure 6.51. Follow the contour of the face, not the nose.

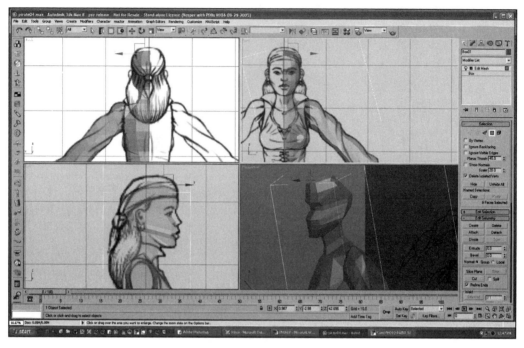

Figure 6.51 Extrude the head of the character.

10. Now for the nose. Adjust the vertices around the base of the nose.

11. Next select the polygons of the nose and extrude them outward, as shown in Figure 6.52.

12. Use the Snap tool, set to Vertex, to pull the top of the extrusion back to the forehead.

13. Weld the top two vertices of the nose to the forehead, as shown in Figure 6.53.

14. Next, extrude the polygons of the upper and lower lips, as shown in Figure 6.54.

15. In Vertex Selection mode, shape the lips to follow the contours of the lips on the template, as shown in Figure 6.55.

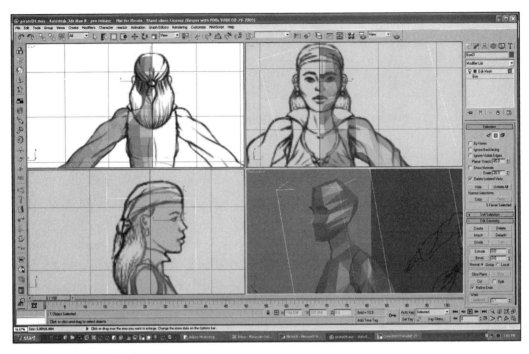

Figure 6.52 Extrude the nose.

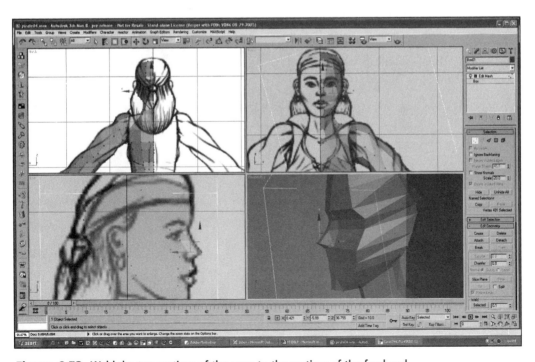

Figure 6.53 Weld the top vertices of the nose to the vertices of the forehead.

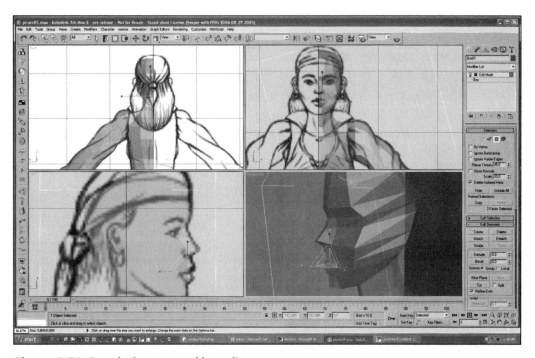

Figure 6.54 Extrude the upper and lower lips.

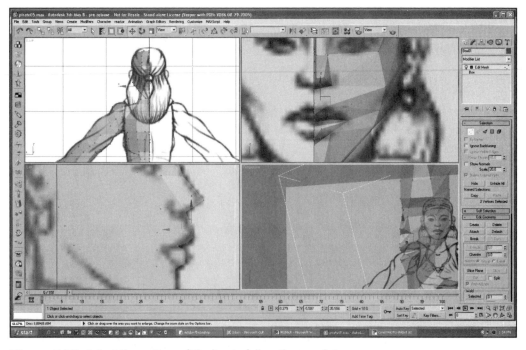

Figure 6.55 Adjust the vertices of the lips to follow the template.

16. Pull the vertices around the top of the head to follow the head back to the knot in the scarf, as shown in Figure 6.56.

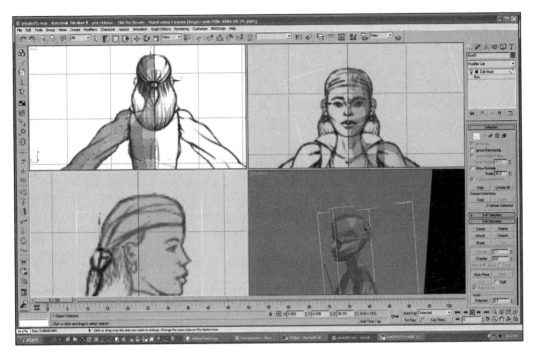

Figure 6.56 Shape the back of the head.

17. You will want the hair to be able to move a little when the character animates. Adjust the back of the character's neck so that you can extrude the hair downward, independent of the neck, as shown in Figure 6.57.

18. Now, extrude the hair down following the contour of the hair on the template, as shown in Figure 6.58.

19. Move the vertices at the bottom of the hair so they are not so flat (see Figure 6.59).

20. Now is a good time to take a look at the model and fix any problems with the shape of the character. Do a little fine-tuning. Your model should look like Figure 6.60 at this point.

21. Now that you are finished with the majority of the model along the mirror seam, you should make sure the vertices of the seam line up perfectly with the center axis of the model. Select the vertices along the seam.

22. Use the Scale tool to flatten the vertices along the center seam.

Figure 6.57 Adjust the vertices of the neck.

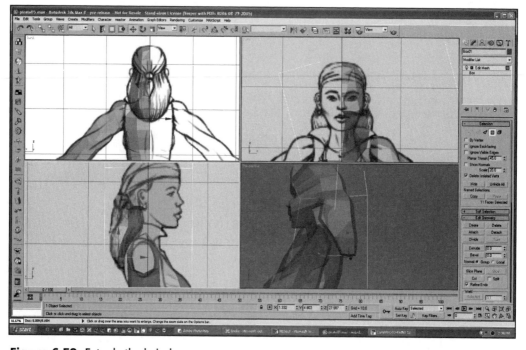

Figure 6.58 Extrude the hair down.

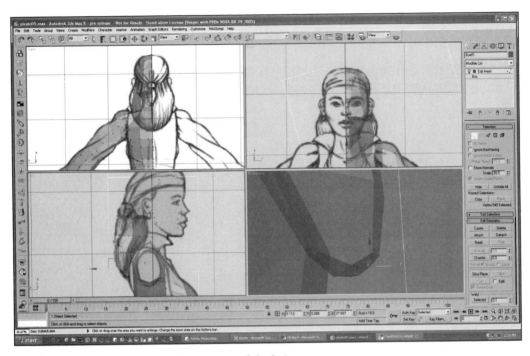

Figure 6.59 Fix the vertices at the bottom of the hair.

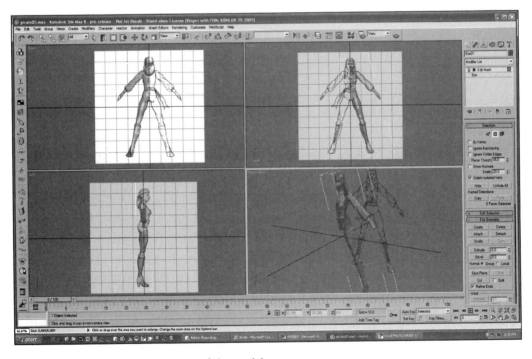

Figure 6.60 Do a little fine-tuning of the model.

23. When the vertices are completely flat, move them so they are flush with the center line, as shown in Figure 6.61.

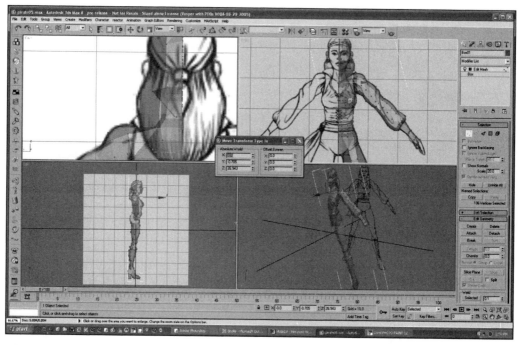

Figure 6.61 Make the vertices along the mirror seam flush with the center.

24. To mirror properly, you need to remove the polygons along the seam. Select them, as shown in Figure 6.62, and delete them. These polygons are not needed in the model and will cause problems later when you try to mirror the model.

25. Now you can go back to modeling the face. You will use the Cut tool in the Edit Geometry rollout to add some needed polygons to the eye of the character. Cut the polygons, as shown in Figure 6.63.

26. When cutting polygons you will often find that the vertices created might not line up perfectly with the vertices already there. After every cut, I always check to see whether there are more vertices than I need. In this case I got an extra vertex inside the nose (see Figure 6.64). I had to remove this vertex.

27. Now you need to move the vertices around the eyes to better follow the shape of the eye. In addition, cut some of the polygons around the nose to give it a more natural shape.

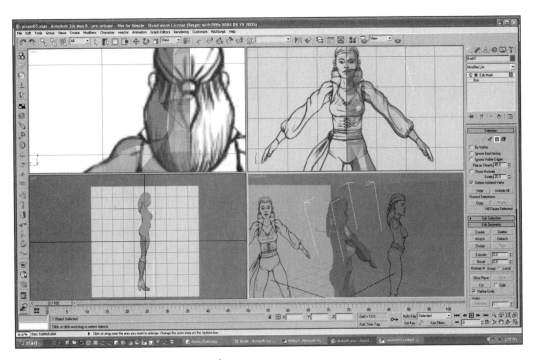

Figure 6.62 Select the mirror seam polygons.

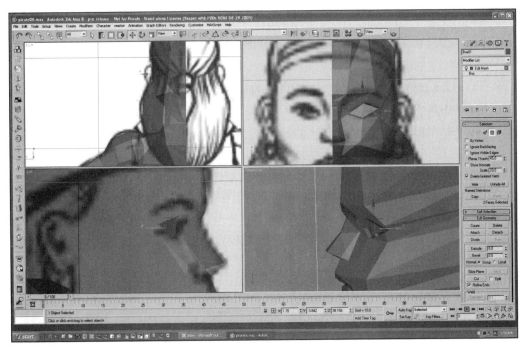

Figure 6.63 Cut some polygons to help form the eye.

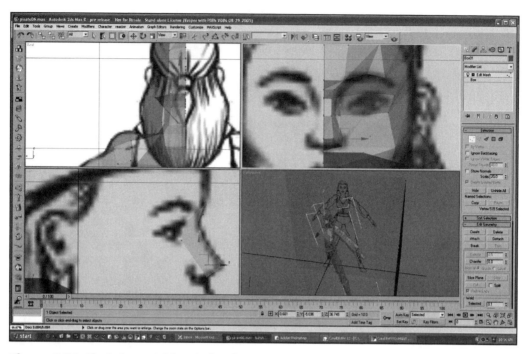

Figure 6.64 Check the model for misplaced vertices.

28. There will be a few vertices that need to be welded together. You can use the Scale tool to bring these vertices together and the Weld tool to join them, as shown in Figure 6.65.

29. Take the center vertex of the eyeball and pull it forward to look more like an eyeball, as shown in Figure 6.66.

30. Now extrude the eyeball inward to give dimension to the eyelids, as shown in Figure 6.67.

31. The head needs a few more polygons around the cheeks and the side of the head to help give it a more rounded shape. Starting from the eye, cut the polygons along the cheek, as shown in Figure 6.68.

32. Cut the polygons along the side of the face from the top of the head to the jaw line.

33. Now you can move the vertices of the face and give your pirate girl a softer, more rounded head (see Figure 6.69).

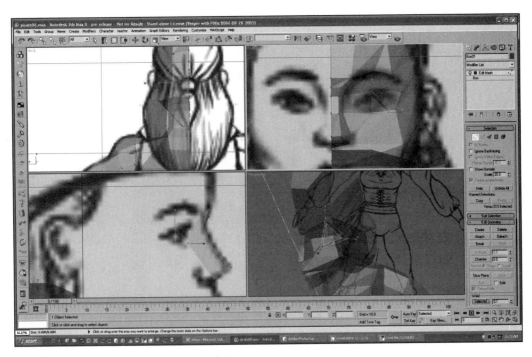

Figure 6.65 Weld vertices where needed.

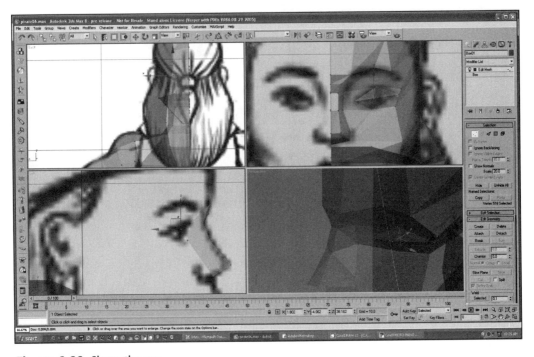

Figure 6.66 Shape the eye.

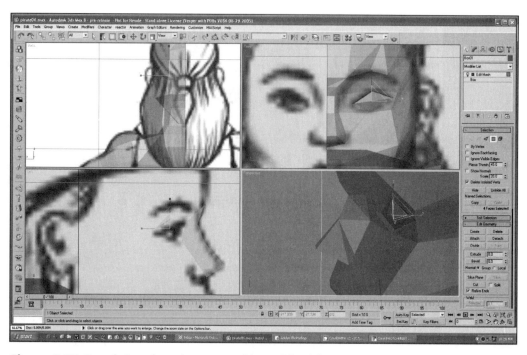

Figure 6.67 Extrude in to form the upper and lower lids of the eye.

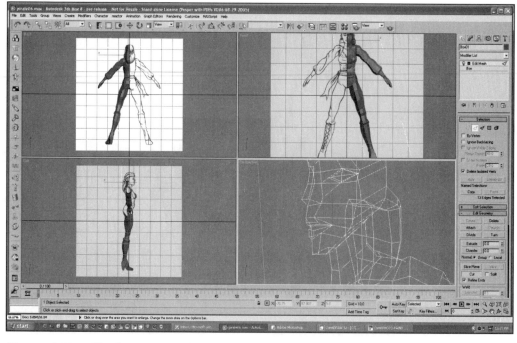

Figure 6.68 Add polygons to the cheek.

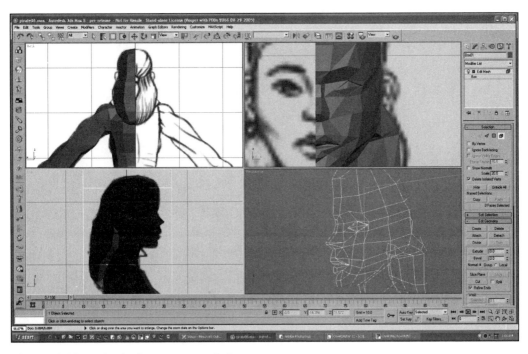

Figure 6.69 Make the face more rounded.

34. Now you need to work on the ear, but the template for the Side view is on the wrong side of your model. Move the side template to a –50 X position with the Move tool.

35. You will need to rotate the template 180 degrees around the Z axis to get it to face the model.

36. Notice that the map is facing the wrong direction. Replace it with the original Side view you had before you flipped it to set up the template. You might need to rotate the image to get it in the right position (see Figure 6.70).

37. In the Side view, move the vertices around the ear so they surround it, as shown in Figure 6.71.

38. Cut the polygons down the center of the ear and adjust the vertices, as shown in Figure 6.72.

39. Cut the polygons of the ear again along the inside of the outer ridge of the ear.

40. Select the polygons of the ear and extrude them outward twice, as shown in Figure 6.73.

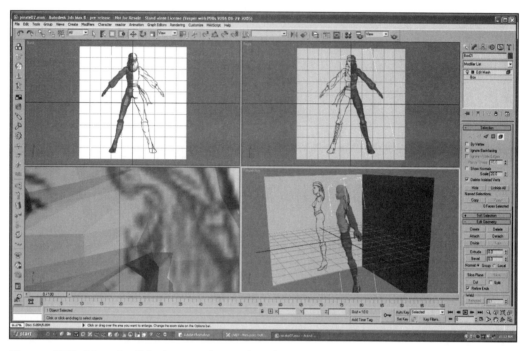

Figure 6.70 Move the Side view template to the other side of the model.

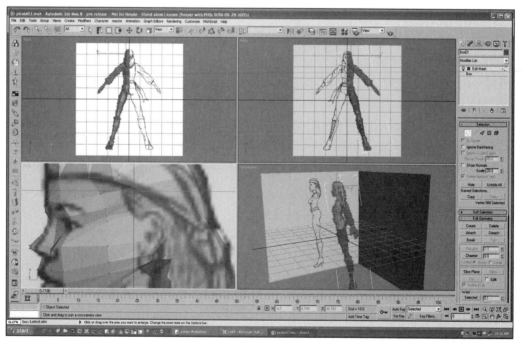

Figure 6.71 Move the vertices around the ear.

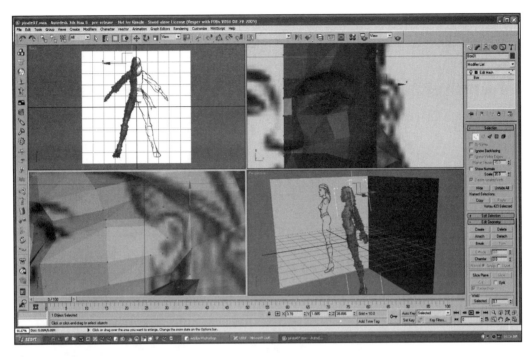

Figure 6.72 Cut the polygons down the center of the ear.

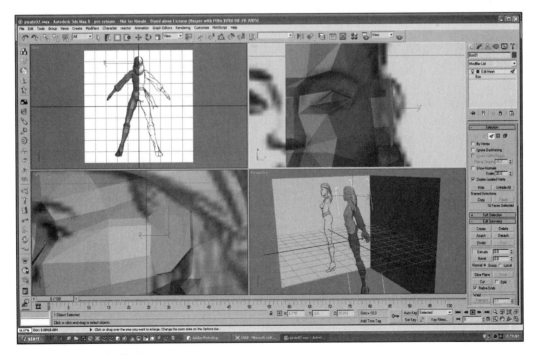

Figure 6.73 Extrude the ear.

41. Snap the extruded vertices along the front of the ear back to the head and weld them in place, as shown in Figure 6.74.

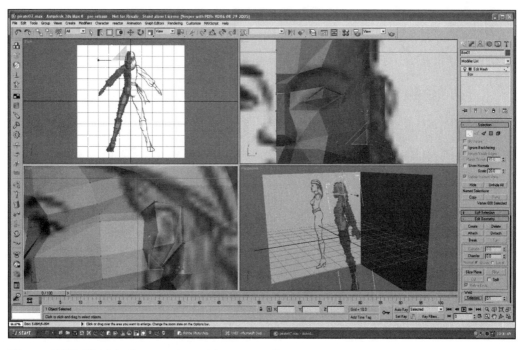

Figure 6.74 Weld the front vertices of the ear together.

42. Make an additional cut to help define the ridge around the inner ear and adjust the vertices, as shown in Figure 6.75. For this and the next few steps I turned off See Through so I could better see the shape of the model.

43. Select the polygons of the inner ear and extrude them in, as shown in Figure 6.76.

44. Weld the vertices along the bottom of the extrusion and on the upper-front of the ear. Refer to Figure 6.77 for how this should look. For games, only the general shape of the ear is needed. Fully modeling the ear is unnecessary.

The head is now set up and ready to go. You are almost done with the model. Just a few more things and you will be finished. Hang in there.

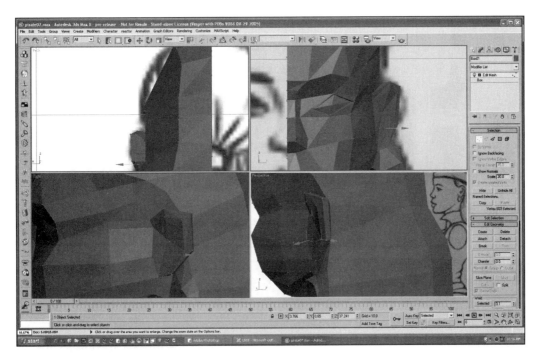

Figure 6.75 Adjust the inside vertices of the ear.

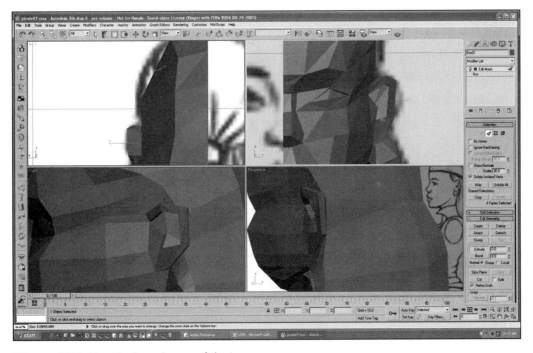

Figure 6.76 Extrude the polygons of the inner ear.

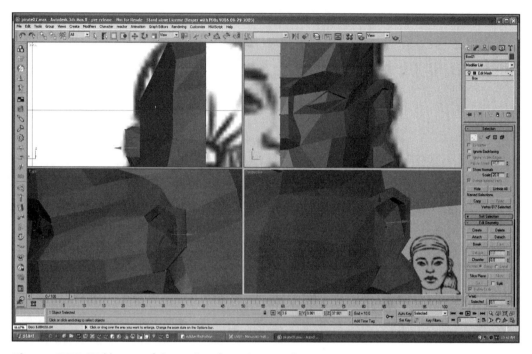

Figure 6.77 Weld some of the vertices from the extrusion.

Finishing the Model

The next thing you need to tackle is finishing the modeling of the hand and fingers. Scroll down to that area of the model to begin.

1. Start with the thumb. Select the polygon along the front of the palm near the wrist and extrude it out, as shown in Figure 6.78.

2. Move the upper vertices down along the thumb to give the base of the thumb a better shape. Refer to Figure 6.79.

3. Now extrude the polygon outward to the knuckle and then to the end of the thumb, as shown in Figure 6.80. Scale the extrusions to taper the thumb as shown.

4. To save polygons we will only give our character two fingers. One finger will be the first finger from the thumb, and the other will be a combination of the remaining three fingers. The three fingers will be defined in the texture. This method allows the character to point and be expressive with her hands without us having to use polygons for each digit. Adjust the vertices of the palm, as shown in Figure 6.81, to prepare for extruding the fingers.

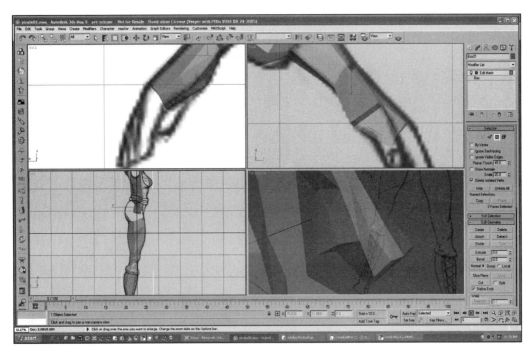

Figure 6.78 Extrude the base of the thumb.

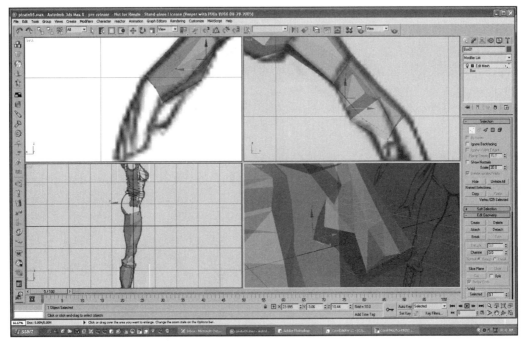

Figure 6.79 Adjust the shape of the extrusion.

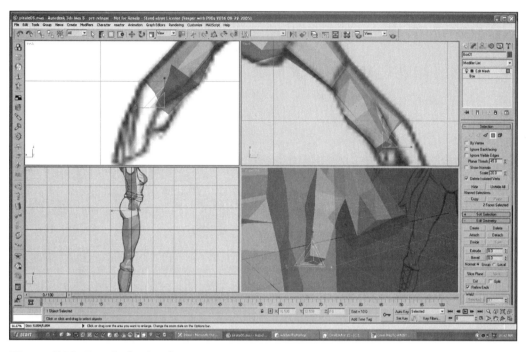

Figure 6.80 Extrude the thumb.

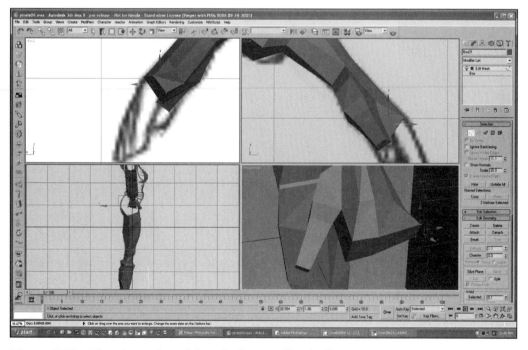

Figure 6.81 Adjust the vertices of the palm for extruding the fingers.

5. Extrude the first finger three times, stopping at each knuckle and the end of the finger, as shown in Figure 6.82. Scale the extrusions to taper the finger.

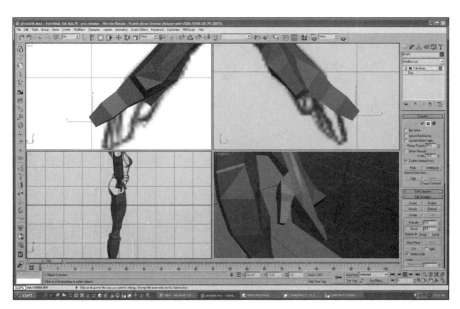

Figure 6.82 Extrude the first finger.

6. Repeat the process for the other three fingers, as shown in Figure 6.83.

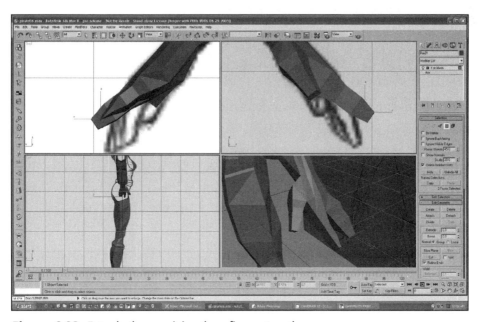

Figure 6.83 Extrude the remaining three fingers together.

7. Now go back in and adjust the placement of the vertices so they form a nicely shaped hand. Look at Figure 6.84 for a reference of how this should look.

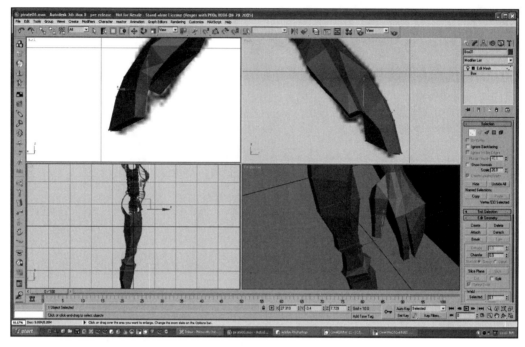

Figure 6.84 Shape the hand and fingers so they look right.

8. Now you can move on to the collar. Cut the polygons to form the base of the collar, as shown in Figure 6.85.

9. Select the polygons of the collar and extrude them up twice, as shown in Figure 6.86.

10. If the character's hair were to remain in one place and not animate, the collar would only need to run into the hair, but because you are making the hair so it can animate, you will need to complete the collar around the back of the neck. Cut and extrude the collar around the back of the neck, as shown in Figure 6.87.

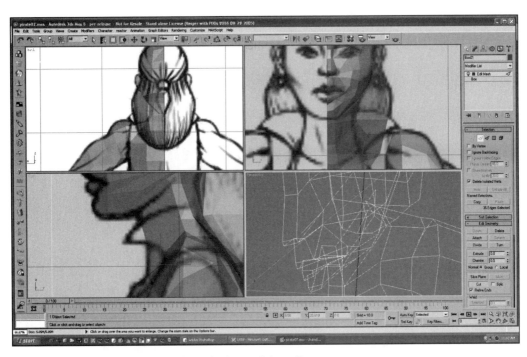

Figure 6.85 Cut the polygons along the base of the collar.

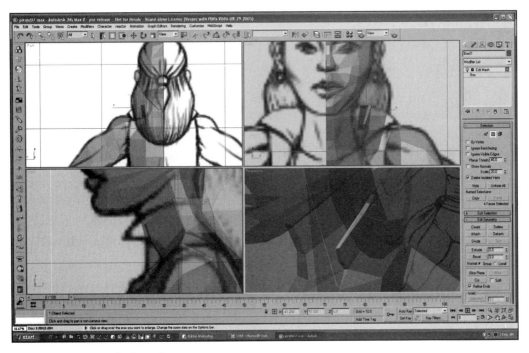

Figure 6.86 Extrude the collar.

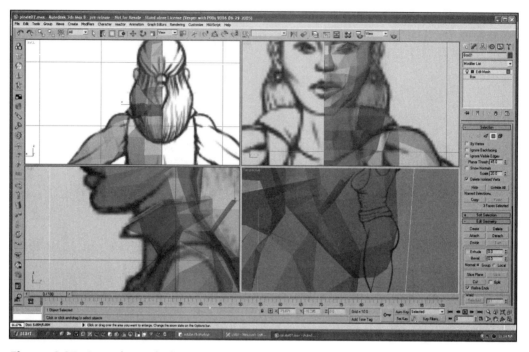

Figure 6.87 Cut and extrude the collar on the back of the neck.

11. Weld the two sections of the collar together and delete the polygons between them.

12. You will also need to delete the polygons of the collar along the mirror seam.

13. Our character has an earring. That will be the next thing you model. Select the polygon of the earlobe and extrude it, but instead of pulling it out from the ear, scale it in, as shown in Figure 6.88.

14. Now extrude the earring out several times, as shown in Figure 6.89. Later, you will rotate the extrusions to make a loop, so make several extrusions.

15. Rotate the earring back on itself to form a loop (see Figure 6.90). The earring adds several polygons to the model, but what is a pirate without an earring?

16. The hair is flat at this point, yet the character has a scarf on her head with a knot in the back. Cut along the back of the hair to where the scarf and hair meet, as shown in Figure 6.91.

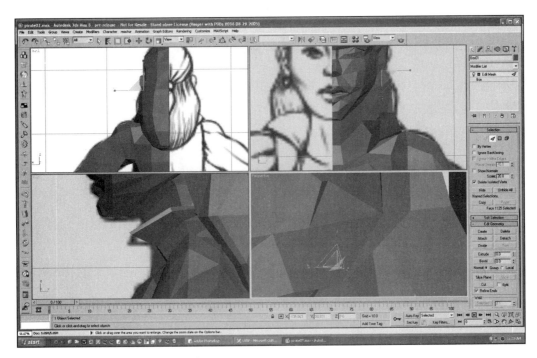

Figure 6.88 Scale the earlobe in for the earring.

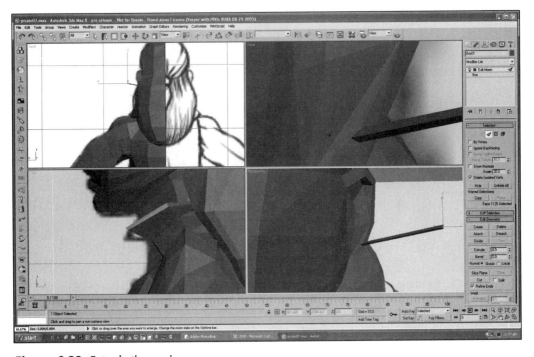

Figure 6.89 Extrude the earring.

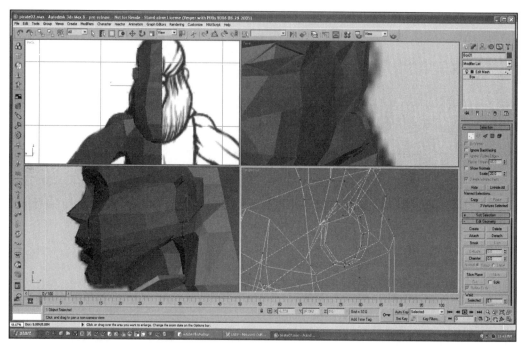

Figure 6.90 Rotate the earring to form a loop.

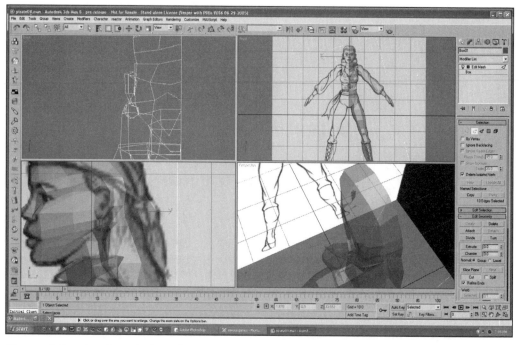

Figure 6.91 Cut along the line of the scarf.

17. Make a second cut along the middle of the scarf.

18. Now shape the scarf, as shown in Figure 6.92.

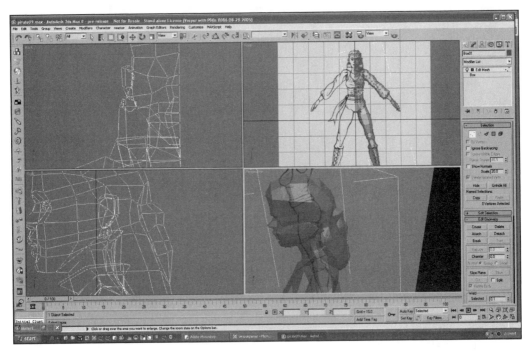

Figure 6.92 Adjust the vertices of scarf and hair.

Now you are finished with the model of your pirate character. Before you go on to create the texture maps, however, it is a good idea to give the character model one final look to see whether any adjustments need to be made. It is better to adjust your model now than to do it when there are a lot of other modifiers on the model. The finished model should look like Figure 6.93.

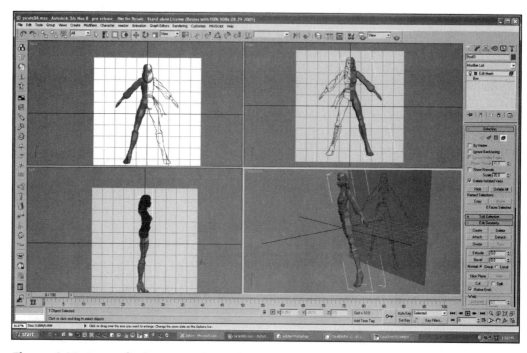

Figure 6.93 Do one final pass over the model, adjusting where needed.

Texturing the Character

Most video games combine the textures of a character into a single texture map, sometimes called a *blanket* or *pelt*. For your pirate girl, you will create a single texture map that measures 512×512 pixels. Before you even start painting, however, you will need to set up the map in 3ds Max so you have a guide.

The pelt for the character will be 512×512 pixels. For now, load a solid black texture map into the next available Sample Slot.

Preparing the Model for Mapping

The first step in preparing the model for mapping is to separate and label the Material ID. A Material ID is a way for you to isolate mapping areas on your model. In Figure 6.94 the polygons of the head are selected. These polygons will later be mapped with a circular projection.

Scroll down the rollouts to Surface Properties and type 1 in the Set ID box, as shown in Figure 6.94. Every polygon on the model needs to be part of a Material ID, even down to the girl's earring, which I have given a Material ID of 2 in Figure 6.95.

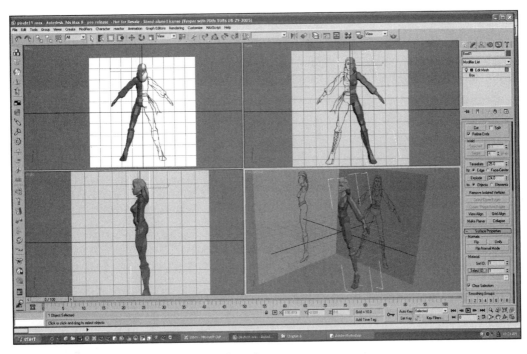

Figure 6.94 The head is given a Material ID of 1.

Figure 6.95 The earring is given a Material ID of 2.

The way you isolate your model depends on the types of mapping projections you will use. Most of the time I like to use circular projections, but in some cases, such as the hands, I use planar projections. In mapping this character I used 10 different Material IDs, as follows.

- Head
- Earring
- Hair
- Collar
- Torso
- Arm
- Hand
- Hip and leg
- Boots
- Heel and sole of boot

Figure 6.96 shows how the torso was isolated. It includes everything from the neck down to the bottom of the sash. The hip could also be included, but I find it much better split the IDs based on hard transitions from one color to another, such as in the pants and the sash, rather than splitting along an area within the pants. It helps to keep painted seams out of the texture.

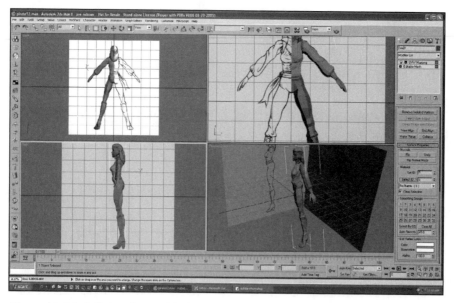

Figure 6.96 Splitting the model along a hard break in color helps reduce seams.

Projecting Maps

To have multiple projections on a single map from a single object mesh, you need to use a special type of shader called a Multi/Sub-Object Material. Bring up the Material Editor, as shown in Figure 6.97, and select the black material you loaded earlier.

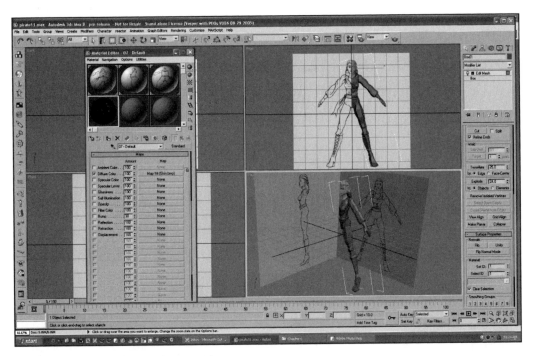

Figure 6.97 Select the black material.

Now click on the box labeled Standard, just below the row of icons in the Editor. This will bring up the Material/Map Browser, as shown in Figure 6.98. Select Multi/Sub-Object from the list, as shown.

You are now ready to start projecting maps to the character.

1. Collapse the stack and set the Material ID selection to 1 so the head is selected.

2. Select UVW Map from the Modifier List to bring up the mapping options.

3. The modifier will come up with a Planar projection, which is the default projection mode. Change the projection to Cylindrical.

4. Change the alignment to X.

5. This next part will be a little tricky. You need to rotate the projector into the right position. Click on the plus sign next to the UVW Mapping line in the stack to access the mapping gizmo. With the gizmo on, you can rotate the projection instead of the model.

6. The projection needs to be lined up so the seam (marked in green on the projection cage) is directly behind the character's head so it will mirror properly. You also need to rotate the projection so its projection cage line runs exactly vertical.

7. Click the Fit button on the Alignment rollout.

8. Now the projection needs to be centered on 0 in the X axis.

9. Scale the projection so it is larger than the mapping area, as shown in Figure 6.99.

10. When you are finished, collapse the stack.

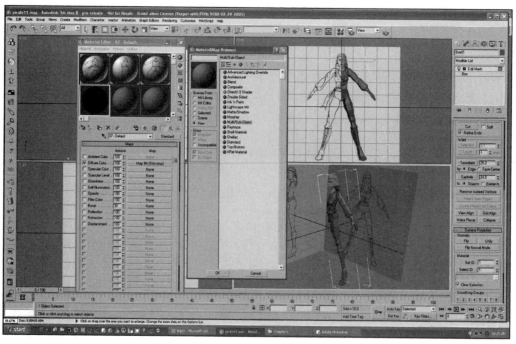

Figure 6.98 Select Multi/Sub-Object from the list.

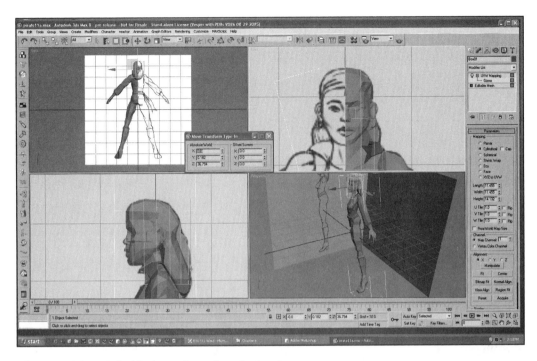

Figure 6.99 A Cylindrical map is used on the head.

That is pretty much it for projection mapping. You will need to go through each of your mapping sets and project a map on each one. With my model I used Cylindrical maps for everything except the hand and the bottom of the boot, where I used Planar maps. Make sure on the torso, collar, and hair that you center to Cylindrical projection on the X axis, as you did with the head. For the arm, leg, and boot, the Circular map should follow the angle of the limb. This might take a little while, but don't worry; this book will still be here when you are done, so take your time.

Unwrapping the UVWs

You must be done projecting maps, if you are reading this. Now comes a really interesting part of the process. You will need to organize the UVWs of the model on your texture area. You will use the Unwrap UVW modifier to do this.

1. Select the model in Object selection mode and then select Unwrap UVW from the Modifier List.

2. Click on the Edit button in the Modifier rollout to bring up the Edit UVWs Editor.

3. You will see all of your projection maps directly over each other in the Editor. It will look a lot like a bowl of spaghetti. Drop back to the Edit Mesh modifier. Ignore the warning pop-up.

4. Now go to the Material ID and set it to 1.

5. The Editor will now only display the first projection of the girl's head laid out flat, as shown in Figure 6.100.

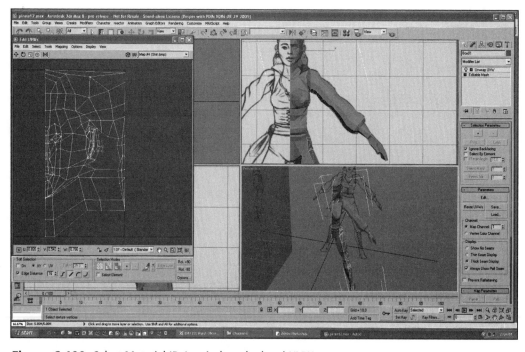

Figure 6.100 Select Material ID 1 to isolate the head UVWs.

6. You need to do two things with the UVWs of the head. First, you need to scale them down so they take up about a quarter of the texture area. You can use the tools on the upper-left panel of the Editor, just below the menu, to move, rotate, and scale selected UVWs.

7. Next, you need to open up any overlapping UVWs in the ear area. Figure 6.101 shows how the UVWs should look after the overlapping ones are flattened out.

Continue working on each Material ID set until you have all of them laid out on the texture and not overlapping. Figure 6.102 shows how mine are laid out.

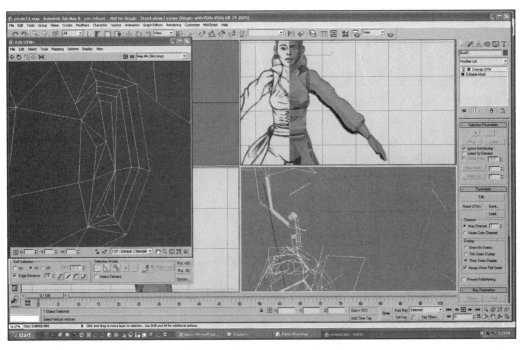

Figure 6.101 Spread the overlapping UVWs out flat in the editor.

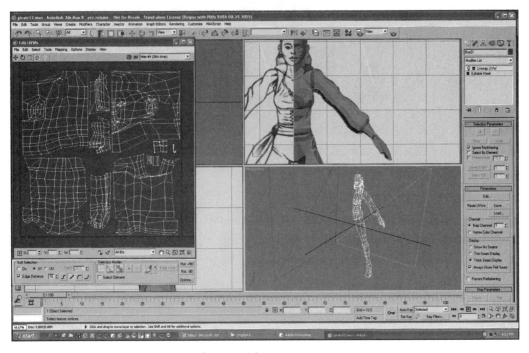

Figure 6.102 Organize the UVWs of the model.

Painting the Texture Map

Now you can use the UVW map as a guide for painting the texture map. First, you will need to get the guide into a 2D painting program, such as Corel Painter. In Edit UVW, go to the Tools menu and then to Render UVW Template. Set the template size to 1024×1024 and then click on Render UV Template at the bottom of the pop-up window. The template will be rendered and can be saved in any file format you want. Alternatively, you can just do a screen grab of the Editor by pressing Print Screen on the keyboard and pasting it into a paint program and cropping it, as shown in Figure 6.103.

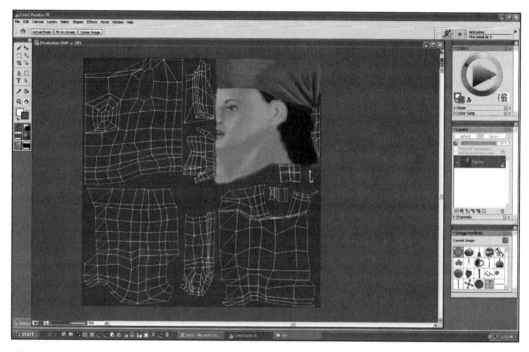

Figure 6.103 Use the guide to paint the texture map.

Continue to paint the texture map until you have all of the texture areas covered. Figure 6.104 shows my final texture map in Corel Painter.

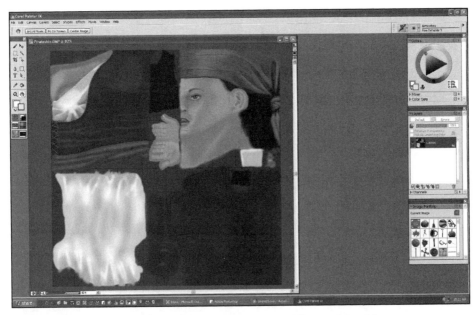

Figure 6.104 Paint each part of the texture map according to the guide.

Applying the Painted Texture Map

When the texture map is finished, you will need to load it into 3ds Max and apply it to the model.

1. Bring up the Material Editor and select the Multi/Sub-Object Material shader (see Figure 6.105).

2. Click on the first sub-material and go to the Maps rollout menu.

3. There will already be a map loaded in Diffuse Color because we loaded the black texture earlier. Click on it.

4. Under Bitmap Parameters, click on the button that has the path to the current bitmap.

5. Browse to the new texture map you just painted and load it. You will see it in the shader sphere.

6. Now you will need to click on two icons in the icon row to apply the texture to the model. First, click on the Apply Material icon, which is the third icon from the left. Next, click on the View Material icon, which is the fourth icon from the right. The face texture should now show up on the model (see Figure 6.106). Alternatively, you can drag the material directly from the Sample Slot to the object.

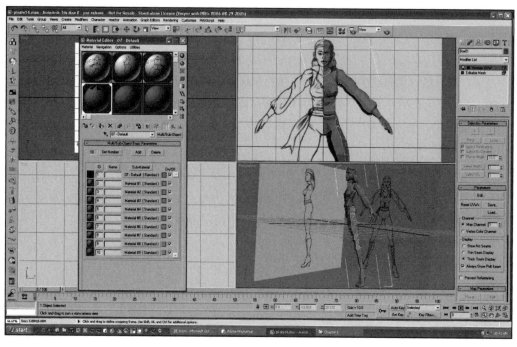

Figure 6.105 Select the Multi/Sub-Object Material shader.

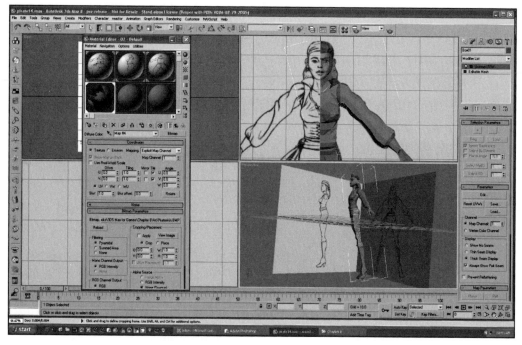

Figure 6.106 Apply the texture map to the model.

7. There is a Go to Parent black arrow icon second in from the right. Click it twice to go back to the Multi/Sub-Object Base Parameters rollout.

8. The next material has not had a map loaded into Diffuse Color, so when you click on the material button you will notice that nothing is loaded there.

9. A series of rollouts will appear. Click on the one labeled Maps.

10. Now click on Diffuse Color to bring up the Material/Map Browser, as shown in Figure 6.107.

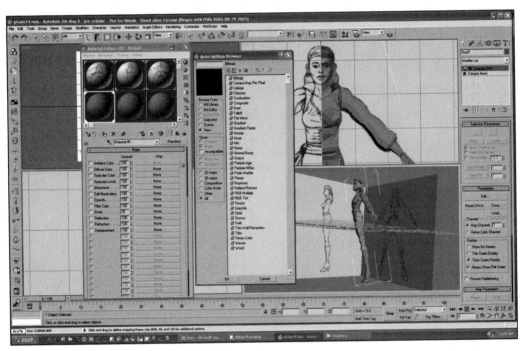

Figure 6.107 Load a bitmap into the second material on the list.

11. Double-click on Bitmap at the top of the list and load the new texture into this slot as well.

12. Apply the texture to the model as you did the first material.

You will need to repeat the process of loading the texture map into each material on the list. Figure 6.108 shows the texture map loaded into all of the slots.

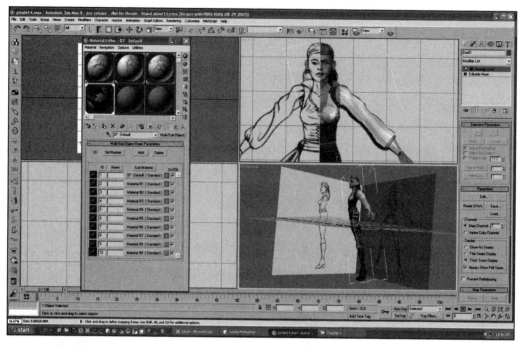

Figure 6.108 Load the texture map into all the material slots.

The model is now textured completely. If you did your painting correctly, the textures should all line up with the UVWs. If you need to adjust any of the textures on the model, you can go back into the UVWs Editor and move the UVWs until they are correct.

Mirroring the Model

Now that the model is built and textured, it is time to complete the other half by mirroring the model. The Mirror function icon is located on the top of the main interface row of icons. It is on the left side and looks like two triangles pointing at each other with a line in between.

1. Collapse the stack so the mirror function works correctly and click on the icon to bring up the Mirror: World Coordinates dialog box, as shown in Figure 6.109.

2. You will need to scroll in closely to the model in the Front view in Wireframe mode to line the mirrored object up with the original. You need to make the object a copy, so select Copy in the dialog box.

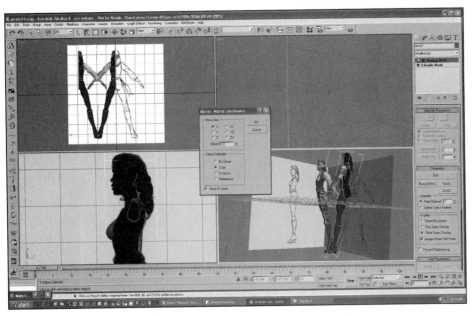

Figure 6.109 Bring up the Mirror: World Coordinates dialog box.

3. The mirrored model is not in the right position, so move it using the dialog box. To do so, type in the coordinates, as shown in Figure 6.110.

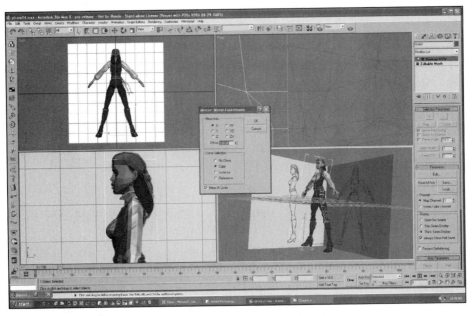

Figure 6.110 Move the copy to line up with the original model.

4. The two halves need to be joined into a single object. Go to the Create tab in the Side Bar and select Compound Object from the pull-down menu. An Object Type rollout will appear. Click on Connect, as shown in Figure 6.111.

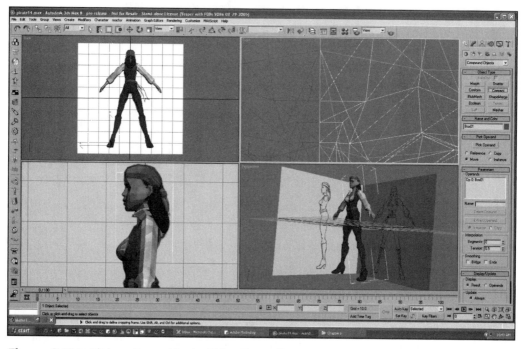

Figure 6.111 Click on Connect in the Object Type rollout.

5. Click on the Pick Operand button and then click on the unselected object of the two mirrored objects, as shown in Figure 6.112.

6. Now that you have a single object, you need to weld all of the vertices along the seam of the two halves. Go back to the Modify tab, collapse the stack, and make the model an Editable Mesh once more by selecting Editable Mesh from the Modifier List.

7. From the Front view, select all of the vertices along the seam of the two halves and weld them together, as shown in Figure 6.113.

8. The model is almost finished. There is just one more thing to do, and that is to smooth the facets of the model. Change the selection mode to Edges and select all the edges of the model. From the Modifier List choose Smooth. Click on Auto Smooth and then change the Threshold to 60, as shown in Figure 6.114.

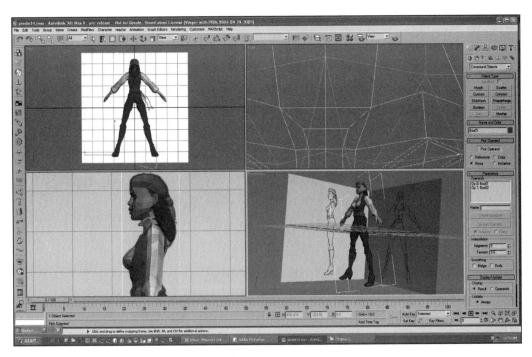

Figure 6.112 Click on the unselected of the two halves.

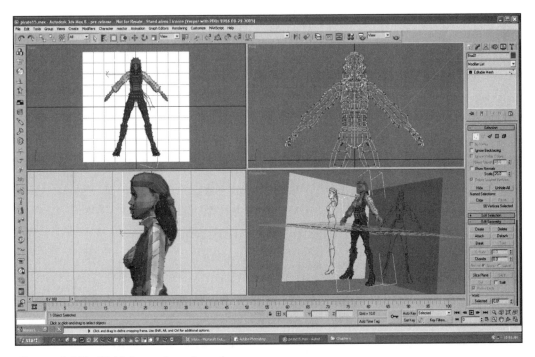

Figure 6.113 Weld the vertices along the seam.

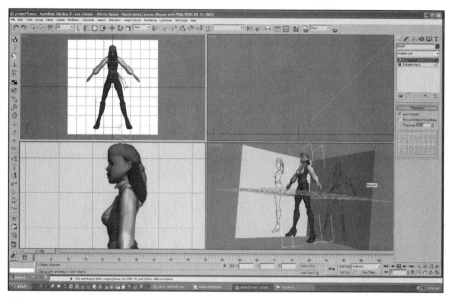

Figure 6.114 Add the Smooth modifier to the model.

There you have it, a finished character model for a game, ready to move on to animation. You should be proud of yourself for making it this far. In Figure 6.115 I have rendered the model to show how it will look in a game. Hopefully yours will look similar. Now that you know how to create a character, try designing a few of your own.

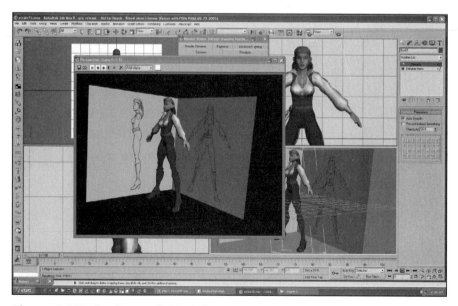

Figure 6.115 Render your finished character.

Summary

Character creation is one of the most rewarding and challenging jobs of a game artist. It is very rewarding for the artist to see a character that she or he designed in a game. It is also challenging to come up with characters that enhance the game design.

This chapter was devoted to character creation. You should now be familiar with many aspects of character creation. In this chapter, we covered several important points.

- Game characters
- Player characters
- Non-player characters
- Enemies
- Character templates
- Polygon budgets
- Character modeling
- Character texturing

Creating good characters for games is a challenging process and takes many steps, yet when the end result is a great game character, the artist can feel satisfied that the outcome was worth all the effort.

Questions

1. Why is character creation important in game design?
2. Who has the main responsibility for creating interesting characters?
3. What are game characters?
4. What is the software that controls characters in games called?
5. A character that is controlled by the player is called what?
6. What do the letters NPC stand for?
7. What makes an NPC an enemy character?
8. Where did the game industry borrow the use of model sheets from?
9. What is a model sheet?
10. What type of art is used to keep the game characters consistent with the designed characters?

11. What is a drawing without perspective called?

12. What tells the artist the number of polygons to use in creating a game character?

13. If all characters in a game had equal numbers of polygons and the budget for characters was 10,000 per frame, how many 2,000-polygon characters could be seen onscreen at any one time?

14. What modifier allows the artist to adjust an object on a sub-object level?

15. Maps are loaded into materials using which Editor?

Answers

1. Because the characters are the focal point of the game

2. The concept artist

3. All intelligent people or creatures in a game

4. Artificial Intelligence

5. Player character

6. Non-player character

7. It can defeat the player.

8. The motion-picture animation industry

9. A template created by the concept artist to help the development team construct accurate models of the designed characters

10. Model sheets

11. An isometric drawing

12. The polygon budget

13. Five

14. Editable Mesh

15. The Material Editor

Discussion Questions

1. Why is the study of figure drawing important in character design?
2. How does simplifying figures into simple geometric shapes help the character artist?
3. Why are characters so important in game design?
4. Why is it important for the artist to maintain a polygon budget for character modeling?
5. What are some good reasons to use a model sheet when building characters?

Exercises

1. Create a model sheet of a favorite character from your favorite game. The model sheet should have enough views to take into account any differences from one side of the character to another.
2. Create a character model based on a model sheet you have created.
3. Create and texture a model of a character for a sports game. Make the character as realistic as possible.

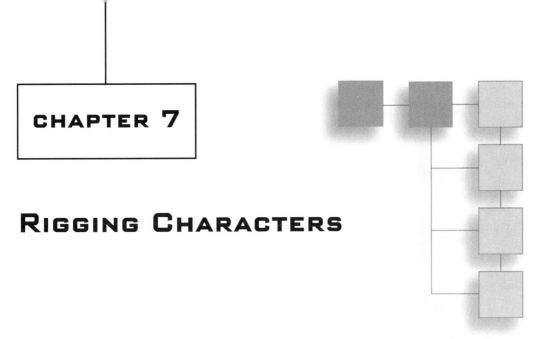

CHAPTER 7

RIGGING CHARACTERS

Rigging is a term used in model creation that refers to the process of attaching a bone system to a 3D model. It is kind of like our own bodies. We have bones and joints that make up a skeleton. Our muscles are attached to our skeletons. By contracting and relaxing a series of muscles we are able to move about.

The human skeletal system of joints, bones, and muscles has its drawbacks. We can only run so fast, jump so high, lift so much, fall so hard, and twist so far. Yet with all its drawbacks the system has worked fairly well for us for the last several thousand years. Is it any wonder that 3ds Max would use the same type of system, or at least one that is similar?

3ds Max has two systems for rigging and animating characters—Bones and Biped. Biped was originally a 3ds Max plug-in called Character Studio, but in version 7 of the software it was incorporated into the main program. This chapter will first cover how to rig a character in Biped, and then it will explore Bones.

The Biped System

Biped is a predefined system for creating skeleton hierarchies for two-legged character models. That was kind of a mouthful, wasn't it? What it really means is that with Biped, you work with a skeleton that is already assembled instead of having to build one yourself. Biped works great for almost all two-legged characters and can even be used for four-legged characters with some modifications.

The advantage of using a Biped skeleton is that a lot of time and effort went into creating a good skeleton that includes systems for muscle flexing and restraints on movement so the knee or elbow doesn't bend the wrong way. Biped skeletons are fully set up with advanced inverse kinematics and flexing mechanisms that it would take hours to create by hand.

A Biped skeleton controls the motion of a model by using a modifier called *Physique* that attaches the model to the skeleton. The attachment is done on a per-vertex basis, allowing every vertex to move independently. In the following example you will see how to add a Biped to the pirate-girl model. You will also scale the Biped to match the frame of the girl, and then you will learn how to attach the Biped skeleton to the model of the girl so she can animate.

1. First, bring up 3ds Max and load the model of the pirate girl.

2. Next, delete the template and change the orthogonal views to Wireframe, as shown in Figure 7.1.

3. Under the Create tab there is a row of icons. Click on the Systems icon on the far right, as shown in Figure 7.2.

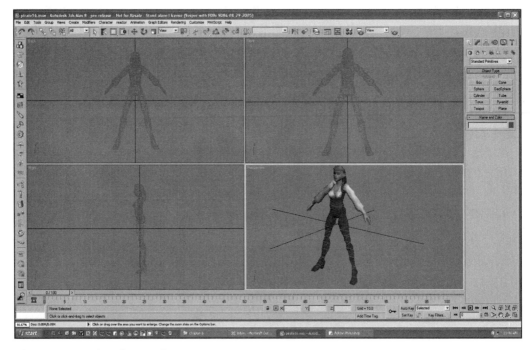

Figure 7.1 Delete the template.

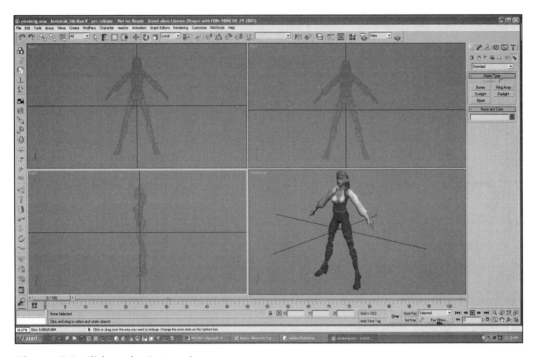

Figure 7.2 Click on the Systems icon.

4. Now, in the Object Type rollout, click on Biped, and in the Create Biped rollout, set the following amounts in the attribute boxes:

- Neck Links: 1
- Spine Links: 4
- Leg Links: 3
- Tail Links: 0
- Ponytail1 Links: 2
- Ponytail2 Links: 0
- Fingers: 3
- Finger Links: 3
- Toes: 1
- Toe Links: 1

5. Place the cursor at the bottom of the model's feet in the Front view and then, holding the left mouse button down, drag upward to insert a Biped skeletal system into the scene. Continue to pull upward until the yellow hip section of the skeleton is positioned properly in the girl's hips, as shown in Figure 7.3.

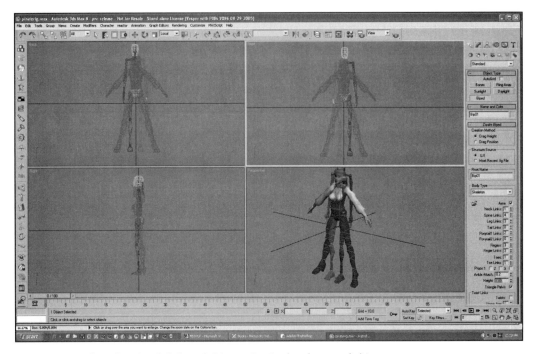

Figure 7.3 Place the Biped skeleton's hip section in the character's hips.

6. If your model is the same size as mine, then the height of the Biped skeleton should be 98.

7. Now you need to line up the Biped skeleton with the model. Go to the Motion tab and click on it to bring up the Motion rollouts, as shown in Figure 7.4.

8. You need to work in Figure mode when scaling, moving, or rotating the Biped skeleton to fit the model. Turn Figure mode on by clicking on the icon of a figure in the Biped rollout.

9. You can now use the manipulator tools to position the Biped skeleton. To move the entire skeleton, select the white diamond-shaped node inside the pelvis. This node is called the COM, which stands for *Center Of Mass*. First, use the Move tool to slide the Biped horizontally to the center of the model, as shown in Figure 7.5.

10. Next, in the Side view, center the pelvis in the hips, as shown in Figure 7.6.

11. Now, you need to work on the legs. Select the skeleton's left thigh link; it is the one colored blue (see Figure 7.7).

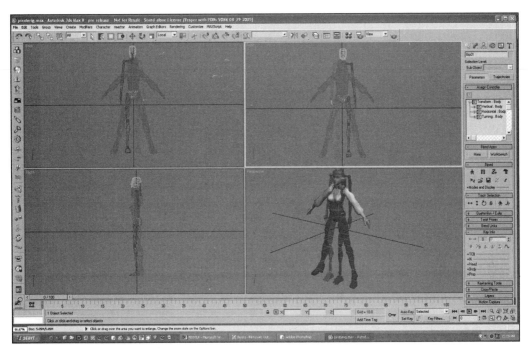

Figure 7.4 Click on the Motion tab.

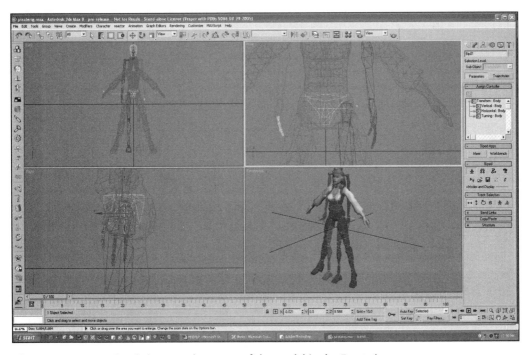

Figure 7.5 Move the skeleton to the center of the model in the Front view.

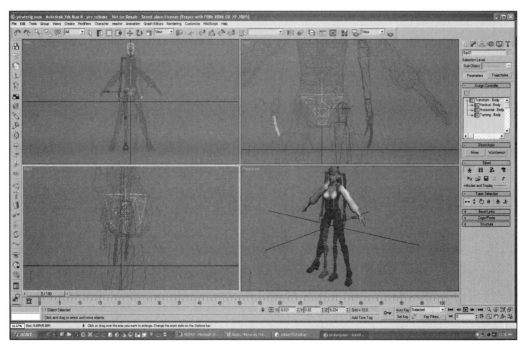

Figure 7.6 Center the pelvis of the skeleton in the pelvis of the model.

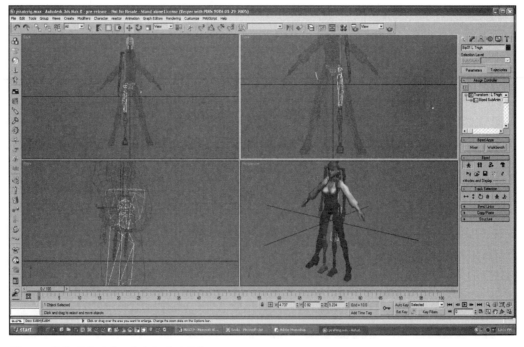

Figure 7.7 Select the skeleton's left leg.

12. Now click on the Symmetrical icon so that whatever action you take with the left leg will be mirrored on the right. The Symmetrical icon is located in the Track Selection rollout and looks like a small human figure with white arms.

13. Using the Rotate tool, rotate the legs out in the Front view. Notice that the rotate action is mirrored across to the right leg (see Figure 7.8).

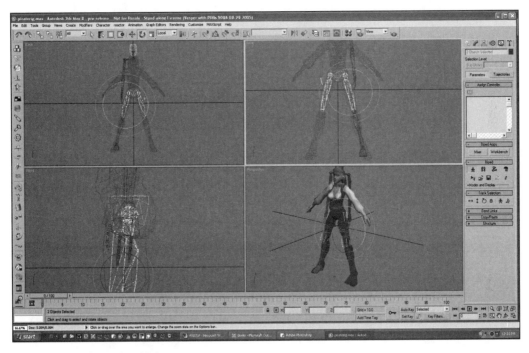

Figure 7.8 Rotate the thighs out.

14. Line up the thighs with the character's legs in the Side view, as shown in Figure 7.9.

15. The thigh links are too long. Use the Scale tool to scale the legs in the X axis so the knee joint lines up with the model's knee. Use Figure 7.10 as a reference.

16. Select the links of the lower leg the same way you did those in the upper leg and rotate them to fit the model, as shown in Figure 7.11.

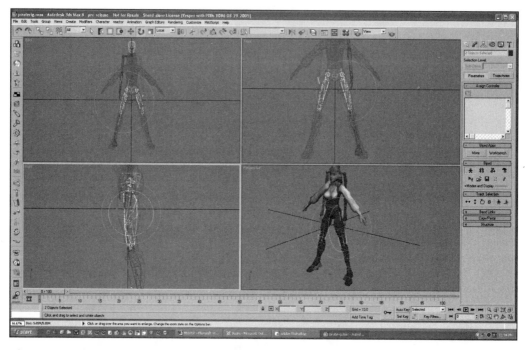

Figure 7.9 Rotate the thighs to fit within the legs.

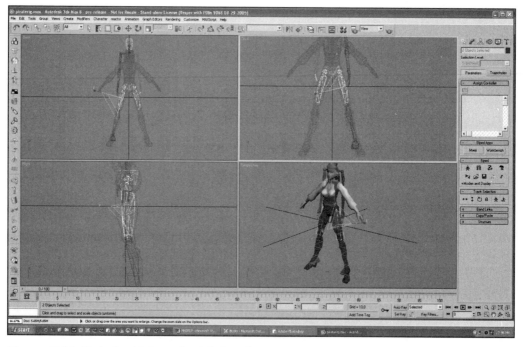

Figure 7.10 Scale the thighs to the right length.

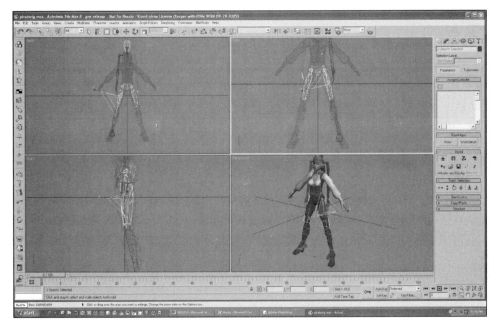

Figure 7.11 Rotate the lower legs into position.

17. The girl is wearing boots with pronounced heels. Select the feet and rotate them forward, as shown in Figure 7.12.

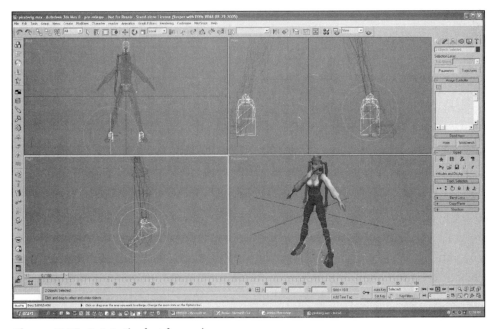

Figure 7.12 Rotate the feet forward.

18. Next rotate the feet out in the Front view to follow the angle of the legs (see Figure 7.13).

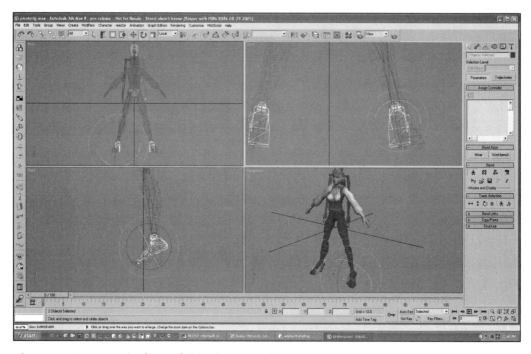

Figure 7.13 Rotate the feet to follow the angle of the legs.

19. The feet also need to be swung out to match the angle of the feet in the model, as shown in Figure 7.14.

20. Select the toe and rotate it so it is level with the toe of the model's boot, and then scale it so it extends slightly beyond the boot, as shown in Figure 7.15. It is always a good idea to have Biped links extend a little beyond the ends of the model so they attach correctly to the model.

21. The skeleton has a series of links for the torso that are too big for the model. Your pirate girl has long legs and a short torso. Select each link of the torso, as shown in Figure 7.16.

22. Scale the selected links down to fit the model, as shown in Figure 7.17.

23. The model has a bow in her back but the skeleton does not. You can adjust the skeleton to match the model by rotating the individual links of the torso from the Side view. First, rotate the bottom link forward, as shown in Figure 7.18.

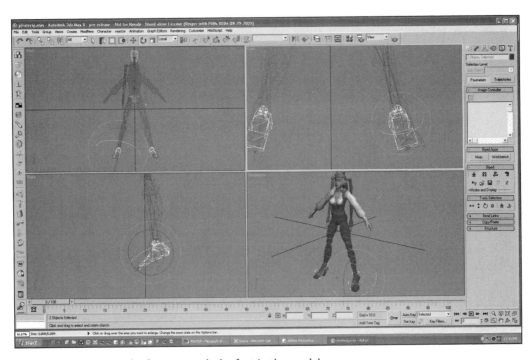

Figure 7.14 Rotate the feet to match the feet in the model.

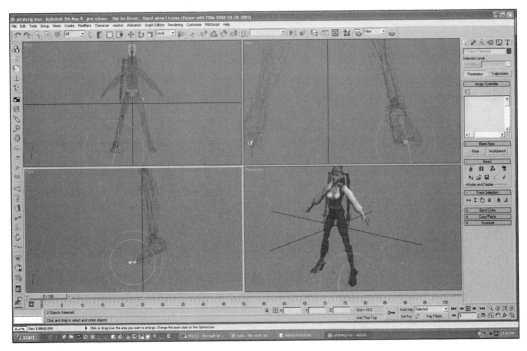

Figure 7.15 Adjust the toe link to follow the toe of the boot.

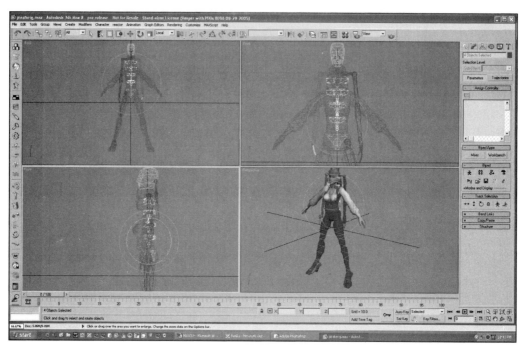

Figure 7.16 Select the links of the torso.

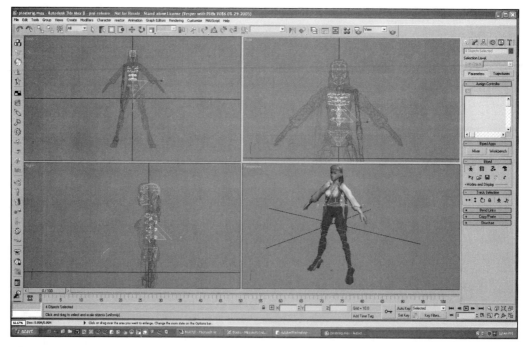

Figure 7.17 Scale the torso links to fit the model's torso.

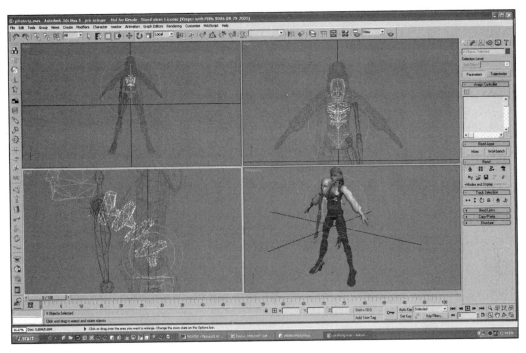

Figure 7.18 Rotate the lower spine forward.

24. Hold down the Ctrl key and click on the lowest link of the spine to deselect it.

25. Rotate the rest of the links of the torso back, following the curve of the model's back, as shown in Figure 7.19.

26. Deselect the lowest link and continue to rotate the skeleton back, as shown in Figure 7.20.

27. Finally, with just the top link of the torso selected, rotate the link forward to line the links of the shoulders and head up with the model, as shown in Figure 7.21.

28. The Biped skeleton is built more for a male figure than a female figure, so the shoulders tend to be wider than necessary for a female character. Select the left shoulder link, and then turn on Symmetrical.

29. Now scale the shoulders in to better fit the female figure, as shown in Figure 7.22.

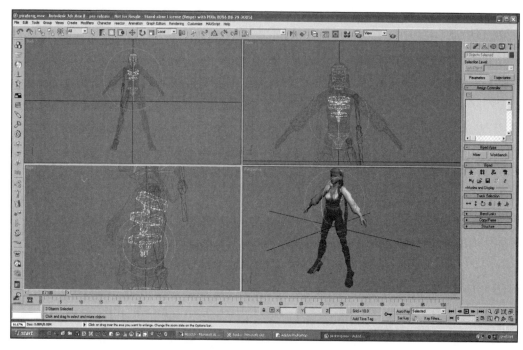

Figure 7.19 Rotate the spine of the skeleton back to follow the curve of the model's back.

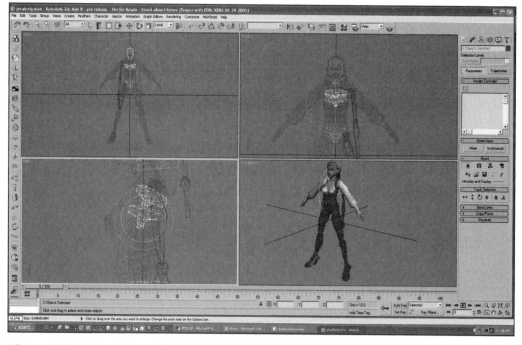

Figure 7.20 Rotate the next link back, still following the model.

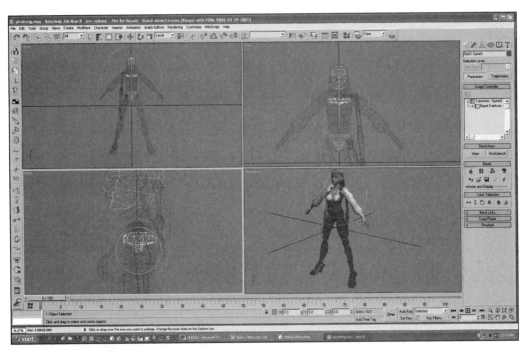

Figure 7.21 Rotate the last link of the torso to line up with the model.

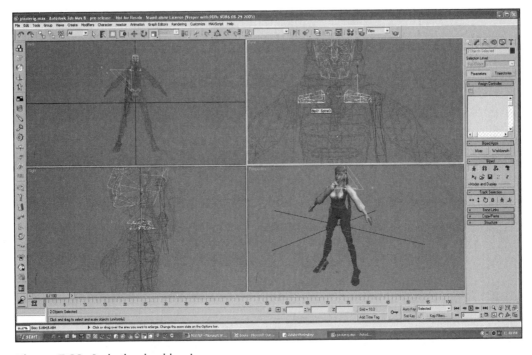

Figure 7.22 Scale the shoulders in.

30. Rotate the shoulders down just a bit to better fit the model (see Figure 7.23).

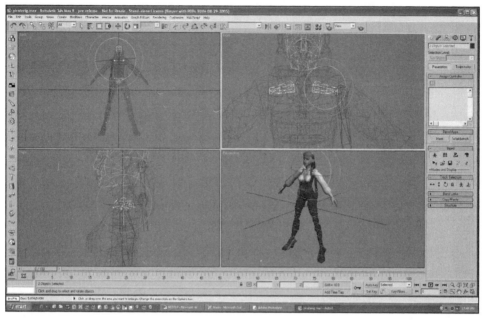

Figure 7.23 Rotate the shoulders down.

31. Select and rotate the arms, similar to how you did the legs (see Figure 7.24).

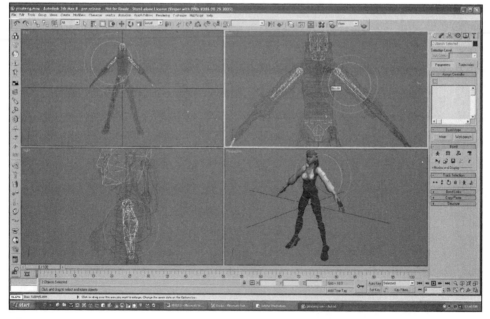

Figure 7.24 Rotate the arms of the skeleton.

32. Make sure the elbow of the skeleton lines up with that of the model, as shown in Figure 7.25.

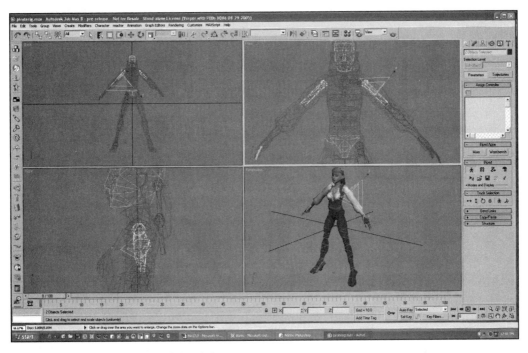

Figure 7.25 Scale the arms of the skeleton.

33. Next, you need to select the lower arms and scale them so the wrists line up with the model, as shown in Figure 7.26.

34. Rotate the lower arm so it matches up with the model's hand, as shown in Figure 7.27.

35. Now you need to work on the thumb and fingers. Start with the thumb. Select the links of the thumb and scale them into the joints of the thumb in the model.

36. Rotate each link to line up with the thumb, as shown in Figure 7.28.

37. Rotate the entire thumb down into the model, as shown in Figure 7.29. It doesn't have to go all the way inside the model, but the closer you can get it, the better the mesh will deform.

40. Scale and rotate the first link of the single finger to fit the model, as shown in Figure 7.30.

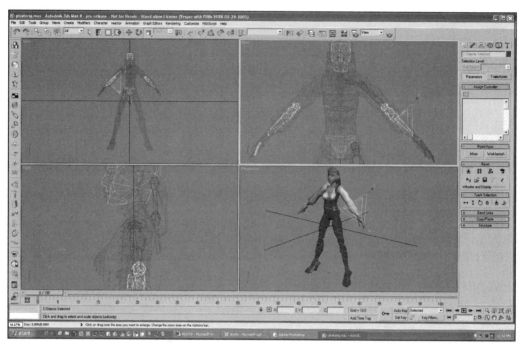

Figure 7.26 Scale the lower arm to fit the model.

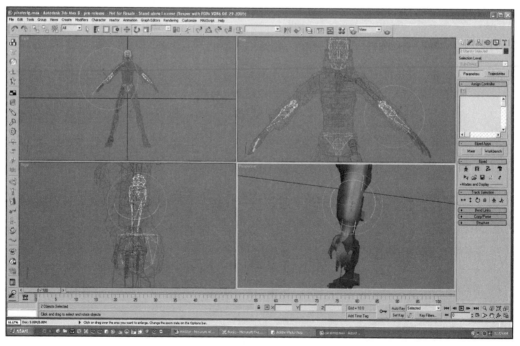

Figure 7.27 Make the hand of the skeleton line up with the hand on the model.

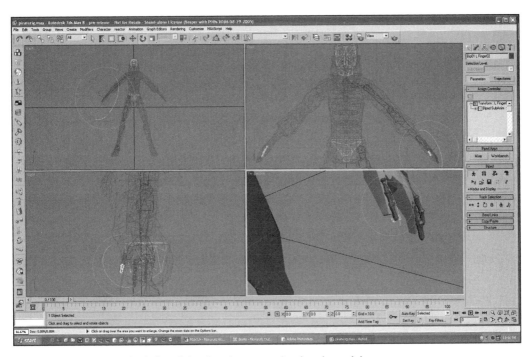

Figure 7.28 Rotate the links of the thumb over to the thumb model.

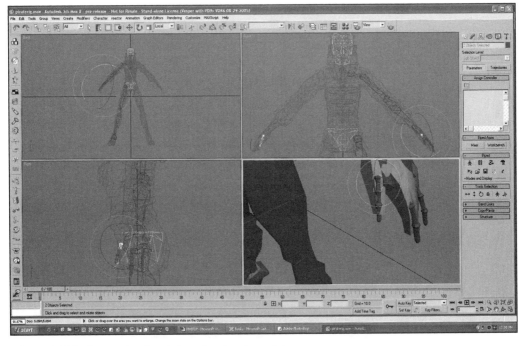

Figure 7.29 Rotate the thumb into the thumb model.

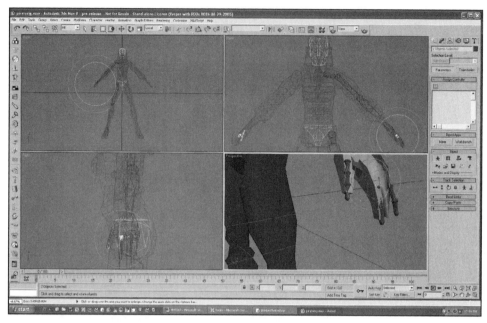

Figure 7.30 Rotate and scale the first link of the finger.

41. Continue on to the second link, lining it up with the knuckle, as shown in Figure 7.31.

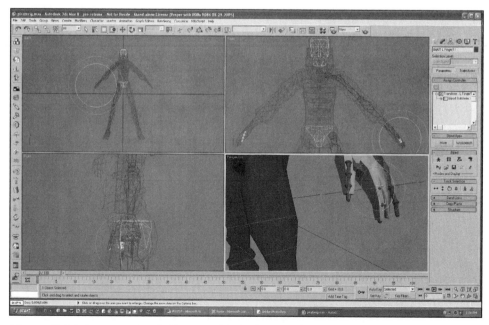

Figure 7.31 Rotate and scale the second link of the single finger.

42. Repeat the process for the third and final link of the finger.

43. Now go to the links that will control the other three fingers. You will not be able to line the links up with all three joints on the model, so just line them up to the middle of the three fingers, as shown in Figure 7.32.

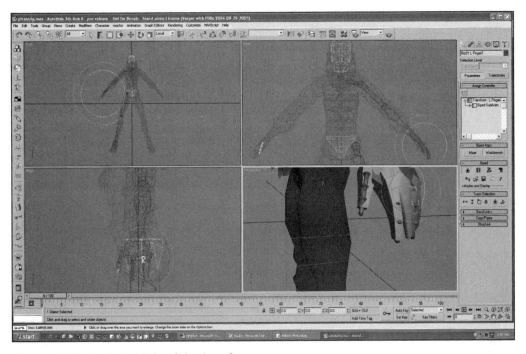

Figure 7.32 Rotate the links of the three fingers.

44. Scale the joints to be just longer than the end of the model, as shown in Figure 7.33.

45. Go on to the ponytail. Rotate and scale the first link of the ponytail, as shown in Figure 7.34.

46. Also, adjust the second link (see Figure 7.35).

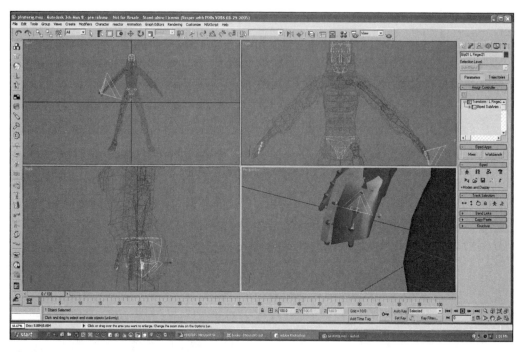

Figure 7.33 Scale the links to fit the fingers.

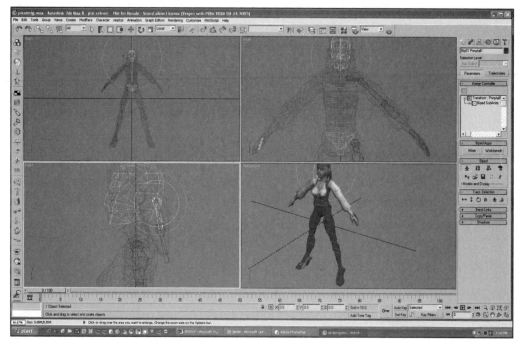

Figure 7.34 Rotate and scale the first link of the ponytail.

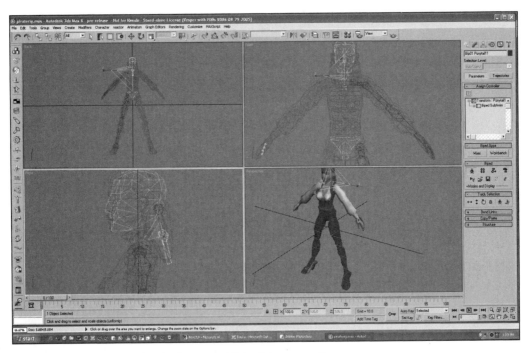

Figure 7.35 Rotate and scale the second link of the ponytail.

Binding Biped to Your Model

Biped skeletons have to be bound to a model before the model can be animated with the skeleton. For this binding process you will use a modifier called *Physique*, which was developed specifically for Biped models and used to be part of Character Studio when it was a separate plug-in. Now Physique is part of 3ds Max, so you can use it for other hierarchies, such as bones or curves.

If you have been following the examples so far in this chapter, you should have a Biped skeleton sized to the model. You can now go forward with attaching the skeleton to the model. Attaching the model is fairly simple. Getting the model to attach correctly is a little more complex.

1. Go to the Modifier panel and click on the mesh to select it (see Figure 7.36).

2. You will notice that the Editable Mesh still has a smooth modifier in the stack. Collapse the stack so you are working from the Editable Mesh. Now your screen should look similar to Figure 7.37.

3. Select Physique from the Modifier List, as shown in Figure 7.38.

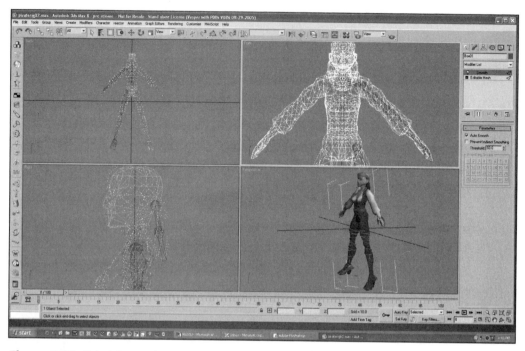

Figure 7.36 Select the mesh.

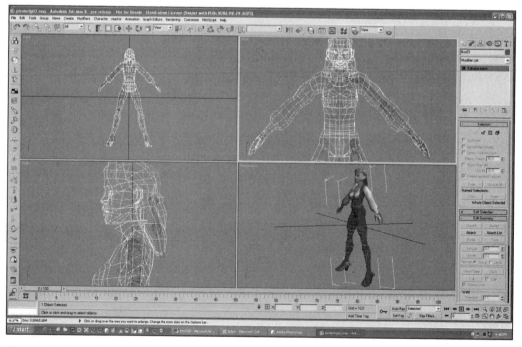

Figure 7.37 Collapse the stack.

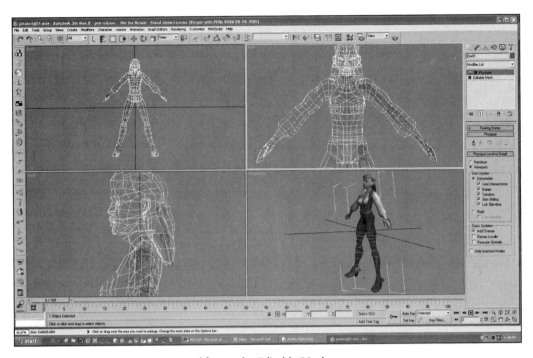

Figure 7.38 Add the Physique modifier to the Editable Mesh.

4. Click on the Attach to Node icon. It is the one that looks like a character with a target.

5. Next select the COM of the Biped, as shown in Figure 7.39. The Physique Initialization dialog box will appear.

6. Click Initialize to complete the attachment. The model will now have an orange line running through it. The line shows the links of the skeleton that are attached to the model (see Figure 7.40).

7. The Biped is now influencing the model. If you select any part of the Biped skeleton and rotate it, the model should move with the rotation of the skeleton. Try moving the arms or legs.

8. First try moving the arms. In the model I constructed, some of the vertices of the arm were outside of the influence of the skeleton and didn't move when the arm moved, as shown in Figure 7.41. These vertices are attached to the root node.

9. Press Ctrl+Z to undo the rotation and place the arm back in its original position.

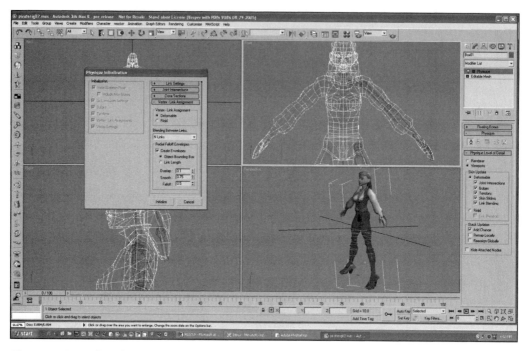

Figure 7.39 Select the COM of the Biped.

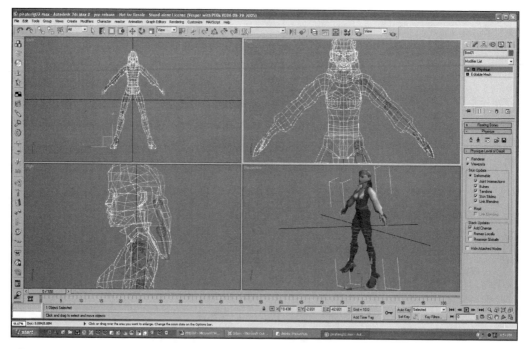

Figure 7.40 Initialize the attachment.

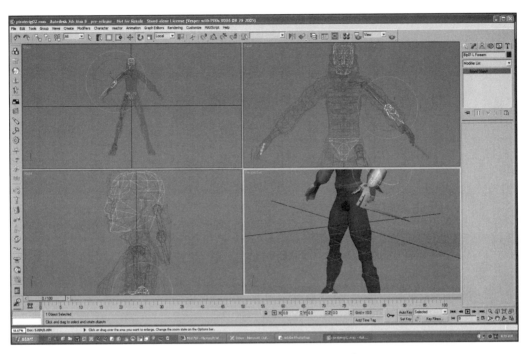

Figure 7.41 Some vertices are not attached to the skeleton properly.

10. Click the plus sign next to Physique in the stack and select Envelope, as shown in Figure 7.42. Physique controls vertex binding through a means of envelopes. Each link has an envelope that surrounds it. If a vertex falls within the link's envelope, it then will be bound to that link.

11. Click on the link of the character's left forearm. The envelope for that link will appear. All of the vertices that are within the envelope will be highlighted, as shown in Figure 7.43.

12. Envelopes in 3ds Max have two types of influences over vertices. Any vertex that falls within the inner envelope is bound completely to the link. Those vertices that fall in the area between the inner envelope and the outer envelope share influences with any other envelope that might overlap with them. Both envelopes can be expanded as needed. You can control the expansion of the envelopes by using the buttons in the Blending Envelopes rollout. The default is Both, but by clicking on Inner or Outer you can scale the individual envelopes independently. For this part of the arm, expand both envelopes using the Scale tool to envelop all the vertices of the forearm, as shown in Figure 7.44.

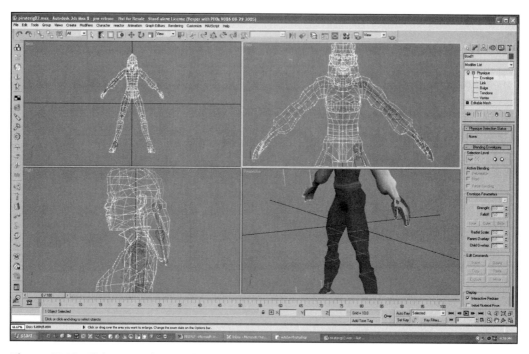

Figure 7.42 Click on Envelope in the stack.

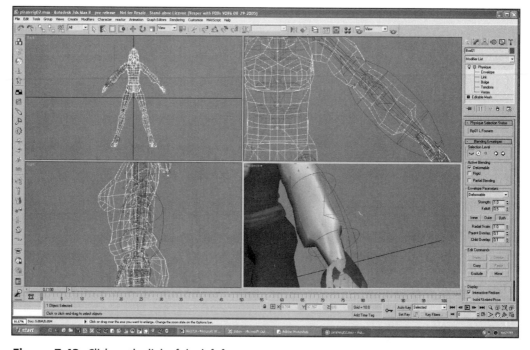

Figure 7.43 Click on the link of the left forearm.

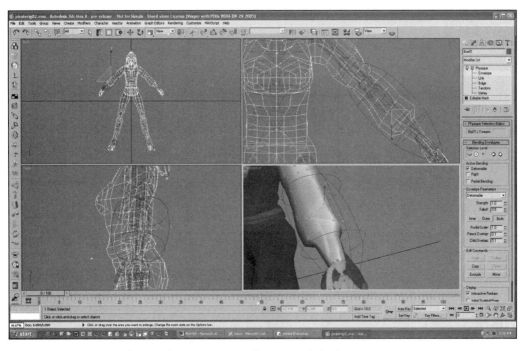

Figure 7.44 Expand the envelope to contain all vertices of the forearm.

13. You can now go to the right forearm and expand that too, but a better way to keep your model consistent from side to side is to mirror the envelope to the other side. To mirror the envelope to the right forearm, first click Copy in the Edit Commands section of the rollout, as shown in Figure 7.45.

14. Now select the right forearm and click on the Paste button. The envelope from the left side will be pasted into the envelope on the right side.

15. The pasted envelope is a direct paste from one side to the other and is not mirrored. Click on the Mirror button to mirror the pasted envelope into the right position, as shown in Figure 7.46.

16. In addition to the arm having a problem, the hand does as well. Move in close to the left hand, select the links that control the three fingers, and expand them to envelop the finger's vertices. Be careful not to expand the envelopes too far so they don't influence the vertices of the index finger (see Figure 7.47).

17. Copy, paste, and mirror each envelope to the right side of the model, as shown in Figure 7.48.

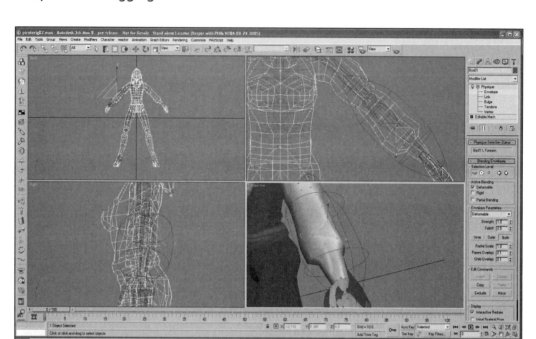

Figure 7.45 Copy the selected envelope.

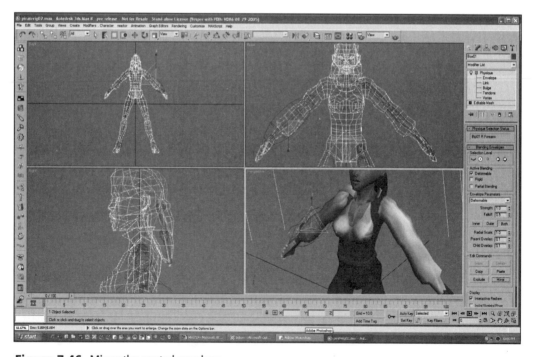

Figure 7.46 Mirror the pasted envelope.

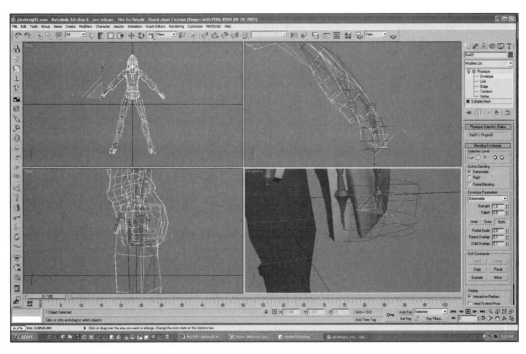

Figure 7.47 Expand the envelopes of the fingers.

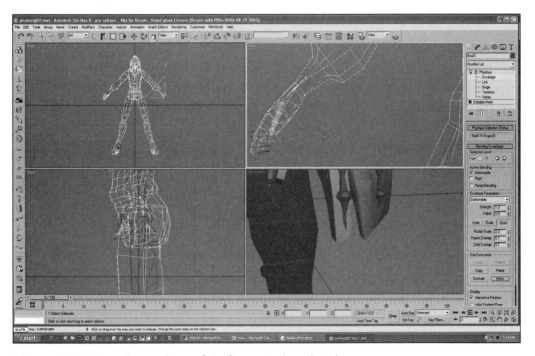

Figure 7.48 Mirror the envelopes of the fingers to the right side.

18. Try testing the model by moving other limbs to see whether there are other problems with the binding of the model. Fix these envelopes as needed by adjusting the envelopes.

19. Even with the envelopes working for all the areas of the model, there could still be problems. Select the lowest link of the torso and rotate it forward. Notice the distortion of the face, as seen in Figure 7.49. The vertices of the face are sharing influences with other links of the model besides the one for the head. You could adjust the envelopes for these vertices, but there is another way to adjust vertices on a vertex-by-vertex level. You will be using this method to fine-tune the influences of the model.

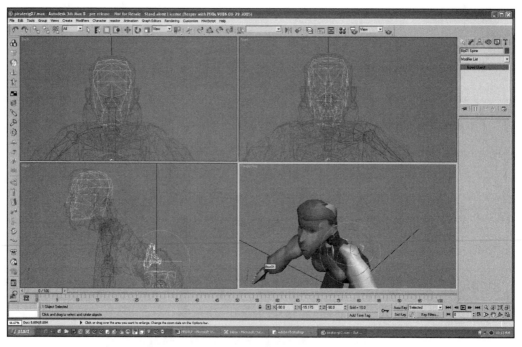

Figure 7.49 The head distorts when the torso is rotated forward.

20. Press Ctrl+Z to restore the torso rotation back to the original position, then select the model and then Vertex in the stack, as shown in Figure 7.50. Each vertex in the model will be designated by a white plus symbol.

21. You can see the vertices that are bound to a link by choosing Select By Link in the Vertex-Link Assignment rollout. Click on the head link with Select By Link to see the vertices that are influenced by that link, as shown in Figure 7.51.

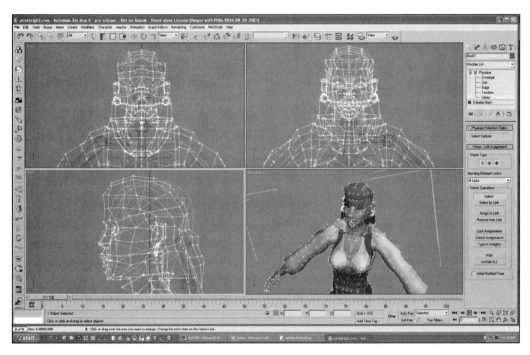

Figure 7.50 Go to Vertex in the stack.

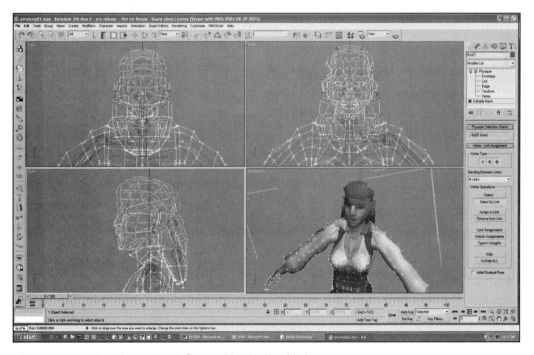

Figure 7.51 View the vertices influenced by the head link.

22. There are several problems with the vertex influences for the head. First, the head is a solid object and does not distort the same way that the torso might. The vertices of the head should be locked to the head. Second, the vertices that are influenced by the head in the shoulder area will cause those vertices to shift position when the head moves. This will cause problems during animation. The influences in these areas need to be removed. Go back to Select and select the vertices of the head above the neck, as shown in Figure 7.52.

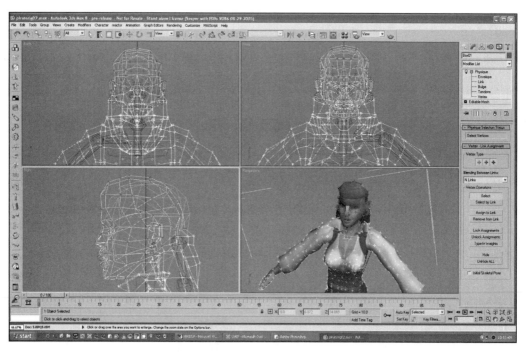

Figure 7.52 Select the vertices of the head.

23. Click on Assign to Link. Notice that when you select this button, the colored plus symbols under Vertex Type change. The blue and green are deselected, but the red remains selected. These buttons control how a vertex is bound to the skeleton. Red vertices are those that can share influences with more than one link. Green vertices are those that are bound to a single link, also known as *rigid binding*. Blue vertices are those that are outside of the influences of any link and are bound to the root node. Change the vertex binding to green, as shown in Figure 7.53.

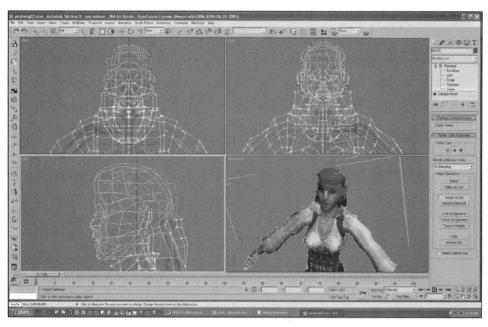

Figure 7.53 Choose Rigid binding by selecting the green plus button.

24. Now click on the head link (see Figure 7.54). All the selected vertices will turn green.

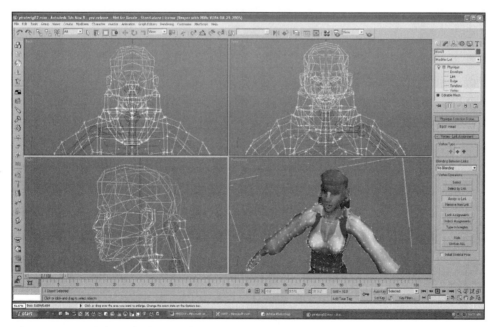

Figure 7.54 Click on the head link.

25. Next, click on the Lock Assignments button. This button locks the vertices so that any other changes you make to the binding of the model will not affect the locked vertices. Locked vertices are designated with a box symbol, as opposed to a plus symbol (see Figure 7.55).

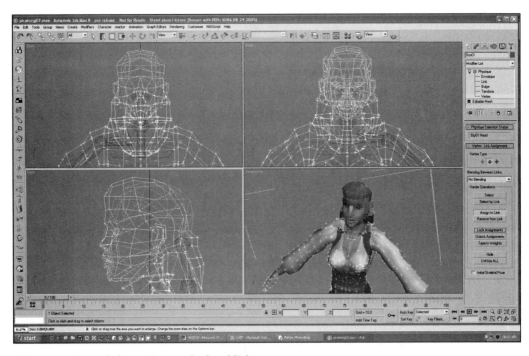

Figure 7.55 Lock the vertices to the head link.

26. The next step is to separate the vertices of the hair from being influenced by the links of the body, and the vertices of the body from being influenced by the hair links. Start with the hair. Select the vertices of the hair below where the hair connects to the head and assign them with a rigid bind to the hair, as shown in Figure 7.56.

27. Now select the lower vertices of the hair and bind them to the lower hair link, as shown in Figure 7.57.

28. Now select all of the vertices of the shoulders and collar area of the model, as shown in Figure 7.58.

29. Click on Remove from Link.

30. Select the links of the head and ponytail, as shown in Figure 7.59. These links will no longer influence the selected vertices.

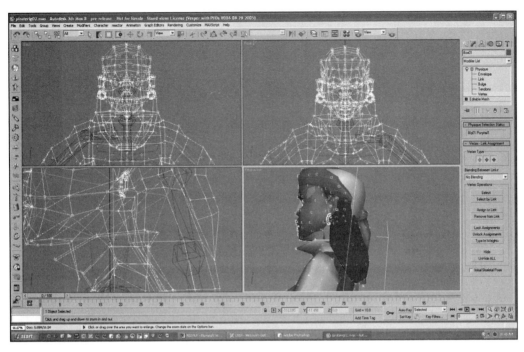

Figure 7.56 Rigid bind the hair to the first ponytail link.

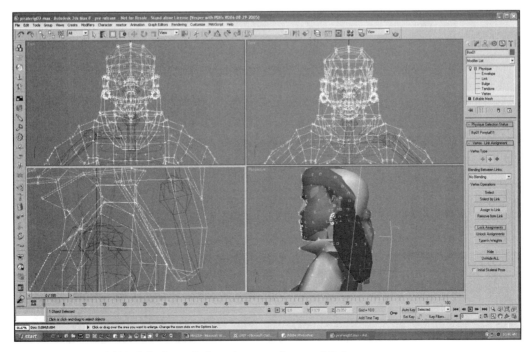

Figure 7.57 Rigid bind the lower hair to the second ponytail link.

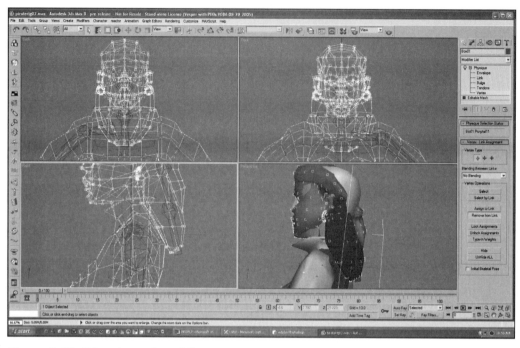

Figure 7.58 Select the vertices of the upper torso.

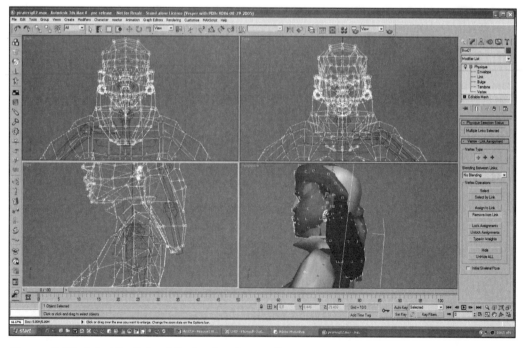

Figure 7.59 Select the links of the head and ponytail.

31. You will notice that when you removed the links' influence, some of the collar vertices turned blue. This is because without the head and ponytail links, these vertices fall outside the influence of any envelopes. You will need to add them to the neck link. Select the vertices of the collar and assign them to the neck link, as shown in Figure 7.60.

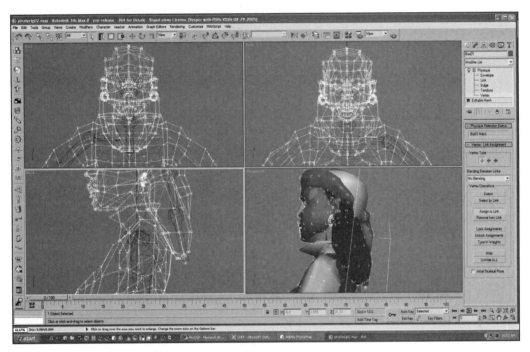

Figure 7.60 Assign the collar to the neck link.

32. While you are in the Vertex mode, you can check for any other unassigned vertexes. They will appear in blue. I found some in the crotch area of the model. Select these vertices and assign them to the pelvis links, as shown in Figure 7.61.

33. There is also a problem with the character's breasts. The vertices are split between two separate links (see Figure 7.62). This will cause some ugly deformations when the character animates, which you can see if you rotate the links. You need to assign all of the breast vertices to one link. It doesn't need to be a rigid bind, but one major influence is best.

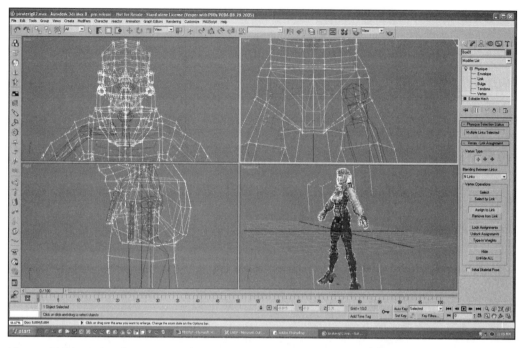

Figure 7.61 Assign the unassigned vertices of the crotch to the pelvis links.

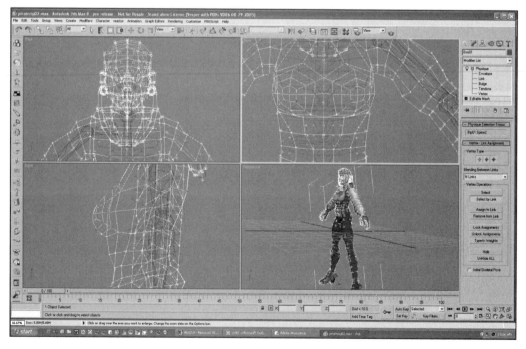

Figure 7.62 The vertices of the breasts are split between two links.

32. Select the vertices of the breasts and remove the lower link, as shown in Figure 7.63. You will want the upper link controlling the movement of the breasts because they should essentially move with the ribcage of the character, and the upper link controls that area of the character.

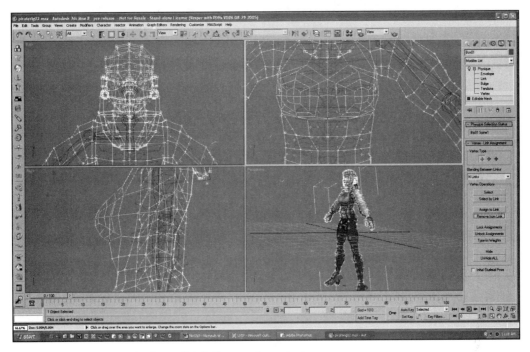

Figure 7.63 Remove the lower link influences from the breasts.

33. Now assign the breasts to the upper link, as shown in Figure 7.64.

34. The model should be ready for animation with Biped. Give it one last check, moving the model around to see whether you missed any vertex assignments.

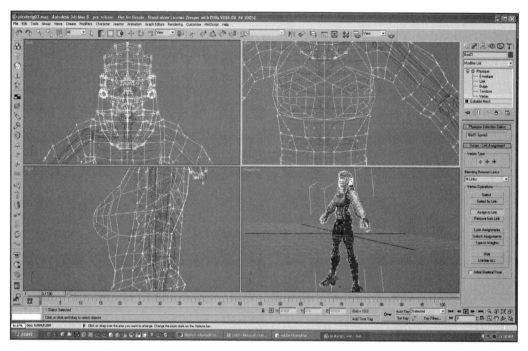

Figure 7.64 Assign the breasts to the upper link.

There you have it; the model is finished and ready for animation. Most character models for games in 3ds Max are animated using Biped, but there are some limitations that you, as a game artist, need to be aware of.

- Some game engines do not support Biped. You need to check to see whether the game technology you will be using for your game supports importing Biped models and animation.

- Some game engines have restrictions for the number of bones used in a character. If you have a bone limitation, you might need to limit the number of links you use in Biped because game engines treat Biped links as bones. You can't delete Biped links, but you can hide them.

- Although Biped works well for most two-legged game characters, it might not have the sophistication you need for a very complex character.

There are times when the Biped system just will not work for a game. In those instances, your best bet is to create your own skeleton assembly using 3ds Max's Bones system.

The Bones System

Bones in 3ds Max, as well as their associated systems of forward, inverse kinematics, constraints, and skinning, are somewhat daunting for the beginning artist. An entire book could be written about the subject and still not begin to cover all of the aspects of character animation with Bones. Because this is a book for beginners, I will present an overview of the Bones system to give you an idea of how it works. As you become more comfortable with 3ds Max, you can explore the possibility of animating with a Bones system.

Creating Bones

Bones are created individually in the viewport. The term "bone" is a little misleading because you are not really creating bones; rather, you are creating joints that are linked with bones. The important element is the joint. Animation happens because joints can be rotated. When you create bones in 3ds Max, you are really placing joints. The bones created represent the areas of non-motion.

Bring up the pirate-girl model without the Biped skeletal system, go to the Systems tab, and click on Bones, as shown in Figure 7.65.

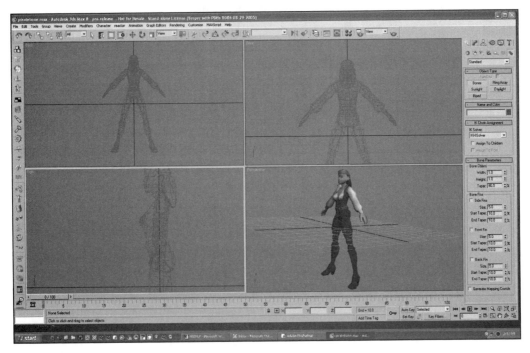

Figure 7.65 Click Bones to create bones.

Notice that I changed the width and height of the bones in the Bone Object roll-out to one instead of ten. Ten is entirely too big for this model. Now you are ready start making bones.

1. In the Side view, move your cursor over the pelvis area of the model and click at the base of the spine, as shown in Figure 7.66. When you release the mouse button, Bones plants a joint in the place where you clicked. Notice that there is a bone now attached to the cursor. The next place you click on the model will determine the location of the next joint.

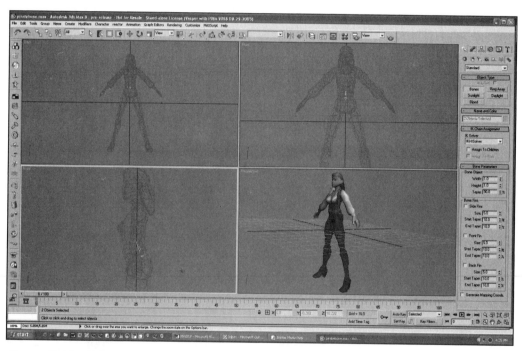

Figure 7.66 Click to create the first joint.

2. Continue to build the spine of the character, placing joints up the spine and ending at the base of the skull where the spine attaches to the head, as shown in Figure 7.67. When you are finished placing bones, right-click to end the chain. 3ds Max will leave a small stub at the end of the chain. Don't worry about this stub right now. The stub is used for applying animation helpers to the bone system. Bones are a hierarchical system. This means that the first bone you place controls all other bones in the chain. If you pivot the spine by rotating the first bone, all of the other bones will rotate with it.

On the other hand, if you select the last bone you made and rotate it, only the one bone will rotate. On the human body, motion generally emanates from the pelvis area, so the pelvis should be the first joint placed in a model. The first joint in a hierarchy is called the *root joint.*

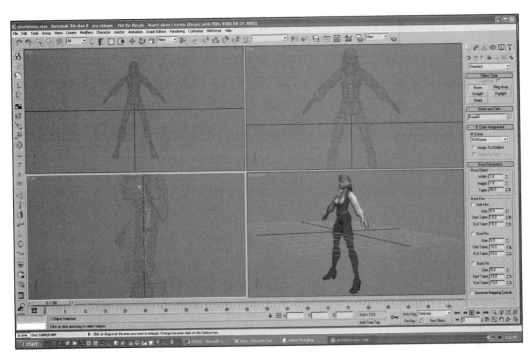

Figure 7.67 Place bones in the spine.

3. You can have more than one bone share the same joint. This is useful when you are working on attaching other bones to the spine, such as the bones for the character's arms. In the Front view, hold the cursor over the bone at the top of the spine just below the neck. You will notice that the cursor will change. Click on that bone. Your current bone chain now originates with that bone's joint, as shown in Figure 7.68.

4. Now you can place the bones in the arm by making joints at the shoulder, elbow, wrist, and base of the fingers, as shown in Figure 7.69.

5. Now you need to position each joint in the other views so it follows the arm. Start with the shoulder. Move it forward, as shown in Figure 7.70.

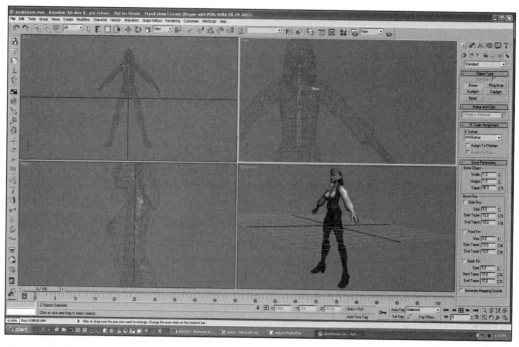

Figure 7.68 Attach the clavicle bone to the spine.

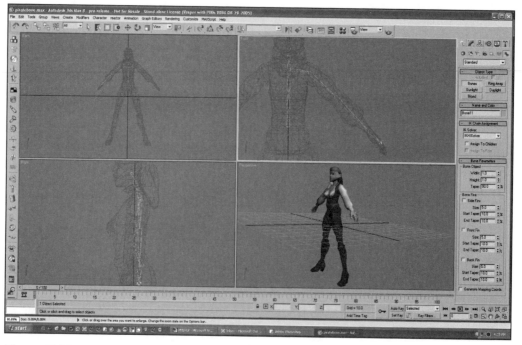

Figure 7.69 Create the joints of the character's left arm.

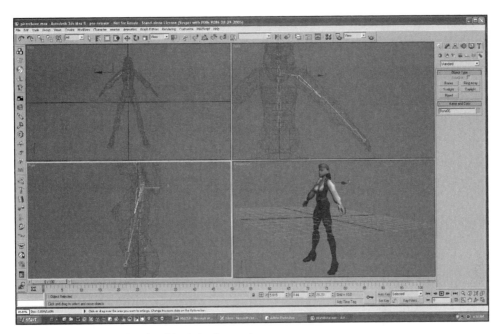

Figure 7.70 Move the shoulder joint forward.

6. Continue to move each joint down the arm to the hand, as shown in Figure 7.71.

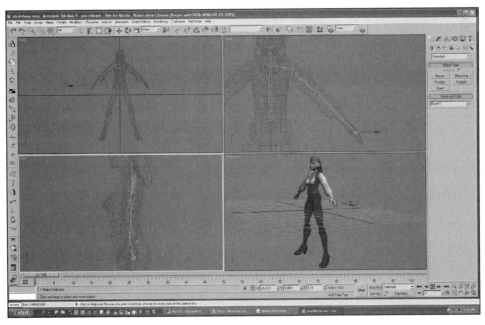

Figure 7.71 Place the joints from the Side view.

7. Because of the position of the thumb, there is no exact way to place the bones. In this example, I placed the bones in the Side view, as shown in Figure 7.72.

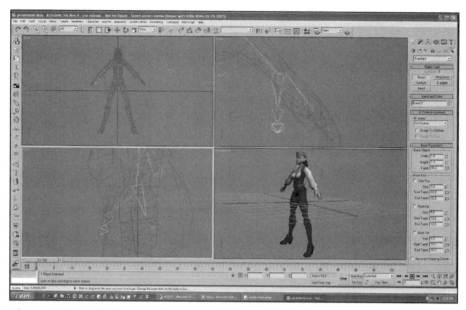

Figure 7.72 Build the joints for the thumb from the Side view.

8. Move the joints of the thumb up in the Front view, as shown in Figure 7.73.

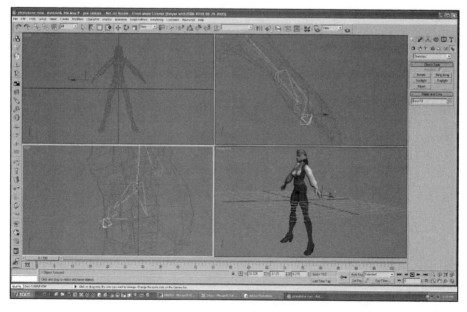

Figure 7.73 Move the joints of the thumb up in the Front view.

9. You can set up the index finger in the Front view, as shown in Figure 7.74.

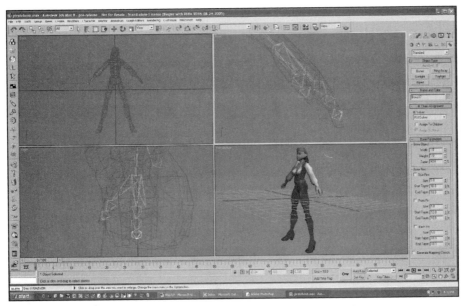

Figure 7.74 Set up the joints of the index finger in the Front view first.

10. Next, move and rotate the joints for the index finger to place them, as shown in Figure 7.75.

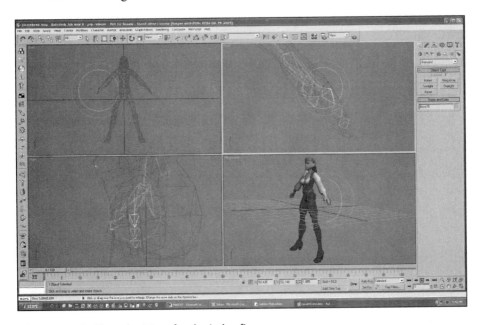

Figure 7.75 Place the joints for the index finger.

11. Last, add the joints to control the other three fingers, as shown in Figure 7.76.

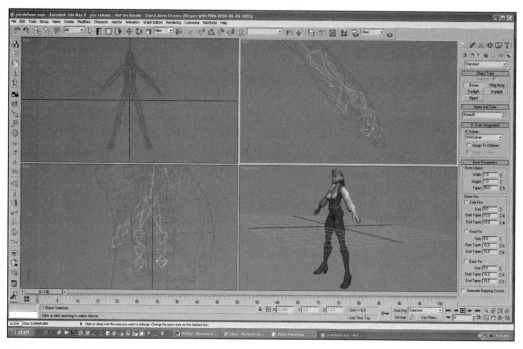

Figure 7.76 Add the last of the joints of the hand.

12. Now you need to set up the bones in the legs. Start in the center of the pelvis and draw the joints down the leg in the Front view, as shown in Figure 7.77.

13. You will want to have the beginning joint placed directly on 0 in the X axis so it is centered on the figure. Right-click on the Move tool and type **0** in the X box, as shown in Figure 7.78.

14. Now adjust the leg joints in the Side view. Use Figure 7.79 as a reference.

15. You can now mirror the arm and leg bone assemblies to the model's right side. Start with the arm. Select all of the bones of the model's left arm and bring up the Bone Tools dialog box from the Character menu, as shown in Figure 7.80.

16. Click on Mirror. The Bone Mirror dialog box will appear. Set the Mirror Axis to X and the Bone Axis to Flip to Y, as shown in Figure 7.81. Click OK to finish.

17. Repeat the process for the leg, as shown in Figure 7.82.

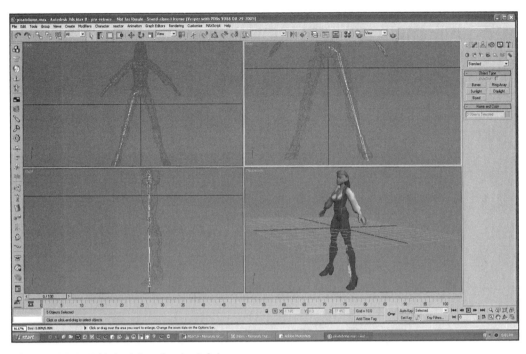

Figure 7.77 Add the joints for the left leg.

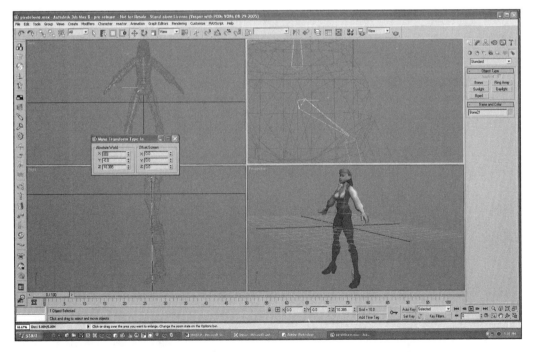

Figure 7.78 Center the first joint on the X axis.

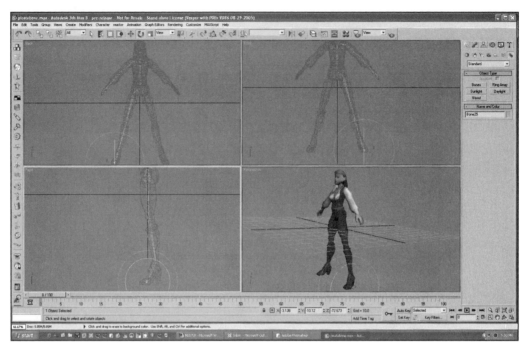

Figure 7.79 Adjust the joints of the leg in the Side view.

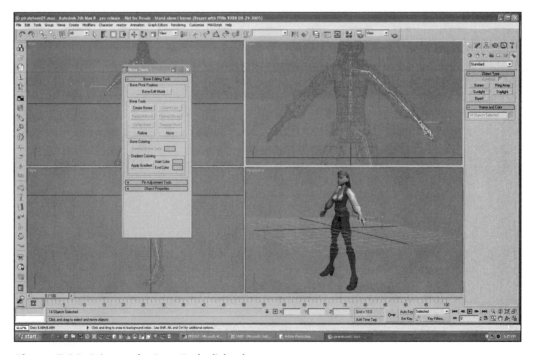

Figure 7.80 Bring up the Bone Tools dialog box.

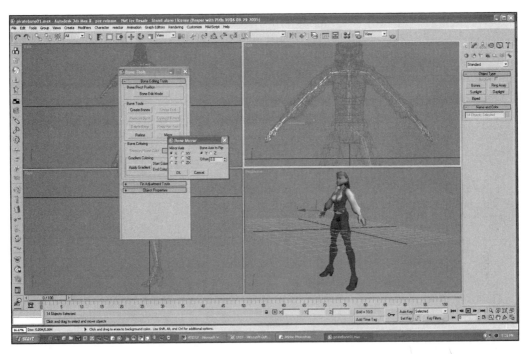

Figure 7.81 Mirror the bones across the X axis.

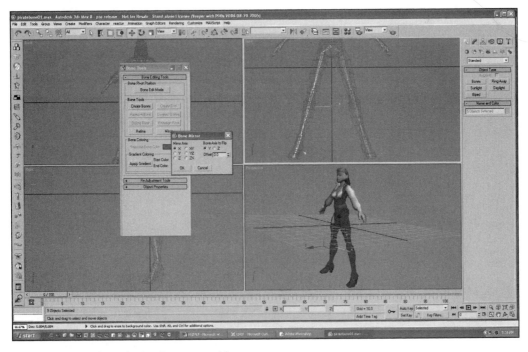

Figure 7.82 Mirror the leg-bone assembly.

That will do it for a simple bone assembly for the character. See Figure 7.83 for a view of how the bones should look. You can, of course, add more bones and helpers, such as inverse kinematics, to the bone structure, but this set of bones should give you a good base for animation. Helpers are used to assist in animating a character.

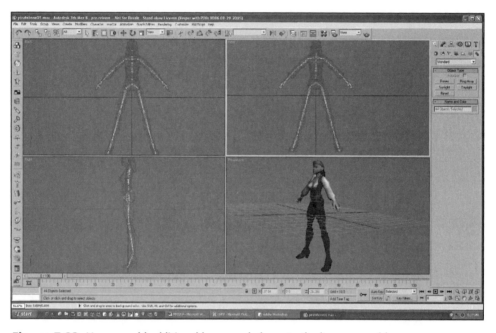

Figure 7.83 You can add additional bones or helpers to the bone assembly.

Once the bones are in place, you will be ready to attach them to the model. You can attach the bones using the Physique plug-in or you can use the Skin modifier. For this example, take a look at the Skin modifier.

The Skin modifier is added to the Editable Mesh. Select it and then choose Skin from the Modifier List, as shown in Figure 7.84.

Press the H key and select all of the bones, as shown in Figure 7.85. An easy way to select just the bones of a scene is to eliminate all other selection types as I did in this case.

All of the bones will be attached to the skeleton and listed in the Bones list box in the Parameters rollout. By clicking on Edit Envelopes and then selecting Bones from the list, you can view and edit the envelopes of each bone segment in the viewports, as shown in Figure 7.86.

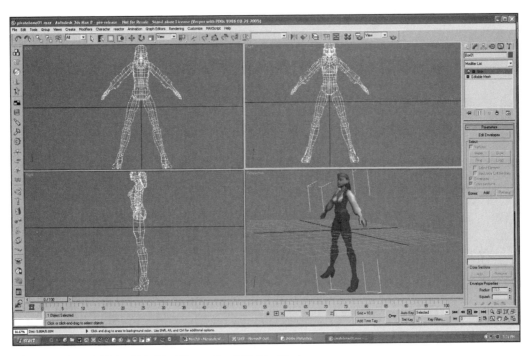

Figure 7.84 Add the Skin Modifier to the Editable Mesh.

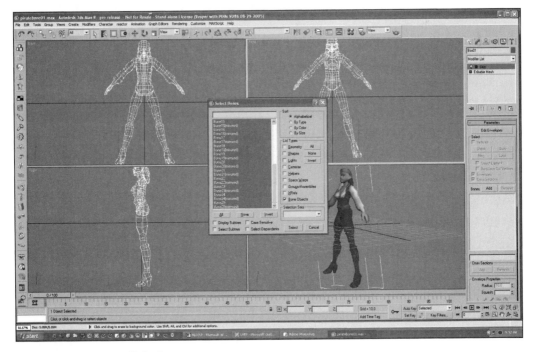

Figure 7.85 Select all the bones.

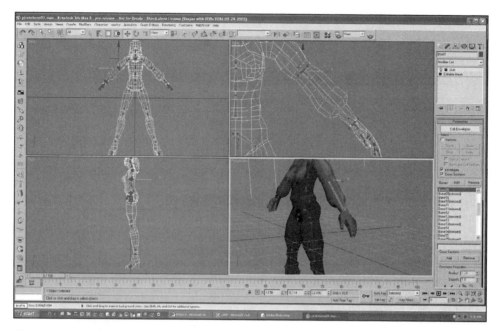

Figure 7.86 Edit the envelopes of the bone assembly.

Edit each envelope to see how the character moves and whether there are any vertices that are not within an envelope.

That was a simple look at the Bones system in 3ds Max. To understand it completely, you will need to spend some time exploring all of the tools and aspects of the Bones system.

Bones in 3ds Max are very flexible. If you understand how to use them, you can have almost unlimited flexibility in animating characters or objects.

Summary

This chapter covered the basics of attaching models to skeletal systems. In this chapter we covered several important points.

- Skeleton assemblies
- Biped system
- Physique
- Envelopes
- Bone system
- Skin

The two skeletal systems for 3ds Max are both useful in game development. Biped offers pre-made skeletal assemblies that you can modify to fit most game characters. The Bones system is extremely flexible and can be customized to meet the needs of any type of character, object, or game engine limitation. If you have a few of your own characters, try using Biped or Bones to prepare them for animation.

In the next chapter, you will learn how to animate your character.

Questions

1. Rigging a model describes what process?
2. What are 3ds Max's skeletal systems similar to?
3. What are the two skeletal and animation systems found in 3ds Max 8?
4. What skeletal system in 3ds Max has a predefined skeletal system for two-legged characters?
5. What is a major advantage of using Biped for animating two-legged characters?
6. What modifiers does Biped use for attaching a skeletal system to a model?
7. What is the COM of a Biped skeletal system?
8. The standard Biped model is more suitable for which type of character—male or female?
9. Physique uses what kind of system for controlling how a Biped system is attached to a model?
10. What happens to a vertex that falls within the inner Physique envelope?
11. How can Physique envelopes be adjusted?
12. What is a rigid bind in Physique?
13. Which system has more flexibility for animation—Bones or Biped?
14. Bones are created by placing what?
15. Which modifier does Bones use to attach skeletal systems to a model?

Answers

1. Attaching a bone system to a model
2. The human skeletal system
3. Biped and Bones

4. Biped

5. It saves production time.

6. Physique and Skin

7. The Center Of Mass

8. Male

9. Envelopes

10. It is bound to a specific link.

11. By scaling the envelopes

12. Vertices are bound to a single link.

13. Bones

14. Joints

15. Skin

Discussion Questions

1. Why might a development team choose to use Biped over Bones for animating characters?

2. Why might a development team choose Bones over Biped for animating characters?

3. Why are Bones systems more flexible than Biped systems?

4. How might a Bones system be used to animate a character's face?

5. Why is it important to check all of the vertices in a model for influences before animating?

Exercises

1. Create and rig a simple character using Biped and Physique.

2. Create and rig a character with four or more legs using Bones and Skin.

3. Rig a Bones character using Physique instead of Skin for binding.

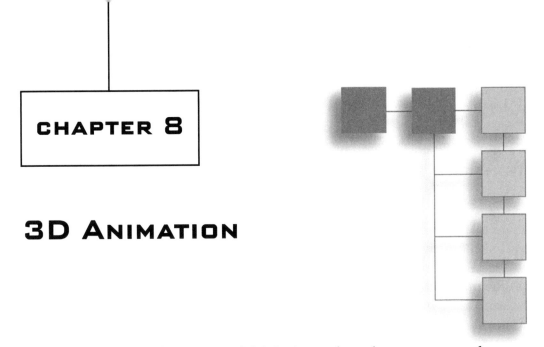

CHAPTER 8

3D ANIMATION

Now that you have a character model, it is time to learn how to get your character to move. For this process you will use 3D animation. 3D animation differs from 2D animation because in 3D animation, you are moving an object or character in a three-dimensional environment, similar to how things move in real life.

Before 3D graphics became popular in games, all animation had to be drawn one frame at a time in 2D. With the advent of 3D graphics, a whole new world opened for animators. Now they could create animation in a 3D environment and view the animation from any angle. Animations became separate elements from the art, making it possible to do one animation and apply it to multiple characters.

Unlike 2D animation that is stored as picture files in a game, 3D graphics are stored as motion files. Motion files can contain data on almost every attribute of a 3D model, including translation, rotation, size, color, and many others. For this chapter you will focus your attention on just a few attributes because not all game engines support the full range of attribute animations.

Understanding Animation

To better understand animation, you should first look at where it came from. Film animation was one of the first forms of drawn movies experienced by audiences. Filmmakers found that if they took a movie camera and shot individual frames of drawings, the drawings appeared to move or animate when viewed on a projector.

It took a little bit of experimenting to get the system to work and to train the animators on how to develop their drawings correctly. Soon, pioneers such as Walt Disney and Charles (Chuck) Jones became well known for their innovative techniques and unique characters, such as Mickey Mouse and Bugs Bunny.

The concept of animated drawings is really quite simple. An animator draws a character in a beginning position. Then, he draws the character in the next major position. For example, the character might start in a standing position and then move to a fighting stance because of an insult or other threat. The two positions are called *key frames* because they define specific movements. If you played a drawing and then immediately played the next one, the action would jump from one position to another, which would make the animation look wrong. The key frames are used as a guide for the frames that go between them. These frames are usually drawn as transitions from one key frame to the next and are called "in-betweens" or "tweens" for short.

The number of in-between frames from one key frame to the next depends on the length of time the action takes to happen. Some movements, such as the preceding example, might take quite a few frames, whereas if the character were to throw a punch, it might not take many frames at all because the punch is a fast movement. Remember that in most games the frame rate is usually 30 frames per second. If it takes a character one second to move from one key frame to another, that would mean there are 29 in-between frames in that motion.

3ds Max has some very powerful animation tools to help animators. The software handles most of the in-between work so the animator doesn't have to. It even gives the animator control over how the in-betweens are developed. In addition, rather than drawing the character at key positions, the animator in 3ds Max can use the same character and just move it into the correct position. Another great feature in 3ds Max is the ability to copy key frames from one frame to another. This helps when the animator is creating a repetitive movement. I won't be able to cover all of the amazing animation tools in 3ds Max in one chapter, but I will give you a good start to learning how animation works in the program.

Animation in 3ds Max

First, you'll take a look at how animation is controlled in 3ds Max. From there, you will work on understanding how to get things to move around and react in a 3D environment. Figure 8.1 shows the animation controls in 3ds Max.

Time slider   Track bar   Animation Keying controls   Animation Playback controls

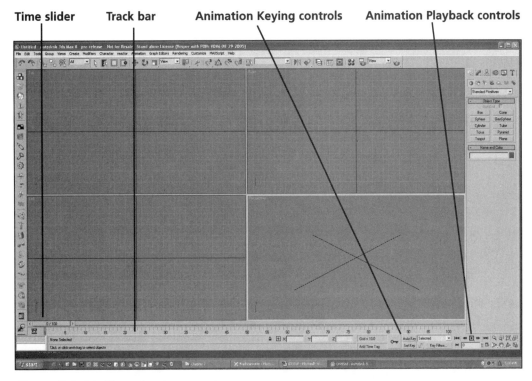

Figure 8.1 3ds Max animation controls

- **Time slider.** Indicates the current animation frame that is shown in the view screen.
- **Track bar.** Shows in a visual sequence the available frames in an animation. The time slider indicator slides along the track bar.
- **Animation Keying controls.** Controls the setting of key frames.
- **Animation Playback controls.** Used to view animations or navigate through animations. These controls are similar to the controls on a DVD player.

So now that you know where the animation tools are, it's time to start working with them.

Ball Animation

You will start with a simple ball-and-paddle animation. The animation will be a little reminiscent of a video game, but this is a video-game art book so that should be okay. You will start by building a couple simple objects and then you will animate them. Bring up 3ds Max and get ready to animate!

1. Start by creating a box. Don't worry about getting the size of the box just right—it only needs to be a narrow box that is quite a bit higher than it is wide, as shown in Figure 8.2.

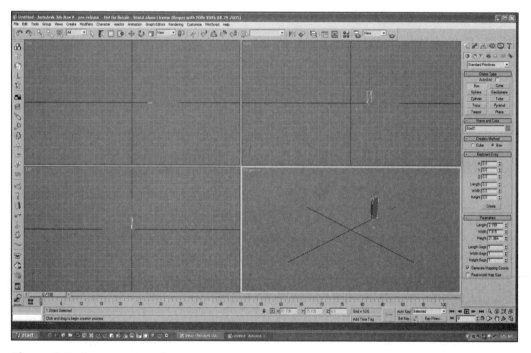

Figure 8.2 Create a narrow box.

2. Next create a sphere that is much smaller than the box. Use Figure 8.3 to compare the sizes to your box and sphere.

3. I created a texture for the box to make it look better. You can create one of your own. The box will be a paddle, like in an early video game. Just make up a texture that looks good to you. Figure 8.4 shows the paddle with the texture.

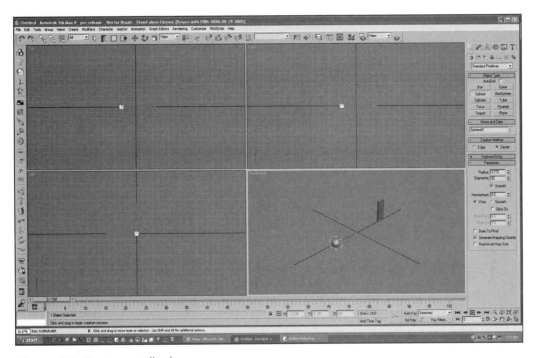

Figure 8.3 Create a small sphere.

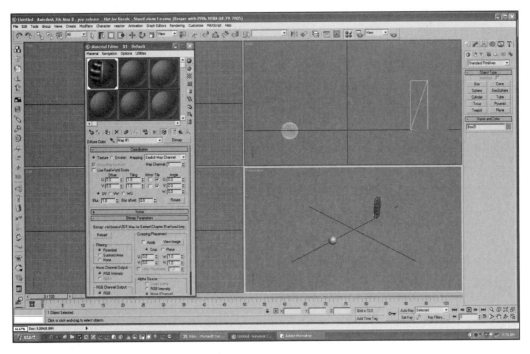

Figure 8.4 Apply a texture map to the box.

4. For the ball you will do something a little different. Instead of using a texture map from a file, you will create a procedural map. *Procedural maps* are generated mathematically in 3ds Max. Select a new material slot in the Material Editor and then go to the Maps rollout. Click on Diffuse Color and select Cellular from the Material/Map Browser, as shown in Figure 8.5.

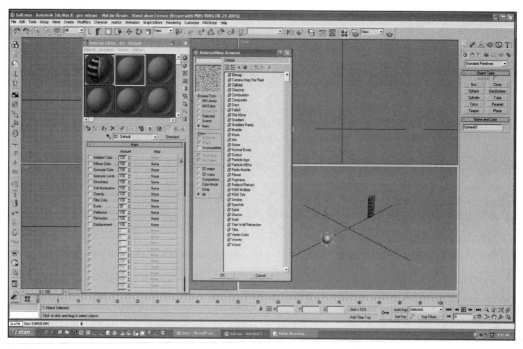

Figure 8.5 Use a cellular material for the ball.

5. The cellular material has several color options available. Click the Cell Color box in the Material Editor to bring up the Color Selector and change the color to a light blue, as shown in Figure 8.6.

6. Now change the top color under Division Colors in the Material Editor to a dark blue (see Figure 8.7). Leave the other color black.

7. Apply the new material to the ball (see Figure 8.8). Procedural materials are different from file texture maps because you can adjust them after they are applied to the object. If you want to change the spacing of the colors or make other changes, you can simply type different numbers into the options in the Material Editor. Try changing a few numbers, such as the Size or Spread options, to see how they affect the texture on the ball.

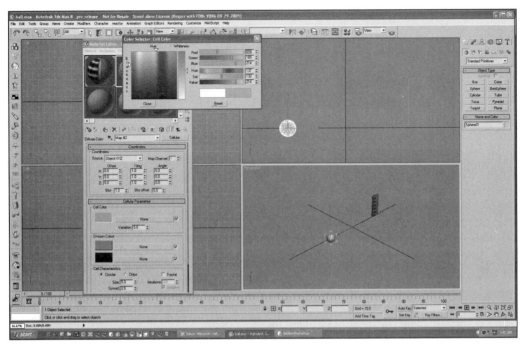

Figure 8.6 Change the cell color to a light blue.

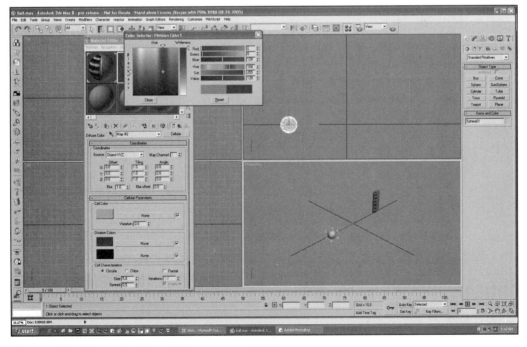

Figure 8.7 Change the first division color to dark blue.

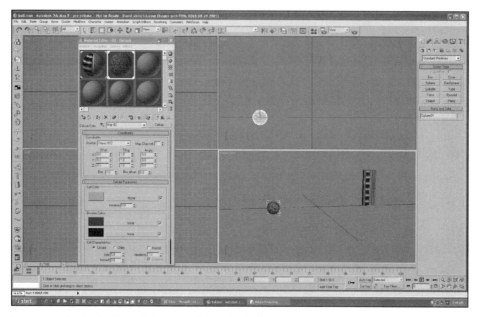

Figure 8.8 Apply the cellular material to the ball.

8. The objects are now ready to animate. Enlarge the Front view by pressing Alt+W with that viewport selected. This will be the view of the animation, as shown in Figure 8.9.

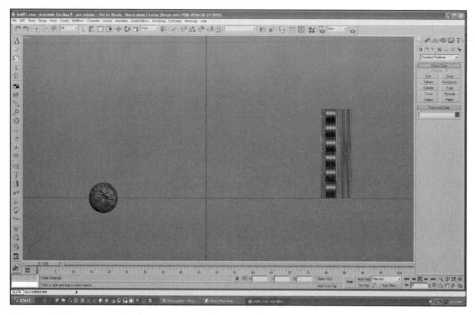

Figure 8.9 Go to a single screen view from the front.

9. Click on the Set Key button to put 3ds Max into animation mode, as shown in Figure 8.10. In animation mode you will be able to set key frames and animate the scene.

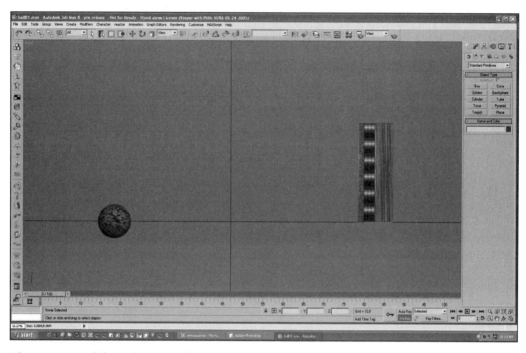

Figure 8.10 Click on the Set Key button.

3ds Max has two systems for setting key frames. The one used most often is the Auto Key system. In Auto Key, any changes in the animation are automatically keyed in the frame where the changes are made. In Set Key mode, key frames are only set by the animator. Auto Key mode is great for developing complex animations without having to worry about setting each key frame by hand, but it doesn't give you as much control over the animation as Set Key mode. In Set Key mode, the animator has the option to change the animation until everything is just right before setting any keys. Set Key mode is mostly for more advanced animators who want the ability to experiment with movements before setting key frames.

10. Pull back from the scene just a little and center the grid on the screen. Make sure the time slider is set at 0.

11. Now move the paddle to the bottom-right corner of the screen.

12. Click on the larger button next to Set Key (the one with the picture of a key on it). This will set a key for the paddle at frame 0.

13. Move the ball into the upper-left corner and set a key for it as well. These will be the starting positions for the two objects (see Figure 8.11).

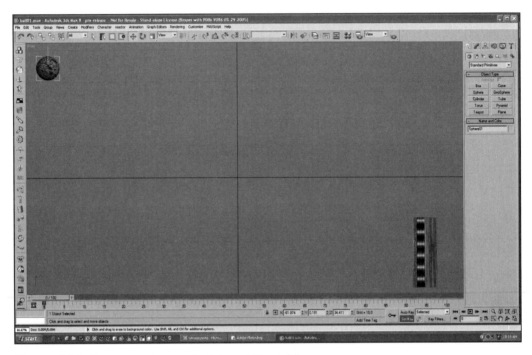

Figure 8.11 Set starting keys for the ball and the paddle.

14. Now move the time slider to frame 30, as shown in Figure 8.12.

15. Move the paddle straight up to the middle of the viewport.

16. Move the ball so that it overlaps the paddle, as shown in Figure 8.13.

17. Set a key frame for both objects at frame 30.

18. Move the time slider to frame 60 for the next key frame.

19. Move the paddle up a little, but not all the way to the top of the screen.

20. Now you need to move the ball to the left side of the screen. Place it near the bottom of the viewport, as shown in Figure 8.14.

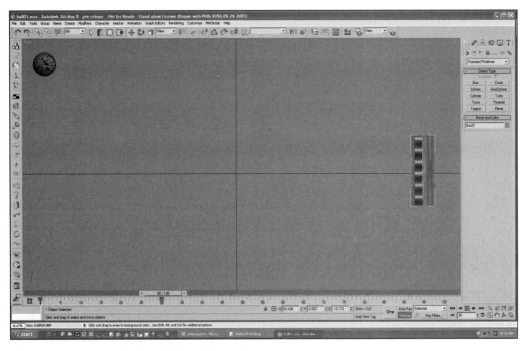

Figure 8.12 Move the time slider to frame 30.

Figure 8.13 Move the two objects so they meet on the right side.

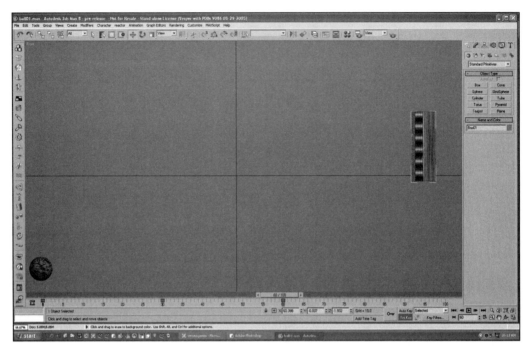

Figure 8.14 Place the ball at the bottom-left of the screen.

21. Set key frames for both the ball and the paddle at frame 60.

22. Now slide the time slider back and forth from frame 0 to frame 60 and watch the movement of the ball and paddle. 3ds Max automatically supplies all of the in-between frames.

23. Go to frame 28. Set a key frame here for the ball, as shown in Figure 8.15. You will be adding some dynamic effects to the ball as it hits the paddle. Frame 28 is close to where the ball first strikes the paddle. The ball needs to stay a constant shape until it hits the paddle. By placing a key frame at 28, you ensure that the ball will stay the same shape to that point.

24. The ball needs to resume its natural state after the impact. Move the time slider to 34 and set a key frame there as well (see Figure 8.16).

25. Now go to frame 30 and scale the sphere in horizontally so that it is just touching the paddle.

26. The ball needs to look like it has the same mass throughout, so you will also need to scale the ball up vertically, as shown in Figure 8.17.

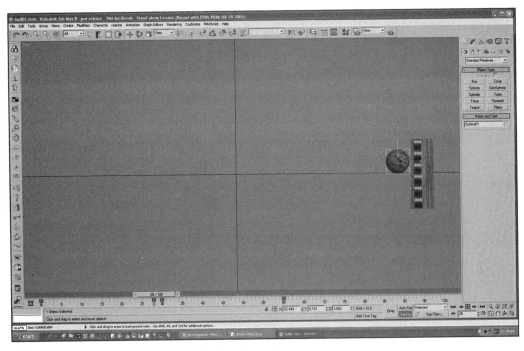

Figure 8.15 Set a key frame for the ball at frame 28.

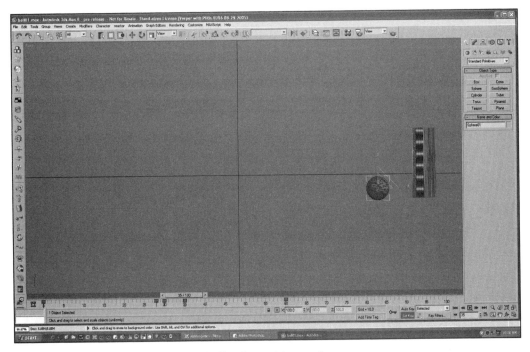

Figure 8.16 Set a key frame for the ball at frame 34 as well.

Figure 8.17 Scale the ball vertically.

Hint

Squashing the ball in steps 25 and 26 is an old animation trick to make the ball seem more alive. It is an exaggeration of an animated element. Exaggeration is commonly used in animation to make the animated characters or objects seem more alive. Animators refer to this as *squash and stretch*.

You just finished an animation in 3ds Max. How do you feel? That wasn't so hard, now was it? Play the animation by clicking on the arrow button in the Animation Playback controls. The ball should start in the upper-left and travel to the paddle, squashing as it impacts the paddle and then rebounding to the lower-left of the screen.

Character Animation

Character animation is more complicated than object animation. In the next section you will learn many of the concepts of animating characters in 3ds Max. Although character animation is complex, it is not difficult if you have a good animation tool, such as 3ds Max. Try the next example and follow it closely.

Freeform Animation

There are two types of animation in Biped: footsteps and freeform animation. *Footsteps* are used for creating common locomotion animations, such as walking, running, or even jumping. *Freeform animation* is for almost everything else, such as crouching, fighting, or swimming.

In the next example you will use freeform animation to have your pirate girl crouch and look side to side as if she is looking for danger.

1. Load the Biped rigged model of the pirate girl from Chapter 7.
2. Press the H key on the keyboard to bring up the Select Objects dialog box.
3. Select Bip01 L Foot, as shown in Figure 8.18. This will select the character's left foot in the Biped skeletal system.

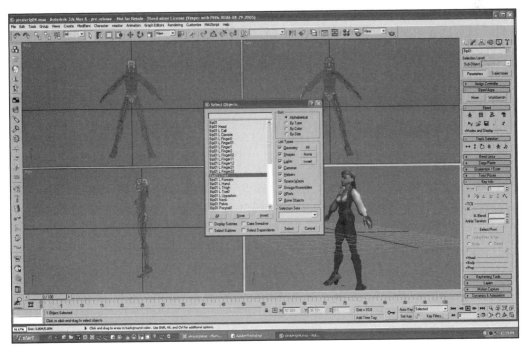

Figure 8.18 Select the character's left foot.

4. Click Select.
5. Now go to the Motion tab and open the Key Info rollout, as shown in Figure 8.19.

Key Info rollout

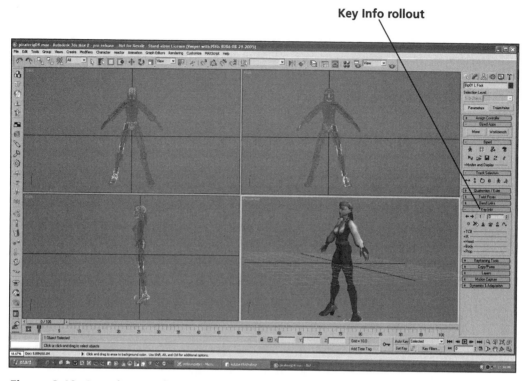

Figure 8.19 Open the Key Info rollout under the Motion tab.

6. You need to plant the foot so that it stays in place for this animation. Click on the icon with the red ball sitting directly on top of the blue rectangle. It is the third one from the left in the Key Info rollout.

7. Repeat step 6 for the right foot, as shown in Figure 8.20.

8. Now you need to have the character bend slightly at the knees. You can do this by selecting the COM and moving it down. The best way to do this is to click on Body Vertical (the up-and-down arrow) in the Track Selection rollout, as shown in Figure 8.21, because it not only picks the track, but it automatically selects the COM as well.

9. Click on Auto Key to turn on the animation features. Now try pulling down in the character. Notice as you pull down that the character bends at the knees. This is because of Biped's built-in inverse kinematics and the fact that her feet are locked to the ground (see Figure 8.22).

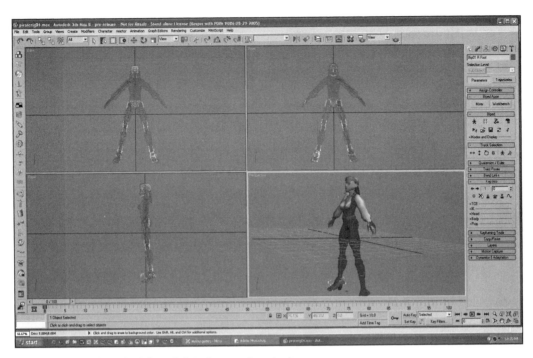

Figure 8.20 Plant the left and right feet so they don't move.

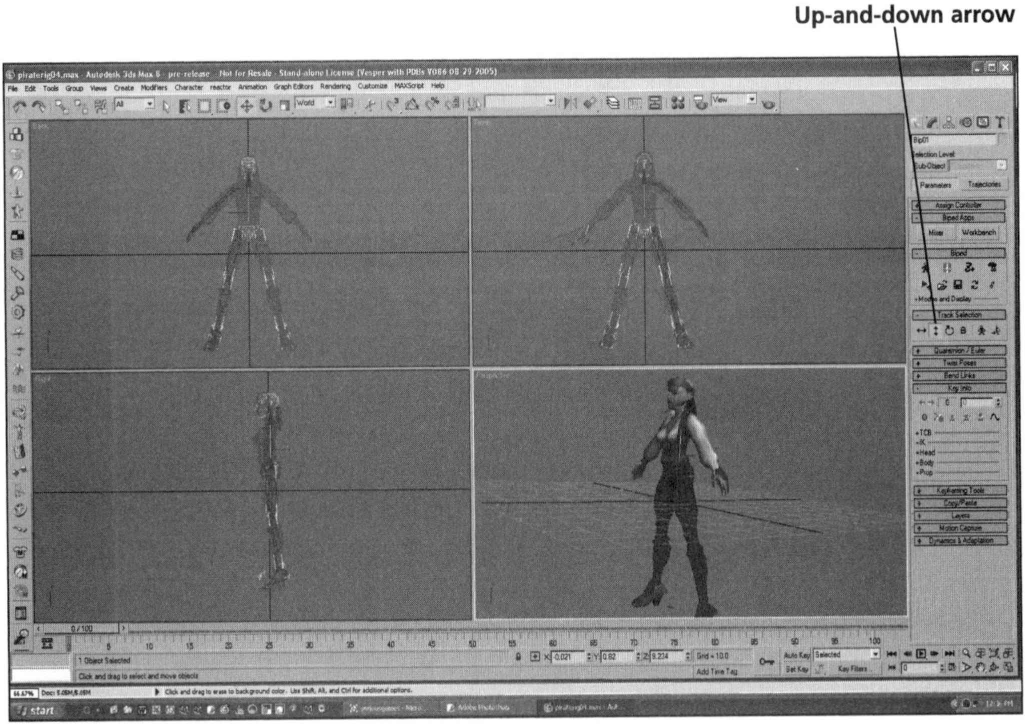

Up-and-down arrow

Figure 8.21 Click on the up-and-down arrow in the Track Selection rollout.

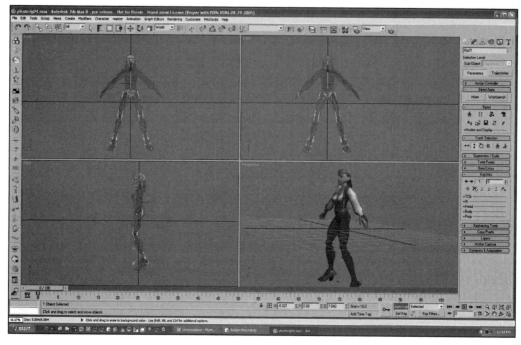

Figure 8.22 Have the character bend at the knees.

10. Press Ctrl+Z to return the character to her normal position.

11. You will be making several other key frames in this animation and you need to make sure the character's feet stay in place. Plant the feet like you did in frame 0 in frames 15, 60, and 75 on the time slider, as shown in Figure 8.23.

12. Have the character bend slightly at the knees as you did before, as shown in Figure 8.24.

13. Now go to frame 15 and have the character bend even more at the knees, as shown in Figure 8.25.

14. You will need to set another frame at the end of the animation so the character will return to a forward position. Move the time slider to frame 75. Click on the red oval in the Key Info rollout to set the key, as shown in Figure 8.26. The red oval is used to set keys in Auto Key mode, instead of using the Key button in the Animation Keying controls at the bottom of the screen because that button is for Set Key mode.

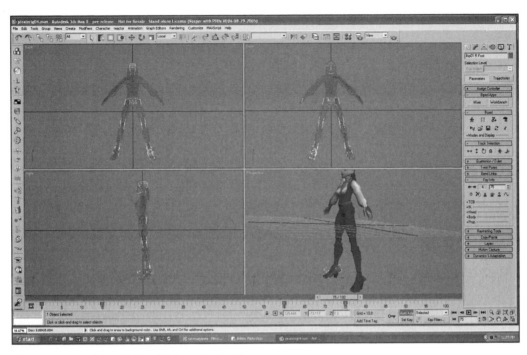

Figure 8.23 Plant the feet in the other key frames.

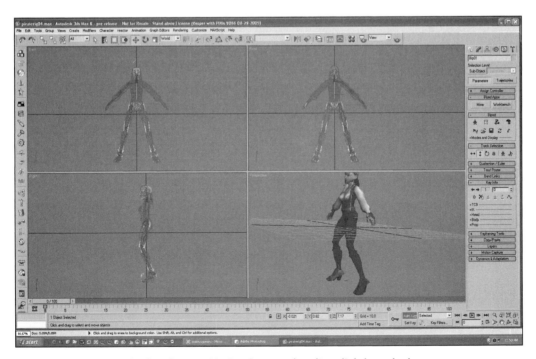

Figure 8.24 Set up the first frame with the character bending slightly at the knees.

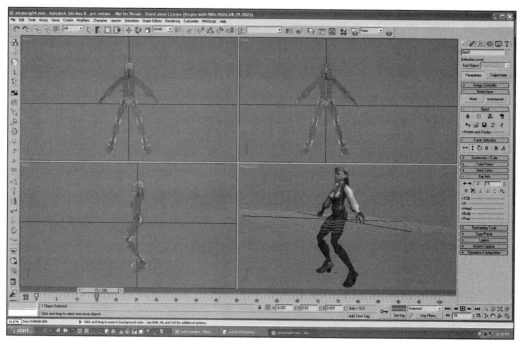

Figure 8.25 Have the character crouch a little more in frame 15.

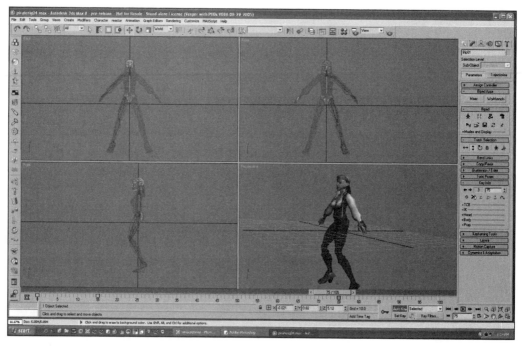

Figure 8.26 Set a key frame at frame 75.

15. Now you need to have the character turn from side to side. Biped has its own controls for moving and rotating the skeleton so it animates correctly. They are called *tracks* in Biped. Change the track to rotate by clicking on the Rotate icon in the Track Selection rollout, as shown in Figure 8.27.

Rotate Icon

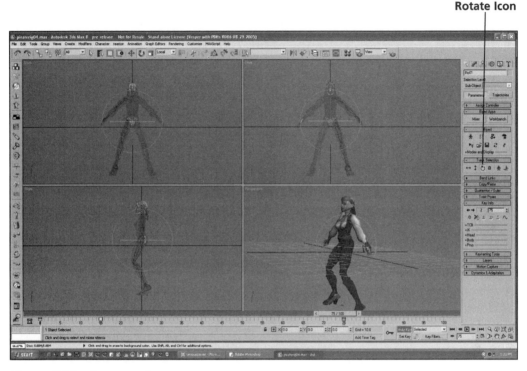

Figure 8.27 Change tracks to rotate.

16. At frame 15 have the character turn to her left by rotating her in that direction, as shown in Figure 8.28.

17. At frame 60 turn the character to her right, as shown in Figure 8.29.

18. Next, you need to work on her arms. Move the time slider back to frame 0. You will animate your character so that as she turns, she will lift her arm as if guarding against danger in the direction she is turning. Select the link of the left upper arm, as shown in Figure 8.30.

19. Click on Symmetry in the Track Selection rollout to select both arms.

20. Rotate the arms back, as shown in Figure 8.31.

21. Select the left forearm link and click on Symmetry to select both arms.

22. Rotate the arms forward to a ready position, as shown in Figure 8.32.

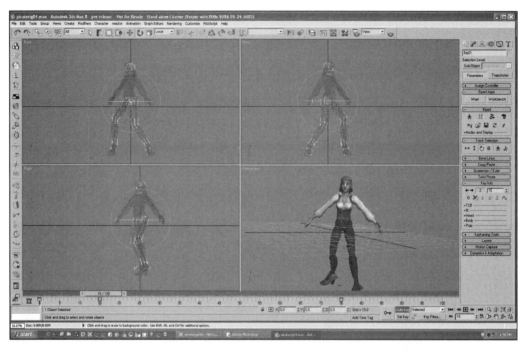

Figure 8.28 Have the character turn to her left at frame 15.

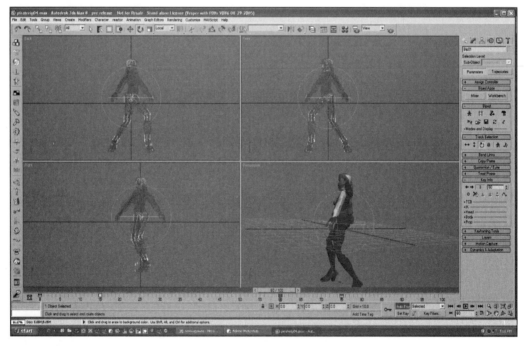

Figure 8.29 Turn the character to her right at frame 60.

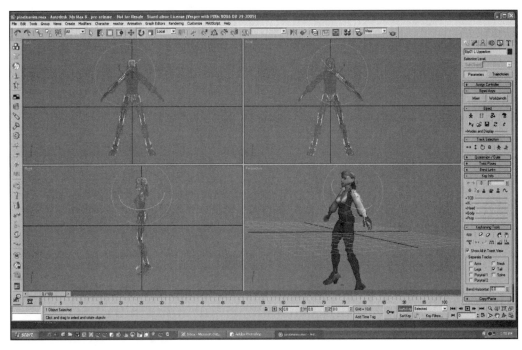

Figure 8.30 Select the left upper arm.

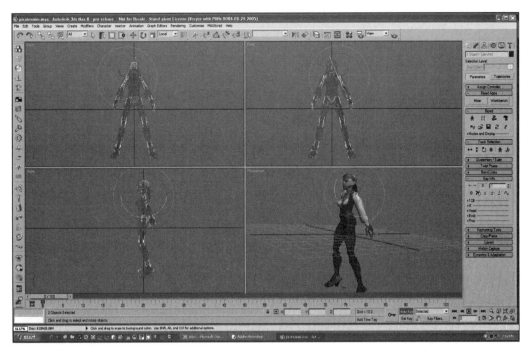

Figure 8.31 Rotate the arms back just a little.

Figure 8.32 Rotate the forearms forward.

23. At frame 15 select the left upper arm and rotate it up as if the character is guarding with that arm, as shown in Figure 8.33.

Figure 8.33 Lift the left arm.

24. Rotate the right arm back and relax it a little, as shown in Figure 8.34.

Figure 8.34 Lower the right arm.

25. Go to frame 60 and relax the left arm, as shown in Figure 8.35. Remember to set a key for each change you make.

Figure 8.35 Relax the left arm at frame 60.

26. Lift the right arm into more of a guarded position, as shown in Figure 8.36.

Figure 8.36 Lift the right arm.

27. Now go on to frame 75 and put the arms back into a ready position, similar to frame 0 (see Figure 8.37). Slide the time slider back and forth to see how your animation is coming along. You still have a ways to go, but it should be taking shape.

28. The major movements of the animation are mostly done now. But you will notice that the character is still very stiff-looking. To soften the stiffness you need to do a lot of little movements that are not as noticeable but that add finesse to the animation. Start with the character's head. Most of the time, the head moves as the body turns. This is because it is easier to turn the head than it is to turn the body. Select the head link in the Biped skeletal system.

29. At frame 15 rotate the head to the left, as shown in Figure 8.38.

30. Do the same at frame 60, only turn her head to the right, as shown in Figure 8.39.

Figure 8.37 The character resumes a ready position at frame 75.

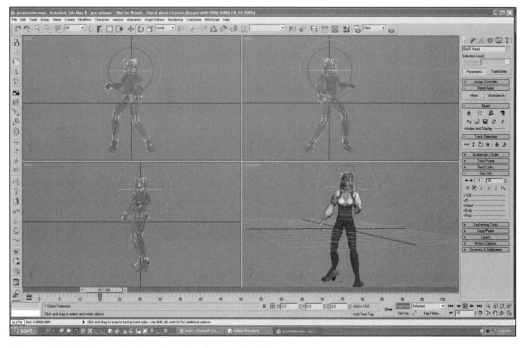

Figure 8.38 Rotate the head to the character's left.

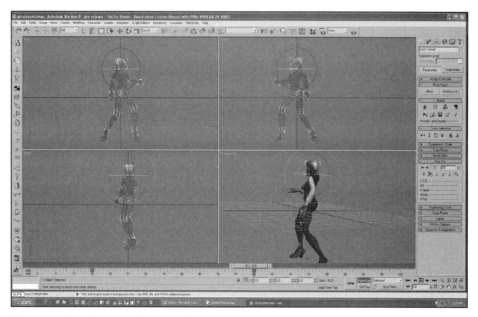

Figure 8.39 At frame 60 rotate the head to the character's right.

31. Now position the head to look straight ahead at frame 75, as shown in Figure 8.40.

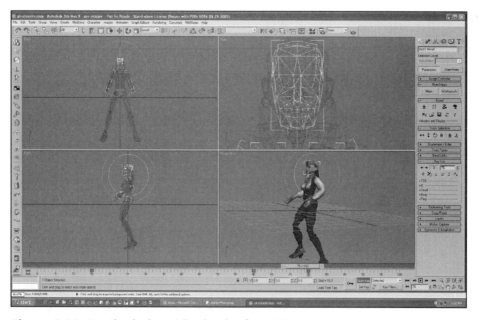

Figure 8.40 Have her look straight ahead at frame 75.

32. You will notice when you review the animation that there is no key frame for the head set at frame 0. That is because we didn't set one there. Often while you are animating, you need to check your animation to see whether you forgot to set a key frame. Go back to frame 0 and position the head to look forward (see Figure 8.41). Because you have Auto Key on, when you rotate the head in frame 0 a key will be set.

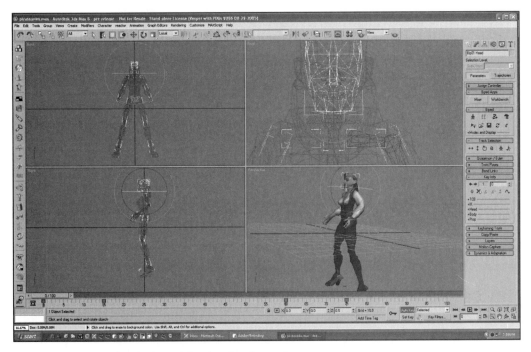

Figure 8.41 Have her look straight ahead at frame 0 too.

33. To look a little more natural the character needs to lean forward just a little when she crouches. The lean gives her a better sense of balance. Select the base of the character's spine, as shown in Figure 8.42, by pressing the H key on the keyboard and selecting it from the list. There are several links in the spine. The base is the lowest link.

34. Rotate the torso forward a little bit. Don't overdo it or she will not look right. See Figure 8.43 for a reference.

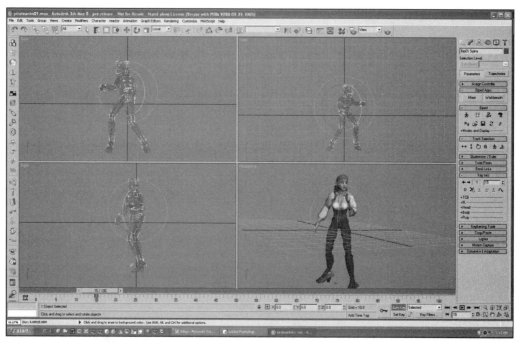

Figure 8.42 Select the bottom link of the spine.

Figure 8.43 Rotate the torso forward to give her a more balanced look.

35. To add even more of a natural look, go to frame 15 again and select Bip01 Spine 2 from the list. Set a frame at 0.

36. Rotate the torso a little to the character's left, as shown in Figure 8.44. The turning to the torso is natural when the body shifts from one side to the other. You already have the hips and head turning in that direction. You need to have the ribcage turn a little as well.

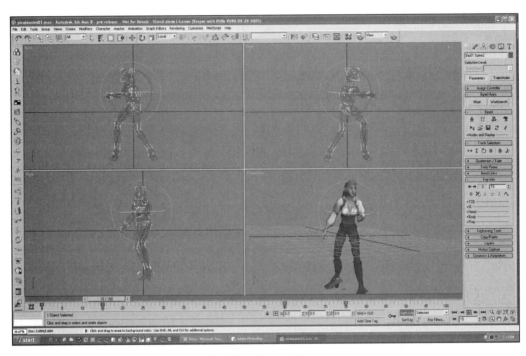

Figure 8.44 Turn the upper torso to the left at frame 15.

37. At frame 60 turn the character's torso to the right.

Most of the animation is now finished. There is, of course, a lot of even more subtle things you can adjust, such as having the character open and close her hands a little or shift her body from side to side as she turns. Animation of characters is a process of refining to take into account a hundred little subtle movements. Good character animation is a process of refining, checking, adjusting, and timing. You need to study movement closely to understand all the aspects and how to get everything to work together.

If you want some study help with human motion, take a look at *The Animator's Reference Book* (Thomson Course PTR, 2005), by Ross Wolfley and myself. This reference manual breaks down many common human movements into a frame-by-frame format from four different angles, using photographs of real people.

Character animation is really the study of motion. If you want to get good at it, you need to spend some time looking at how people move. Sit on a park bench and watch people as they walk by. If you look closely, you should notice that the way people stand and walk is very different. These differences give individuals personality.

Another aspect of character animation is exaggeration. In the first example in this chapter, you exaggerated the squashing effect of the ball hitting the paddle. Exaggeration in the right places can improve the personality and sense of life in an animation. Exaggerations that will help give life to characters might include adding a little more spring in the characters' steps or increasing the characters' reactions to movement. For example, if a character is going to throw a punch, exaggerate both the windup and the punch, emphasizing the extremes of the motion.

Animating with Footsteps

Biped has a number of predefined animations that can be added to a character using the Footsteps tool. Footsteps control the movement of the character's feet but they also influence the entire body to give the character a natural motion, including shifting of weight from one foot to the other and counterbalancing the arms. Footsteps can create a natural-looking walk, but the walk is generic and lacks personality. It does provide a good base, however, for adjusting a walk with freeform animation.

1. It is often easier to work on a Biped model if you hide the mesh so you can see the model better. Select the mesh and right-click to bring up the floating menu. Choose Hide Selection, as shown in Figure 8.45.

2. Press the H key and select Bip01 from the list, as shown in Figure 8.46.

3. Open the Motion panel and, in the Biped rollout, turn on Footstep mode by clicking on the icon that looks like two footprints next to each other.

4. A new set of rollouts will appear. Go down to the Footsteps Creation rollout and click the Create Multiple Footsteps button. It is the third one from the left. The Create Multiple Footsteps: Walk dialog box will appear, as shown in Figure 8.47.

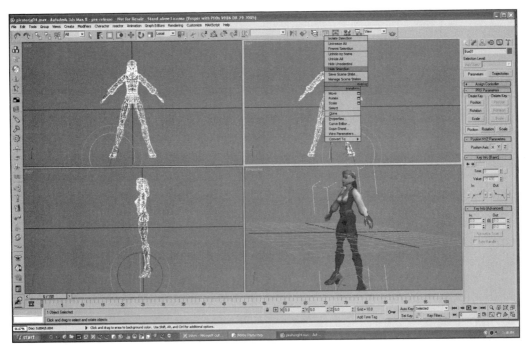

Figure 8.45 Hide the mesh.

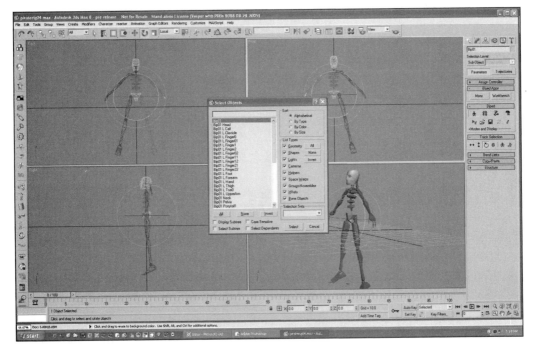

Figure 8.46 Choose the Biped COM.

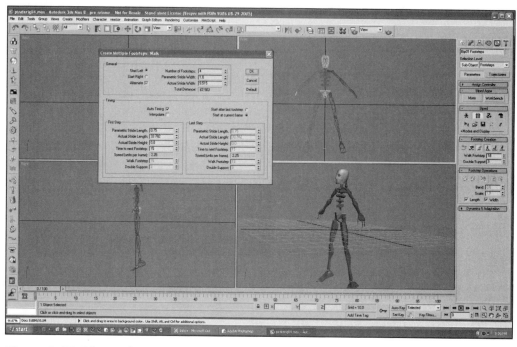

Figure 8.47 Bring up the Create Multiple Footsteps: Walk dialog box.

5. Change the Number of Footsteps value to 6 in the General group of the dialog box and click on OK.

6. Now you can create the keys for the walk by clicking on the Create Keys for Inactive Footsteps button, which is the first button from the left in the Footsteps Operations rollout. The biped will change to line up with the footsteps, as shown in Figure 8.48.

Hint

If you can't see the Footsteps in the viewports, you can turn them on by clicking on the Show Footsteps and Numbers button in the Display group of the Biped rollout, as shown in Figure 8.49.

7. Run the animation to see the Biped walk. Notice that the Biped changed dramatically when placed in the key frames. The motion will need to be adjusted to offset these changes.

8. You will need to adjust the keys of the walk to fit the model. Bring back the model by going to the Display tab and accessing the Display panel, then clicking on Unhide All in the Hide rollout. The mesh will reappear, as shown in Figure 8.50.

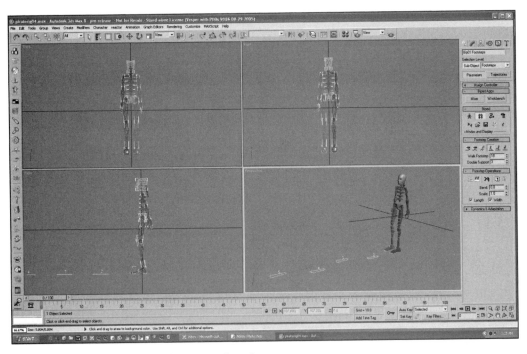

Figure 8.48 Create keys for the new walk cycle.

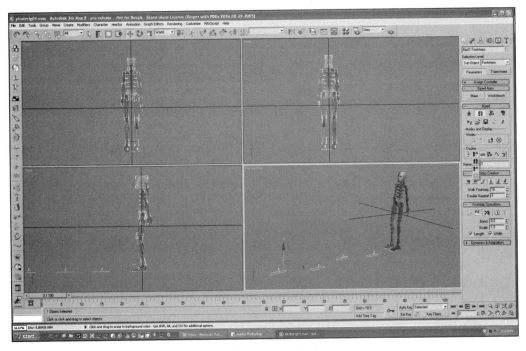

Figure 8.49 Click on Show Footsteps and Numbers to display Footsteps.

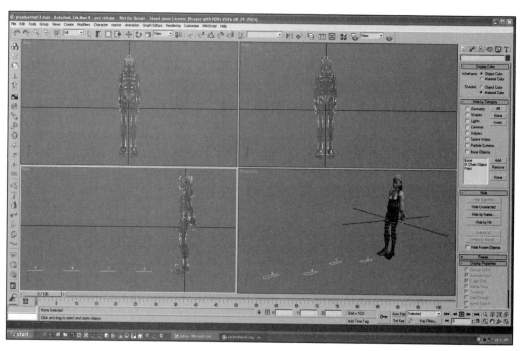

Figure 8.50 Unhide the mesh.

9. Go back to the Motion tab and turn off Footsteps mode.

10. With the mesh now in place, two problems are immediately noticeable.
    The first problem is that the boots are protruding through the floor. This is
    because you rotated the feet in the rigging process to account for the boots'
    long heels. The second problem is that the pirate girl's chest is collapsed.
    This is due to the adjustments of the back you made during the rigging
    process. First you should deal with the boot problem. Click on Body Verti-
    cal and raise the COM six units in the Z axis. The easiest way to raise the
    COM is to type the new number in the Z box located just below the track
    bar (see Figure 8.51).

11. Notice that there are several keys already set for the COM in the track bar.
    To fix the problem with the boots, you will need to move the COM up six
    units at each key; otherwise, the character will sink back to the original
    height.

12. Slide the time slider along the track bar to check each key, as shown in
    Figure 8.52. An easy way to go from key frame to key frame is to use the
    Next Key and Previous Key buttons in the Key Info rollout.

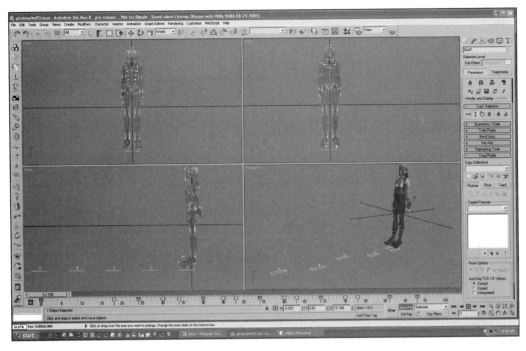

Figure 8.51 Move the COM up six units.

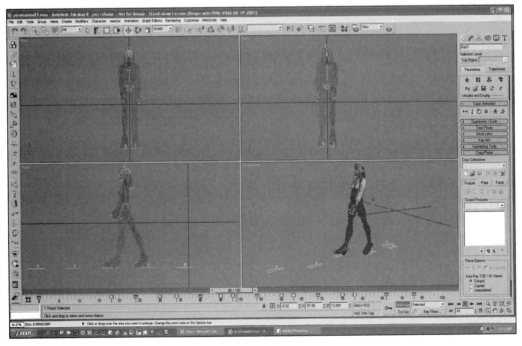

Figure 8.52 Check each frame to make sure the boots do not protrude into the ground.

13. The feet are not at the right angle; they need to be rotated forward. Select the left foot and click on Symmetrical to select the right foot too.

14. Rotate the feet forward, as shown in Figure 8.53.

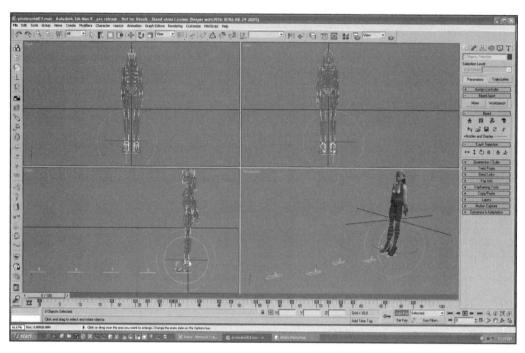

Figure 8.53 Rotate the feet forward so they line up with the ground.

15. You will need to rotate the feet for every key frame in the sequence, as shown in Figure 8.54.

16. Now for the girl's chest. Press the H key and select Bip01 Spine2 from the list.

17. Rotate the spine to the right in the Side view about 22 degrees.

18. Rotate the spine link for each key frame, as shown in Figure 8.55.

19. Although the girl's chest is not collapsed, she still does not look right because she is leaning too far back. Select Bip01 Spine and rotate it forward 15 degrees for each key frame, as shown in Figure 8.56.

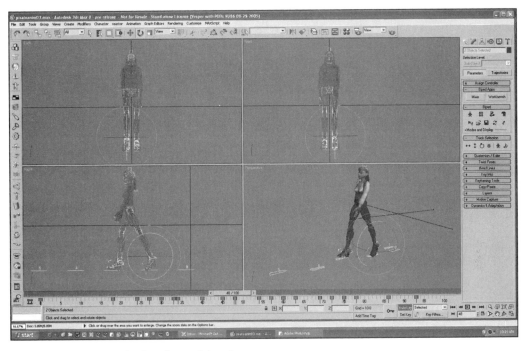

Figure 8.54 Rotate the feet for each key frame.

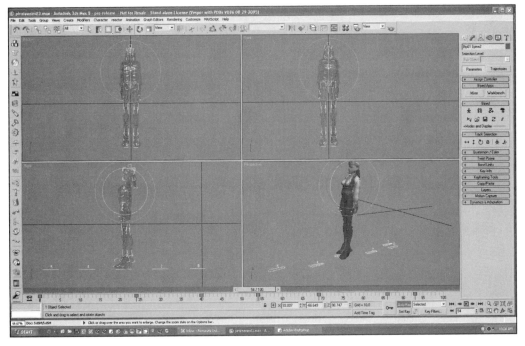

Figure 8.55 Rotate the spine to lift the chest.

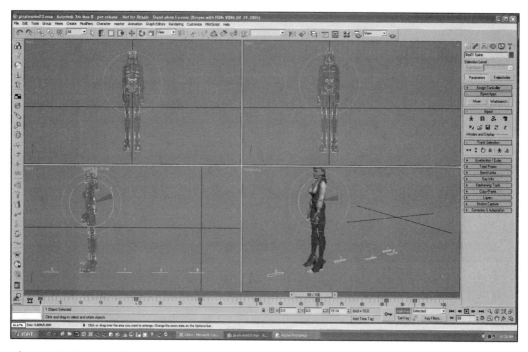

Figure 8.56 Rotate the lower back forward.

There—it is not perfect, but the major problems are gone. The character now walks correctly on her high-heeled boots. She also stands with some pride instead of hunching over. You can continue to refine the walk in any way you like. Try a few experiments to see how the walk can be changed.

Summary

This chapter covered concepts dealing with animation. In this chapter we covered several important points.

- 3D animation
- Understanding animation
- 3ds Max animation tools
- Object animation
- Squash and stretch
- Freeform character animation
- Study of motion
- Footsteps animation

This chapter and this book were only the beginning in the study of a program as deep and complex as 3ds Max. You should now be familiar with many of the basic concepts of the program. Hopefully you have followed the examples and are now ready to go on to some more advanced concepts.

You have made it through this book—congratulations! (Unless, of course, you skipped to this section—in which case you need to go back and read the rest of the book. I can't very well congratulate you if you didn't actually read the book, now can I?) But if you did make it this far, congratulations! Well done! I hope you were able to gain a lot from the examples and instruction. Good luck in your work.

Questions

1. What kind of files do games use for animating characters and objects?
2. Before 3D, how were characters animated in games?
3. What is the advantage of separating motion from the art?
4. The initial drawings of a movement at the extremes of the movement are called what?
5. If the animation runs at 30 frames per second and a motion lasts for 1.5 seconds, how many pictures need to be drawn for the motion?
6. What is the name of the device that moves the animation from frame to frame?
7. Where are the Animation Playback controls located in 3ds Max?
8. What two systems does 3ds Max use for setting key frames?
9. A more experienced animator who wants to experiment with a motion before setting the key frame will most likely use what system for setting key frames?
10. Why might an animator squash a ball on impact with another object?
11. What should an animator study to learn about character animation?
12. What two types of animation are used with biped models?
13. Footsteps control what part of the Biped character?
14. Which type of animation would an animator use for a swimming animation?
15. What does an animator have to do to give a Footsteps animation more personality?

Answers

1. Motion files
2. They were drawn by hand.
3. Animation can be applied to multiple characters.
4. Key frames
5. 45
6. The time slider
7. In the lower-right corner
8. Auto Key and Set Key
9. Set Key
10. To make the ball motion seem more dynamic
11. Human motion
12. Freeform and Footsteps
13. The placement of the feet
14. Freeform
15. Adjust it using Freeform animation.

Discussion Questions

1. How is game animation different than film animation?
2. Why are key frames important in animation?
3. Why should an animator pay attention to the timing of a movement?
4. What are some good ways to learn about human and animal motion?
5. Why is it important to give game characters distinctive animation?

Exercises

1. Animate a character running using Biped.
2. Animate a character climbing a wall using Freeform animation.
3. Give a Biped character a limp.

INDEX

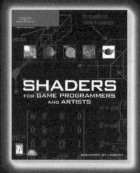

License Agreement/Notice of Limited Warranty

By opening the sealed disc container in this book, you agree to the following terms and conditions. If, upon reading the following license agreement and notice of limited warranty, you cannot agree to the terms and conditions set forth, return the unused book with unopened disc to the place where you purchased it for a refund.

License:

The enclosed software is copyrighted by the copyright holder(s) indicated on the software disc. You are licensed to copy the software onto a single computer for use by a single user and to a backup disc. You may not reproduce, make copies, or distribute copies or rent or lease the software in whole or in part, except with written permission of the copyright holder(s). You may transfer the enclosed disc only together with this license, and only if you destroy all other copies of the software and the transferee agrees to the terms of the license. You may not decompile, reverse assemble, or reverse engineer the software.

Notice of Limited Warranty:

The enclosed disc is warranted by Thomson Course Technology PTR to be free of physical defects in materials and workmanship for a period of sixty (60) days from end user's purchase of the book/disc combination. During the sixty-day term of the limited warranty, Thomson Course Technology PTR will provide a replacement disc upon the return of a defective disc.

Limited Liability:

THE SOLE REMEDY FOR BREACH OF THIS LIMITED WARRANTY SHALL CONSIST ENTIRELY OF REPLACEMENT OF THE DEFECTIVE DISC. IN NO EVENT SHALL THOMSON COURSE TECHNOLOGY PTR OR THE AUTHOR BE LIABLE FOR ANY OTHER DAMAGES, INCLUDING LOSS OR CORRUPTION OF DATA, CHANGES IN THE FUNCTIONAL CHARACTERISTICS OF THE HARDWARE OR OPERATING SYSTEM, DELETERIOUS INTERACTION WITH OTHER SOFTWARE, OR ANY OTHER SPECIAL, INCIDENTAL, OR CONSEQUENTIAL DAMAGES THAT MAY ARISE, EVEN IF THOMSON COURSE TECHNOLOGY PTR AND/OR THE AUTHOR HAS PREVIOUSLY BEEN NOTIFIED THAT THE POSSIBILITY OF SUCH DAMAGES EXISTS.

Disclaimer of Warranties:

THOMSON COURSE TECHNOLOGY PTR AND THE AUTHOR SPECIFICALLY DISCLAIM ANY AND ALL OTHER WARRANTIES, EITHER EXPRESS OR IMPLIED, INCLUDING WARRANTIES OF MERCHANTABILITY, SUITABILITY TO A PARTICULAR TASK OR PURPOSE, OR FREEDOM FROM ERRORS. SOME STATES DO NOT ALLOW FOR EXCLUSION OF IMPLIED WARRANTIES OR LIMITATION OF INCIDENTAL OR CONSEQUENTIAL DAMAGES, SO THESE LIMITATIONS MIGHT NOT APPLY TO YOU.

Other:

This Agreement is governed by the laws of the State of Massachusetts without regard to choice of law principles. The United Convention of Contracts for the International Sale of Goods is specifically disclaimed. This Agreement constitutes the entire agreement between you and Thomson Course Technology PTR regarding use of the software.